Organising Learning in the Primary School Classroom

To be

Organising Learning in the Primary School Classroom

Fourth edition

Joan Dean

Routledge
Taylor & Francis Group
LONDON AND NEW YORK

First published 1983 by Croom Helm Ltd

Second edition published 1992 by Routledge

Third edition published 2001 by RoutledgeFalmer

Fourth edition published 2009 by Routledge
2 Park Square, Milton Park, Abingdon, Oxon, OX14 4RN

Simultaneously published in the USA and Canada
by Routledge
711 Third Ave, New York, NY 10017

Routledge is an imprint of the Taylor & Francis Group, an informa business

© 1983, 1992, 2001, 2009 Joan Dean

Typeset in Sabon by
Bookcraft Ltd, Stroud, Gloucestershire

British Library Cataloguing in Publication Data
A catalogue record for this book is available
from the British Library

Library of Congress Cataloging in Publication Data
Dean, Joan.
   Organising learning in the primary school classroom / Joan Dean.
     p. cm.
   Includes bibliographical references and index.
   1. Education, Elementary—Great Britain. 2. Education, Elementary—
Curricula—Great Britain. 3. Elementary school teaching—Great Britain.
4. Classroom management—Great Britain. I. Title.
   LB1556.7.G74D43 2008
   372.941—dc22   2008007504

ISBN13: 978-0-415-46519-9
ISBN10: 0-415-46519-2

Contents

List of Reviews and Figures

Reviews

Figures

Chapter 1

Introduction

Janet Rogers was in her second year of teaching and was working with a Year 4 class. She enjoyed her work and had settled into her school well. She was sometimes made conscious that she was living in a fast-changing world when there seemed to be a continuous flow of government edicts and documents requiring new ways of doing things. She was also concerned about climate change and felt that it wasn't being sufficiently considered in primary schools. She found it hard to fit in all the demands of the National Curriculum and worried that she found it difficult to find time to work with children with special educational needs and the few very able children she had in her class. At the same time, she just loved her job and hoped that life would get a little easier as she grew more experienced.

She talked all this over with Mary, the deputy head, who had been her mentor in her first year. Mary suggested that Janet should set aside some time in the coming Christmas holiday to think carefully about her philosophy of primary education – the things she felt were really important and those that were less so – and also to consider the ways in which she felt happiest teaching, which could help her to define her teaching style. She could then go on to define her objectives more clearly, determine the skills and knowledge she needed to achieve them and analyse some aspects of her work carefully, looking at where she might be able to make improvements.

The reflective teacher

This book sets out to do just that – to help you to reflect on your philosophy of education and your preferred teaching style and with these in mind to analyse what is actually happening in your classroom. We will look at the skills and knowledge you need and how best to organise your work in the classroom, given your particular aims, interests and abilities and the needs of your class. Good teachers are reflective teachers.

Osterman and Kottkamp (1994: 46) suggest that 'Reflective practice is viewed as a means by which practitioners can develop a greater level of self-awareness about the nature and impact of their performance, an awareness that creates opportunities for professional growth and development'. Reflective teaching also involves thinking about the feelings that are aroused by classroom situations. Osterman and Kottkamp suggest collecting observational data and analysing and reflecting on this, asking yourself questions such as 'Why did events take place as they did? What ideas and feelings prompted my actions? Did my actions correspond with my intentions? Did my actions lead to the outcomes I intended?'

Pollard and Tann (1987: 1) make the following statements about the nature of reflective teaching:

- Reflective teaching implies an active concern with aims and consequences, as well as with means and technical efficiency.
- Reflective teaching combines enquiry and implementation skills with attitudes of open-mindedness, responsibility and whole-heartedness.
- Reflective teaching is applied in a cyclical or spiralling process in which teachers continually monitor, evaluate and revise their own practice.
- Reflective teaching is based on teacher judgement, informed partly by self-reflection and partly by insights from educational disciplines.

Reflective teachers need to be self-critical and analytic

You need to take time every so often to evaluate your current work in relation to your philosophy of primary education – the things you feel are really important and those which are less so. You also need to consider the ways in which you feel happiest teaching and appear to get the best results, not only in terms of children getting the right answers but also in the extent to which you have been able to stimulate enthusiasm and interest and help children to become effective learners. What do you do to encourage children to have good ideas? What skills are they developing? Are they able to work together in pairs or groups? The answers to these questions will, of course, depend on the age of your class, but they are important skills for future learning. From there you can go on to define your objectives and plan your work, perhaps analysing various aspects of your work to see if there are ways in which they could be improved.

Managing children's learning

Every teacher is a manager of children's learning. As a teacher you influence the children you teach in many ways. Because of you, many of them will learn things that they will remember for the rest of their lives. It is a considerable responsibility.

How you discharge this responsibility does not depend only on the person you are and the relationships you are able to build with the children and colleagues, important as these are. The actual teaching skills you possess, your ability to organise children's learning, your ability to observe, select and present material, lead discussion, assess and evaluate and reflect on your performance and so on are crucial. They make all the difference between a group in which most of the children come near to achieving their full potential and one in which most are underachieving.

School management and effectiveness in the classroom

The way a school is managed has a considerable effect on what happens in individual classrooms, but research into effectiveness suggests that the classroom is the place where the quality of teaching and learning determines how effective the school actually is. In recent years teachers have done much more work together, planning and making decisions which affect what happens in their classrooms. Many schools which are large enough also have teachers co-ordinating the work in different subjects and for special educational needs, although this poses problems for really small schools. This could mean that individual teachers lose some autonomy but this may be offset by the support of a colleague who has made a study of a particular aspect of the curriculum or of special needs.

Different teachers have different styles of working. This provides variety in the school, which can be valuable and keeps the teaching dynamic in many classes. It means that there will be a variety of opportunities for children to learn during their time at school. However, some styles are more effective than others and you need to be constantly assessing the way you work to ensure that children are learning as effectively as possible.

Each chapter in this book contains suggestions to enable you to review your particular situation in the area of work dealt with in that chapter. These review suggestions are intended to help you to highlight the areas in which you most want to see development in your work and could lead on to you making plans in the light of your conclusions. You may like to work through the book chapter by chapter, thinking out your point of view as you go along. Alternatively, you may like to select particular areas of your work to consider and analyse.

Recent developments in primary education

Education rarely seems to be out of the news. Our government places a good deal of emphasis on education and teachers and schools have had to cope with many new developments in the recent past and there will, no doubt, be many more to come.

Every Child Matters

An important development has been the 'Every Child Matters' agenda. This was introduced in 2004 and has affected many subsequent developments. It lists five outcomes as a key to well-being in childhood and later life. These are being healthy, staying safe, enjoying and achieving, making a positive contribution and achieving economic well-being. This development has led to the Primary Strategy, described below.

Excellence and enjoyment: a five-year strategy for primary schools

This development was first published in May 2003 and sets out its aims as:

- helping children to develop as confident, enthusiastic and effective learners;
- providing opportunities for all children to fulfil their potential through a commitment to high standards and excellence within an engaging, broad and rich curriculum.

The strategy started by acknowledging that many primary schools were working very successfully and 'delivering very high quality education as part of a rich and fulfilling primary experience' and Ofsted have judged two-thirds of nursery and primary schools as good or better. Future government plans for primary education include the following:

- continued improvement in literacy and numeracy;
- a broad and balanced curriculum in all primary schools;
- ensuring that every subject in the curriculum is well taught;
- provision of a wide range of in- and out-of-school activities like dance, sport and drama;
- extended services including childcare;
- schools working closely with parents;
- improvement in schools which are weak at present;
- better teaching and a more personalised approach across the curriculum;
- the introduction of modern language teaching into all primary schools by 2010.

The amalgamation of children's services and education

This development should lead to a situation in which schools will have access to a much broader picture of the children coming into the reception class: both those working in early years provision and those working in schools have much to learn from each other. It should enable schools to build more easily and fully on children's earlier experiences.

All these developments will have an impact on staff in schools and it will be important to ensure that they are not yet more burdens for school and pre-school staff, but opportunities which support them.

Reviewing your work

All teachers need to review their work at fairly frequent intervals and provision for this is built into each chapter in this book.

The review on the next few pages is designed as a starting point for your thinking and as something to come back to after you have read this book. This is why it is substantially longer than any of the other reviews suggested in other chapters.

All teachers have their own style of teaching, based on their own philosophy of education and their own ideas of the best way of working for them and for the particular children they teach; they organise their work to take into account their own preferences and skills. Review 1.1 is designed to help you identify your own organisational preferences so that you can keep them in mind as you work through this book. This is entirely a question of personal preferences. None of the options suggested here is intended to represent an ideal view, and although each list tends to be in the order in which development in primary education seems to be going for the future, this doesn't mean that the later items are wrong in any way if you can make them work really well. There is no reason for not choosing them if they represent your preferred way of working. You may find it interesting to see if you change your original ideas after considering the assessment suggestions as you work though the text.

Review 1.1 Profile of organisational preferences

Tick the statement in each section which most nearly represents your views.

Pattern of daily programme

1   Each child in my class has an individual programme matched to his or her needs. I then withdraw groups for specific teaching and do some whole-class work when it seems appropriate.
2   My main emphasis is on group work with a good deal of individual work and some class work.
3   I like to spend some time working with the whole class, some on group work and some with individuals.
4   I divide the time available about equally between class and group work and pay attention to individuals as seems necessary.
5   I work with the whole class for most of the time, following this up with group and individual work as seems necessary.

The teacher's use of time

1   I work with the whole class as part of the literacy and numeracy hours but for the rest of the time I work mostly with small groups or individuals, extending their thinking and helping them to plan their work.
2   I spend about half my time in whole-class teaching and the other half with small groups and individuals.
3   I spend more than half my time in whole-class teaching with some group teaching and follow this up with individuals.
4   A high proportion of my time is spent in whole-class teaching with occasional group or individual work.

The children's use of time

1   I encourage children to plan the use of their time and try to create opportunities for them to do this.
2   I aim to have an even balance between work which matches the needs of individuals and also to offer children some choice in the order in which work is done, and also to try to balance the amount of work undertaken by the whole class and group work.
3   I expect the majority of children to work at the pace of the class, but I try to arrange for the slower children to have extra time on aspects of work they find difficult. I let children choose the order of some pieces of work upon occasion.
4   Almost all my children spend the same amount of time on each aspect of curriculum and do similar work, with help if necessary.

My assistant's use of time

1 We plan before the lesson how she will observe during the whole-class part of the work, noting the reactions of different children.
2 We agree the things she will observe during that period.
3 We agree that when the children are working individually or in groups she will work with individuals or groups whom we know wil need help.
4 We plan to meet later in the day to exchange information about what happened.

Choice of activity

1 Much of the children's work allows choice within a carefully structured framework. I try to teach children to choose intelligently.
2 I think it is important for children to learn to choose and I build opportunities for this into the programme.
3 I like to provide a certain amount of choice as well as some compulsory activity.
4 I try to provide some choice but the majority of the work I give children to do is compulsory.
5 I keep choice to a minimum because I believe that every child should experience a similar curriculum.

Use of competition and co-operation

1 I believe that it is important for children to learn to work together and I plan a good deal of co-operative group work. I try to avoid competitive situations. I spend some time discussing with children how they can best work together.
2 I try to encourage co-operation but use competition occasionally in situations where it seems unlikely to do any harm.
3 I use competition when I think it will motivate children. I also do some work designed to encourage co-operation.
4 I find that competition is valuable providing it doesn't get out of hand. I provide occasional opportunities for co-operation.
5 Competition is an important incentive in the classroom as in life and I believe that children need to learn to fail as well as to win. I would like to foster co-operation but don't feel that there are many opportunities for doing so within normal classroom work.

Grouping of children

1 Children often work in groups that are usually formed on a friendship basis and I aim to train them to work co-operatively.

2 I use group work a good deal, forming groups according to the needs of the work in hand. I aim to have children working together.

3 I have some work in interest groups, some in friendship groups, some in ability groups and some in groups I have structured so that they are heterogeneous. Children are encouraged to work together.

4 I normally do core subject work in ability groups. I also have occasional interest groups in topic work.

5 I prefer to work with children in ability groups when I am not working with whole class.

Use of space

1 I use all the space I can and allow children to work in other parts of the school and move freely about the classroom.

2 I allow children to move about the classroom to collect things and occasionally I allow them to work outside the classroom when this seems necessary.

3 I prefer children to stay in their places except for practical work. I rarely let them work outside the classroom.

4 I like children to be in their places where I can keep an eye on them.

Use of resources

1 I want to ensure that all my children are computer literate by the time they leave my class. I therefore plan a lot of work designed to make this possible.

2 I try to make the maximum use of resources to foster individual learning. I try to select and make teaching materials which can be used independently of the teacher. I try to organise so that the computers are in use most of the day. I use the whiteboard every day with the children.

3 I like to have some good individual materials as well as materials to use with the whole class and I buy and make both types. I aim to ensure that the children make good use of the computers.

4 I like to have some good individual textbooks for core subject work, but prefer to have a variety of books for other subjects.

5 I use textbooks a good deal, supplementing them with other materials when necessary. I am conscious that I have still a lot to learn about computers but want the children to learn about them.

6   The main resources in my classroom are my own voice, the board, pictures to help the children's understanding and some good textbooks. I allow the children to use the computers occasionally.

Records and assessments

1   I keep a forecast of my work and aim to keep a detailed record of each child's work and progress through the National Curriculum and in social and personal development and I involve the children in this process.
2   I keep a forecast/record of my work, record each child's progress in National Curriculum work and note other things as necessary.
3   I keep a forecast/record of my work and a check-list of children's progress in the core and foundation subjects.
4   I keep a forecast/record of my work and a mark list showing each child's marks in the core and foundation subjects.
5   I keep a forecast/record of my work and try to look back at it when planning the next piece of work.

Work with other teachers

1   I like to work with other teachers in a teaching team or sharing thinking and materials. I learn a lot that way.
2   I like to do some work with other teachers.
3   I work with other teachers occasionally, usually when we take a group out.
4   I discuss work with other teachers but we are each responsible for our own work and development.
5   I prefer to work with my own class all the time, but I take part in staff discussion from time to time.

Work with parents

1   I like to get to know all the parents of the children in my class and try to meet them as soon as I can and take note of what they say about their children.
2   I tell them about the work we are doing and suggest ways in which they can help at home. I also like to have parents helping in the classroom.
3   I try to get to know some of the parents of children in my class and I have carefully selected parents helping in the classroom.
4   I get to know the parents of the children in my class as far as I am able but I am not keen to have parents in the classroom.
5   I believe teaching is a professional task which should be left to professionals.

Equal opportunities

1   I am conscious that it is all too easy to treat boys and girls, children from different cultures, middle- and working-class children and children with disabilities in different ways and to be prejudiced about what they can do.

2   I check myself frequently to see that this is not happening and aim to teach my children to value people as individuals whatever their background.

3   I am conscious that it is easy to show prejudice without being aware of it and I do my best to avoid treating any group or individual differently because of race, gender, social class or disability. I discourage any expression of prejudice from the children.

4   I try to avoid treating any individual or group differently because of race, gender, social class or disability.

5   I try to treat all children in the same way.

Chapter 2

Preparing for a new class

Your ability to observe children and interpret their behaviour is a basic teaching skill which provides you with the knowledge you need to teach them. Unless you teach in a very small school you are likely to have a new class of children each year. This chapter is concerned with ways in which you can prepare for a new class.

Learning about the children

When you get a new group of children, you need to spend time finding out about them in order to be able to teach them effectively. In the past, teachers have sometimes taken the view that they wanted to see new children with fresh eyes and they were therefore not interested in what other teachers had to say about them. While this view is understandable, it is one which is no longer tenable. A teacher who wishes to start afresh is quite properly taking the view that he or she may relate differently to a child or group of children from the previous teacher and does not want to prejudice the relationship by looking at the children through someone else's eyes. Where a record is only concerned with a teacher's opinion about a child and his or her potential, it makes a certain amount of sense to want to see with fresh eyes, but a factual record of the child's achievement and the stage he or she has reached is important information for the next teacher and all members of staff need to work together to see that each of the records you are keeping is really likely to be useful to the next teacher.

There are many things you need to find out in advance if you are to make the most of your first days with a new class and you would be wise to do this, if possible, by the end of the previous term so that you can do some preparation for your new class. Review 2.1 suggests a number of things you might ask the previous teacher about the children who will be coming into your class. It is sensible to prepare by getting all the factual information you can from the previous teacher about the children you will be teaching. This is different from getting opinions, because you want to avoid biasing your views, although all assessment has an element of subjectivity. It will be

Review 2.1 Finding out about children who will be coming into your class

You need to talk with the children's previous teacher(s).

1 Ask for any factual information about work attempted and achieved.
2 Enquire about teaching approaches and materials used. Which seemed to be the most effective and showed the best results?
3 Were there any children who posed particular behaviour problems? What worked best with them?
4 Find out all you can about the particular problems of any children with special educational needs, what they can actually do and what they actually know and what seem to be the best ways of helping them.
5 Find out if there are any children of exceptional ability and ask what has been done to extend them and any particular interests or skills that they may have.
6 Ask if there are any children with particular problems, such as poor knowledge of English, or a background of serious illness.
7 If there are children from different racial backgrounds, ask about any problems they pose or difficulties they experience and what the previous teacher has done about them.

Review 2.2 Looking at records

Where children are coming into your class from another class within the school, or a feeder infant school, their records should be studied for factual information.

1 Look for evidence of general ability, especially standardised test results and SATs; note exceptionally high or low performance and any apparent discrepancies between ability and attainment.
2 See if any of the children have physical problems, such as poor sight, hearing or poor co-ordination and note any children who should wear glasses or hearing aids, and any with conditions such as asthma, diabetes or epilepsy which may need special care.
3 Note any children with other learning problems, including gaps in schooling, frequent changes of school, non-English-speaking background
4 Note any children with home problems likely to affect the child in school. and so on.

particularly helpful to find out the level each child has reached in the National Curriculum and, where relevant, how he or she has performed in the Standard Assessment Tasks (SATs). You also need to know such things as the books each child has read or is reading, the phonic knowledge each of the younger children possesses, the mathematical skills each has acquired and so on.

This information will give you some starting points when the children come to you next term and should enable you to plan some lessons for them. You are also bound to get some of the previous teacher's opinions about the children and you need to try not to let these influence you too much, so that you can form an independent opinion of each child when you get to know him or her.

If possible, visit the children you will be teaching in their own classroom the previous term, perhaps arranging this by asking their teacher to change classes with you for a short time (see Review 2.3). Use this opportunity to get a feel for the class as a group. How do they respond to questions? Are they quick with ideas and suggestions? Do they talk enthusiastically about what they have been doing?

This is only a broad preliminary to studying further all the children, but it alerts you to those who may most need study and those whose needs are likely to be different from those of the majority. It will also colour some of your overall planning and help you to remain sensitive to the fact that your class is composed of individuals. On the other hand, it is important not to let your initial summing up of children colour your expectations too much. The evidence suggests that when teachers are open about their expectations children can do very much better than when teachers' expectations are more limited. It is very easy to label children prematurely. They could turn out to be very different from your initial impression and you need to keep this well in mind.

Review 2.3 Classroom visit: things to find out

1 Identify children about whom it might be wise to know more.
2 Talk with the children about what they have been doing.
3 Look at the work of children who will be coming to you and make a special note of any who appear to be having difficulty or whose work appears to be outstanding.
4 Look at the general level of presentation of work and at what appears to be common practice.
5 Look for anything unusual, such as the child whose presentation of work is poor but whose ideas are good; unusual ideas, points of view or use of language; unusual but persistent errors.

Make a note of the children's ages

At this stage of planning it may be a good idea to look at children's ages. You need to be aware of the different ages of the children in your class and make some allowance or difference in provision for the younger ones. It is easy to see the younger children as less able, although in reality they are progressing as well as older children but are at an earlier stage of development. More recent research suggests that the youngest children in a class often do less well than their older peers, but over time, they can be seen to make above average progress when their age is taken into account. This is something you need to remember and it would be wise, before starting work with a new class, to look at their ages and make a mental note of age differences.

Note information about individual children

It may be helpful at this stage to start a loose-leaf ring file with a page for each child on which you can note things that happen which give you teaching information. In the first instance you will be noting points which have arisen as a result of your preliminary investigations. It is particularly important to do this for children who have special needs or are unusual in any way, whether exceptionally able or with particular kinds of problems or abilities. This may be the start of your record of these children.

If you teach a reception class you may have a more difficult task in getting to know the children who will be coming to you except where your school has a nursery class. Other nursery classes and playgroups will also be ready to pass on information about the children. Most schools with reception classes invite parents and children to visit the school on one or more occasions before they actually start and this may give you the opportunity to find out something about them, particularly if you get the chance to talk to the parents. If you can find out something about individual children's interests and their families you can at least start with some information which will help you to talk to new children and help them to feel at home.

Whichever age group you teach, your organisation for the first few days – and perhaps weeks – needs to be very flexible so that you can adapt to the children as you go along. The assessments you received from the previous teacher and those you make as you go along of language and literacy, mathematics, personal and social development, knowledge and understanding of the world, physical development and creative development will all be useful in planning teaching and also give you a reference point for assessing how far children have progressed by the end of the term and year.

Planning for your new class

Whatever the age group you teach you will be making plans before the new school year starts. Try to plan for the first week with diagnostic work in mind. Plan fairly broad topics with work at a variety of levels and some open-ended questions. Choose, where possible, areas in which all children are likely to have a reasonable opportunity for success but which still provide challenges at various levels. For example, a story which provides a variety of work may be a good idea. It is likely to interest the children if the level is right and does not require complicated plans for organising work at a time when you are only just getting to know the children.

If you have a chance to meet with your teaching assistant before term starts, use this opportunity to talk over the things that you will be looking for in the first days and weeks with the class and suggest things that she could observe for you.

This early work may give you some opportunities for finding out the children's interests and abilities in school work and possibly related activities out of school hours. If you were able to obtain good prior knowledge of the able children and those with problems, this should enable you to pitch the work at a reasonable variety of levels and it is at this stage that your class file becomes useful. Note relevant points as they arise but don't try to do too much at once.

Initial observation of children

During the first few days with a new class you will be observing things such as the way children settle down to work, their comments and replies to questions, their first piece of writing and so on. These clues will quickly identify any problems and you will be noting the kind of responses which particular work evokes from different individuals. If you have a class other than reception, you will have information about each child's prior achievement in the National Curriculum and this will enable you, if you wish, to group children for any particular work on an ability basis.

If you have a reception class, you will be noting the children who settle into school easily and those for whom it is a traumatic change from home. You will also be getting to know parents as they bring and collect their children and using the opportunities to learn from them about each child and the parent's view of how he or she is settling into school.

In the classroom you will be noting which children choose which activities and the level of interest and concentration shown by individuals. You will be getting information from the baseline assessments you will be making and this will guide you in selecting work for the children. The need for baseline assessment means that you must be systematic in finding out about every child, studying a small number each day and recording your findings carefully and using this information to plan work.

With an older group you will need to go on from your preliminary observations to check some of them. At an early stage you can check things such as ability to concentrate and whether a child is right- or left-handed. You will want to hear each child read, and you will probably find out a good deal from the errors each child makes. Collecting and noting errors in written work and looking for patterns in the kind of mistakes made is also useful.

Further observation and testing

If previous records do not tell you a great deal about children's prior achievement it may also be useful – at a fairly early stage but after you have started to get to know the children reasonably well – to undertake some testing. For example, group spelling tests designed to cover all the possible phonic variations may be helpful and will enable you to check phonic knowledge. Tests in mathematics can be designed to give you information about children's knowledge and skills. There is much to be said for devising your own diagnostic tests for a number of aspects of the National Curriculum, so that you can become aware of what a child needs to learn, although it is wise not to do too much testing. A group of teachers might well spend time together devising test material for different aspects of the National Curriculum. Testing needs to be backed up by observation of how children actually tackle tasks in a subject such as science.

Your observation of children may also lead you to check sight and hearing if you see a child peering to see or holding his or her head in a way which suggests he or she isn't hearing too well. A simple check on sight is to ask a child what he or she sees at a distance and what close to. You can check hearing by standing behind a child and asking him or her to repeat what you say. If you find a child who has difficulty with either of these two senses it should be reported and parents informed about the problem as soon as possible.

A useful part of this preliminary observation process is an opportunity, in the previous term, to meet the parents of the children who will be coming to you and get their views of, and their hopes for, their child. This may give you some idea of what motivates a particular child and help you to identify attitudes. It may also offer you an opportunity to enlist the parents' interest in what their child will be doing at school next term and also to enlist their support.

Matching work to children

The task from then on is one of matching work to individuals and small groups. This is not an easy task especially if you have a large class. It is very easy to underestimate the able children and overestimate the less able. You will find some help with this in a number of chapters in this book, but particularly in Chapter 19, Providing for individual needs.

Review 2.4 Looking back at the end of term on what has happened

1   What do I now know about my children that I didn't know at the beginning of term?
2   What do I feel has gone well and needs to be continued?
3   What am I less happy about and what should I do to improve this next term?
4   What do my children think about what has happened since they came into my class? What have they really enjoyed and what have they disliked? Have I asked them these questions?
5   Their previous teacher told me about some of the problems s/he found with these children, did I too find them to be problems?
6   What will be the important things to prepare for and do next term?

Chapter 3

The children

Education at school is about children learning. Children are different from one another and are likely to respond differently to different approaches and treatment. Any group of children, however homogeneous, is a collection of different and often very different, individuals. This is even more true in schools today than it was in the more distant past. A school may have children from a variety of cultures, speaking different languages and behaving in different ways from native British children. This development is making enormous demands on teachers.

Much has been said and written recently about personalised education and while it is not really possible or efficient for children to be taught individually for much of the time, you do need to give careful consideration to children as individuals. If, as a teacher, you are to help them all to learn, giving some consideration to individual needs, you must first find enough common strands to enable some work to take place in a group or as a class. It is then possible to get the majority started and use this as an opportunity to work with individuals. It may also be the case that some really able children have ideas of their own which they want to pursue and if you can fit in enough discussion with them about these ideas and how they want to investigate them and you are happy with what they are suggesting, this may offer a good opportunity to work with other individuals who need more help from you in other areas.

As the children grow older they can become increasingly aware of their own learning styles, particular interests and ideas they would like to develop. They will also gradually become more aware of their own learning needs with help from you and can then do more to seek out the ways of learning which suit them best.

Starting school

The differences among children are particularly evident at the beginning of schooling, whether this is in a playgroup, a nursery class or a reception class. They come to school with different ideas and interests and ways of looking at things and with differing experience. They also have to cope with the shock of leaving home and mother.

Cohen and Cohen (1988: 49) note that children starting at infant school for the first time have to adapt to the following:

- being part of a crowd of children, particularly in the playground;
- presence of fewer adults or unfamiliar adults at playtime and dinner time;
- organisational processes such as lining up, queuing or waiting;
- competition for adult attention – involves waiting and fewer opportunities for one-to-one conversation;
- being addressed as one of a group or class;
- restrictions on movement and noise;
- organisational constraints on time, the possibility of being last or left behind.

There may also be some children coming into a reception class who have not previously experienced leaving their home and mother and you need to be especially aware of them and try to gauge how they are feeling.

These aspects of school are less likely to cause problems now than formerly because of the greater pre-school provision than in the past, but as a reception class teacher you need to be very conscious of the kinds of experience which will be new to the children. This will be particularly important in the case of immigrant children who not only have the same problems of leaving home as the other children but also the language problem of not understanding what anyone is saying. They may be more or less managing by copying what others are doing. In their case, it will be wise to try to use the same words fairly frequently when telling children what to do, so that they gradually learn what they mean. It also helps both you and them if you can learn a few words of their language.

Children changing schools

If you teach Year 3 you may also have the problem of children coming from another infant school, who may need some help in settling in. If you normally have a considerable number from the same school it will be wise to set up a scheme for finding out what you want to know about these children. If it can be arranged it would be a good idea to visit the school and meet the children who will be coming to you. This will give you an opportunity to talk to their teacher and get some useful information about them and it will also help the children to know what you look like.

A very important consideration for teachers at all stages of primary education is the degree of experience that children bring to their learning. A child will only understand what you say if s/he can bring relevant experience to the interpretation of your words. In preparing for any new piece of work you need to start by thinking about the experience which children will bring to it and the experiences to which you will introduce them. It is very easy to overestimate the experience which children already have and to assume that because they use some particular words they have the experience which enables them to understand their meaning.

The process of organising children's learning so that curricular aims can be achieved involves bringing together the needs, ideas, interests, experiences and characteristics of the children with your own knowledge, skill, experience and preferred ways of working and those of your assistant within a given environment. It is therefore very important to consider what your children are like and how they learn.

Having an assistant is a considerable advantage in getting to know the children, in that there are two people talking with them and observing them. You will both see different things and discussing them will extend the knowledge you both have.

Child development

Teachers of children at the primary stage of education are usually very conscious of the children's development, partly because development at this stage is so rapid and partly because in the past a good deal of emphasis has been placed on child development in initial teacher training. This will be particularly important in the case of immigrant children, who may have no English and whose parents are also non-English-speaking. It may be that a social worker or someone else from the local authority may have some information about their background, but where there is none, you will just have to 'play it by ear'.

The importance of this knowledge for the teacher lies in the decisions which have to be made about suitable times and methods for enabling particular children to learn particular things.

There will also be differences in the amount and kind of English language skills a child may have and you will gradually discover this as you work with them; there will need to be many opportunities for children to talk together and also many opportunities for you to talk with them as individuals. Some children will start school with a wide vocabulary and well able to express themselves clearly. Others may have a more limited ability and many schools nowadays have some British-born children of immigrant parents who may still start school with very little knowledge of spoken English.

Boys and girls

There is now a great deal of information about the differences between boys and girls. Boys tend to be behind girls in development all the way through the primary school and they also tend to get more attention from the teacher, possibly because they are more demanding.

Professor Gerard (2005), from New York University, used international data to show that boys fail to match girls' achievements regardless of how they are taught or the schemes used to close the attainment gap. Girls are better at reading in all the countries that are members of the Organisation for Economic Cooperation and Development. He also found that the number of single-sex schools in a country had nothing to do with the size of the gap. He says that from 1975 onwards the gap was one of about 2% and this figure remained relatively static until 1988/9 when GCSEs were introduced in Britain. At this point the gap widened to about 10% and has remained fairly static ever since.

The gap may also have something to do with boys' ideas of masculinity. Another researcher, Ann Phoenix, said 'We found that 11–14 year olds believed you could not be masculine and be seen to be working hard in school'.

There are also differences in developmental level, which mean that boys are behind the girls in language work in particular, although they usually do well in mathematics and any technical subjects. Boys tend to be at the extremes of the ability range more often than girls and there are usually more boys than girls with special needs. Docking (1990) in a study of junior school children found that gender was significantly related to the length and quality of children's writing in the first year of the junior school with girls outperforming boys, and this initial superiority was maintained throughout the junior years.

Mortimore *et al.* (1988) found that girls had a more positive attitude to school than boys and more positive self-concepts. Far more boys than girls were rated by their teachers as having behaviour problems. Docking (1990) also found that, in each year of the junior school, boys expressed a much less positive view of school than girls and boys were much less likely than girls to rate themselves highly on items concerning personal anxiety.

Some researchers have found that when young children were playing both boys and girls tend to play as would be expected for their gender, but when they felt that they were not being observed, they played happily with cross-gender toys – the boys with dolls and dishes and the girls with trucks and aeroplanes, but when someone started to watch them they reverted to 'gender-appropriate' toys.

It has also been noted that teachers often have stereotypical views about gender which tend to affect the way they treat children. They may tend to encourage the behaviour they believe exists, for example by complimenting boys on their strength but not complimenting the girls on anything.

Some writers argue that schooling has tended to become feminised, especially at the primary stage where a large majority of teachers are women. This feeling may be influencing the materials chosen and the behaviour rewarded and encouraged.

Most teachers have encountered the child who initially has some difficulty in tying shoelaces or forming letters who, six months later, performs these tasks easily. The problem is that in any given class there will be children at a variety of stages of maturity, varying abilities and varying language use. Somehow the teacher has to see that they all learn. This isn't easy!

A child comes into the world with a legacy of inherited abilities, tendencies and characteristics. Throughout the early years each child is developing as an individual person and this continues when s/he starts school. Home and school environment interact with the child's inherited abilities and tendencies and s/he discovers personal talents and abilities, interests and limitations. The adults and children around provide models and a child will test out behaviour in play and in everyday living, persisting with some kinds of behaviour and modifying or abandoning others in the light of the responses which come, either from the teacher or assistant or from another child.

Children have also developed ideas about the world by the time they start school and these will be continually modified by their experience in and out of school. In science in particular, the ideas children have developed may be a barrier to observation and reasoning. Young children often cling to their own ideas in science even when experience shows them to be incorrect. In a similar way the mathematical knowledge which most children have on entry to school, while useful as a starting point, sometimes creates problems because children do not relate their existing knowledge to the language of school mathematics. It is therefore important for you as a teacher to become as aware as you can of children's ideas as a starting point for new learning. This makes discussion with them at an early stage very important, giving you a picture of their ideas and enabling you to direct their observation and thinking in ways which will help them to develop these ideas further.

Physical development

A child's physical attributes will have an effect on his or her emerging personality. A child who develops early will be at an advantage in being able to do things which others find difficult and will become more confident as a result.

This is particularly relevant in relation to the time of year when a child was born and the point at which he or she starts school. A child born in September may well be physically among the most developed in the class because s/he will be among the oldest. A child born in June, July or August is likely to be less well developed because s/he is among the youngest. We saw in the previous chapter that there is some evidence that teachers may attribute differences in children's performance to differences in ability, when the differences may simply reflect a difference in the stage of development. It is important to continue to bear in mind the age differences of the children in your class and make appropriate allowances for them.

Teacher expectation is known to be important in motivating children, and, if children begin to think of themselves as less able, this is likely to affect the effort they put into their work and this in turn will affect their performance. In any case children who start school in the summer term have less time in the infant school than those who start in the autumn, and it is important that their developmental stage is taken into account.

Sight and hearing

Some particular aspects of physical development have a good many implications for teachers. Sight and hearing are not fully co-ordinated when a child starts school, and co-ordination may pose problems which will later solve themselves. It is also important for teachers of young children to be on the lookout for defects not yet noticed. For example, a child may have very short or very long sight but will not realise that this is different from the norm until he or she makes comparisons with what someone else sees. Much the same is true of hearing. Colour blindness is also comparatively common in the population and most teachers will encounter a colour-blind child at some time in their career. Children who have difficulty in distinguishing colours will have a number of problems in the classroom and the sooner this is recognised the better.

Self-awareness

The DfES paper *Excellence and Enjoyment: Conditions for Learning* (2004) suggests that 'self-awareness refers to the capacity we have to understand our own thoughts and emotions – what we think and why we do things'. This can help children make sense of what they think and feel and develop the ability to manage, organise and direct their thinking, feeling and learning and support their achievement and attainment. As they grow older it can lead to the ability to plan their learning, thinking ahead about what they might need and anticipating obstacles. Young children tend to be very emotional and this can often affect both their learning and their relationship with you and with other children. You need to spend time talking with them about how they react to different people and different situations.

Intellectual development

Inhelder and Piaget (1958) describe the child's cognitive development as involving a number of stages which all children pass through at their own pace. The very young child, up to about two years of age, is in what they call the sensorimotor stage, when he or she is learning to co-ordinate movement and is discovering the world around. Children then enter the pre-operational stage, which lasts until about seven years in most children.

They are becoming more social but still tend to see the world as revolving around themselves. From about seven years of age children enter a stage of concrete operations when they begin to see the world more logically but still need to see or do things to understand them.

Finally, often by the age of about eleven, but sometimes much later, children reach a stage of formal and abstract operations when they can reason and think systematically. They may regress to earlier stages in the face of some situations and problems. Although Inhelder and Piaget wrote about this fifty years ago it still holds true today.

Piaget (1952) also suggested that intellectual behaviour was always involved in each person's adaptation to his or her environment. In the process of adapting, the individual uses two processes, *assimilation* and *accommodation*. In assimilating new information the child first takes it in and then tries to relate what s/he perceives to existing knowledge and understanding, which is accommodation. This may mean making adjustments to how s/he thinks about his or her existing knowledge or adjusting the new knowledge to fit with what s/he knows already. Once again an old study remains true and useful after more than half a century.

Gardner (1983) suggests that human beings have a number of different kinds of intelligence. These include linguistic, musical, logical-mathematical and scientific, bodily-kinaesthetic, which includes art, and personal intelligence or ability to get on with other people. In planning the programme for children, you need to be aware of the possibility that individuals may have different types of intelligence and allow opportunities for these to develop.

As you gradually get to know your children you will begin to see that they learn in quite different ways from one another. Some children are visualizers, who learn best by looking and will also learn from touching and handling things. They like to make pictures in their minds from what they have seen and touched. Learning will often be helped by discussion, talking about something with someone else helps to fix it in your mind. Some of them will learn best from listening both to you and to other children, watching one another and imitating each other. All children learn by doing. It may be particularly true in the case of immigrant children who may find it easier to learn by doing things because this is less affected by language barriers.

It is also important to remember that children have different learning styles. Cullingford (1995) notes that 'recognising that fact and diagnosing the style of each pupil is at the heart of true assessment and individual help'.

Emotional development

Emotional responses are a primitive response to danger and are controlled by a different part of the brain from that which controls rational thinking. Human beings respond emotionally more quickly than they respond intellectually, and children have to learn to control their emotional responses and teachers need to help them with this. This is particularly true of the youngest children who respond emotionally to a situation before thinking about it.

Goleman (1996: 34) makes the point that emotional intelligence probably plays a larger part in how we do in life than intelligence quotient (IQ). He suggests that 'At best, IQ contributes about 20 per cent to the factors which determine life success, which leaves 80 per cent for other forces'. Other characteristics are also important:

> Abilities such as being able to motivate oneself and persist in the face of frustration, control impulse and delay gratification; to regulate one's moods and keep distress from hampering the ability to think; to emphasise and to hope.

He notes that:

> Much evidence testifies that people who are emotionally adept – and who know and manage their own feelings – are at an advantage in any domain of life, whether romance and intimate relationships or picking up the unspoken rules that govern success in organisational politics.
> (Goleman 1996: 36)

Goleman (1996: 43) also suggests the following aspects of emotional intelligence:

- knowing one's own emotions – self-awareness – recognising a feeling *as it happens*;
- managing emotion;
- motivating oneself; emotional self-control; marshalling emotions in the service of a goal;
- recognising emotions in others
- handling relationships.

Recognising emotions in others involves interpreting body language. We all use a good deal of non-verbal communication. It is something we tend to do instinctively and subconsciously but not everyone is equally competent at reading this language; it is therefore a good idea to talk about it with children from time to time. This will be something which on the one hand can be very useful to immigrant children in that they will probably learn to respond to body language more quickly than spoken language, but they will also have their own vocabulary of body language which may be quite different from ours and they are likely to be very puzzled by our lack of understanding of it.

If you are to help children to develop emotional control and under-standing, you need to find time to discuss feelings with them on a number of occasions as they grow older. Such a discussion could start with children thinking of an occasion when they felt happy or sad and you can go on to discuss situations when children felt angry. Anger can be an overwhelming feeling, particularly for young children, and many want to hit out at someone when they feel angry. It helps to discuss possible alternative ways of behaving by asking children to try to remember a situation when they felt angry and then to think about what they did about it and what happened at the time, asking themselves if there might have been a better way of dealing with their anger. It may be a good idea to ask them in pairs to discuss possible good ways to cope when you feel angry and then go on to discuss this further as a class. Aim, if possible, to establish some ideas about dealing with personal anger, both in yourself and with anger in others. This discussion could be useful to recall when you have to deal with issues like bullying and aggression.

Empathy

Children need to develop the ability to empathise with others, trying to understand their points of view and how they are feeling. *Excellence and Enjoyment* (DfES 2004: 50) suggests that:

> Being able to empathise involves understanding others, anticipating and predicting their likely thoughts, feelings and perceptions. It involves seeing things from another's point of view and modifying one's own response, if appropriate, in the light of this understanding.

You need to build a relationship with all your children, by being empathetic and showing that you really care about them. You need to be a good listener and learn as much as you can about them so that you know them as individuals.

Children who not only manage their own emotions but also are sensitive to the feelings of others tend to make better relationships with their peer group and are more popular. Children need help with recognising the ways others are feeling and you can help this by discussing with them the ways in which people show their feelings. It can be useful to refer to empathy when discussing body language with children, helping them to understand ways of knowing how someone is feeling from the way s/he stands and moves.

They may also need help in developing social skills and learning the non-verbal language of social behaviour. You can discuss how best to get involved in a game you want to join, how to deal with someone who is angry with you or is rude to you. Discussion of bullying can be part of this.

Many schools use *circle time* as a means of involving children in discussion of these kinds of issues. This is a discussion period where the teacher asks open-ended questions to get the children to talk about matters which are important to them. This is all part of personal and social education.

Review 3.1 Children's development

1   How conscious am I of differences in children's ages? Do I sometimes assess a child as not being very intelligent when s/he is just younger than many of the class?
2   Have I any children with sight or hearing problems? How can I best help them?
3   Have I any immigrant children in my class who do not speak English? What can I best do to help?
4   What kinds of intelligence do my children show? Reasoning ability? Language ability? Ability in art or music? Social skills?
5   What evidence is there among my children of emotional development? Do some children become angry or impatient easily? How well do they get on with others?
7   Am I making enough opportunities to discuss feelings and how to manage them? Can my children recognise the feelings of others?
8   How well do my children read body language? How aware are they of the way people express themselves through movement?

The development of the self-image

Docking (1990: 7) describes the self-concept or self-image as follows:

> The self-concept is the picture of ourselves which we carry around and it incorporates all those things which are important to us – relative and friend relationships, status, material possessions, other skills and hobbies. It is learned in detail as we grow up and glean information from what others do or say to us … The self-concept is learned … It is vital that early experiences are predominantly positive and that children can come to see themselves as accepted, loved and successful.

The behaviour and response of other people towards a child help to develop his or her self-image. Initially parents start this process. A child whose parents praise and encourage him or her becomes confident in the ability to do things and is more likely to become a confident and competent adult than the child whose parents behave in a more negative way for much of the time.

The positive and negative effects of praise

When the child starts school, teachers continue this process and at the primary stage much is happening that is important for the development of the self-image. The extent to which a child is praised or scolded or is acknowledged to achieve success or failure influences his or her attitudes and behaviour. All of us react positively to praise when we know it is genuine and deserved, and activities in which other people tell us we have succeeded are those most likely to be repeated. Conversely, failure tends to make us want to avoid the activity in which we have failed. In this sense the teacher may reinforce some kinds of learning and also act negatively by identifying the behaviour to be eliminated.

This is an idea which you should share with your assistant, who will also have opportunities to praise and encourage children.

Askew and Wiliam (1995: 18) suggest that what is important for praise to be effective is that it is:

- *Contingent* the praise must depend upon some particular thing the pupil has done, rather than the pupil's general performance;
- *Specific* the praise should identify the specific behaviour being praised, so that the pupil is aware of what aspect of his or her work is being singled out for praise;
- *Credible* the praise must be sincere; praise that follows a formula (that is, it is always expressed in the same way) or which sounds insincere is likely to be ineffective because pupils can 'see through' such praise very quickly.

Your task, as teacher, is to find things that you can genuinely praise for each of your children. You may not be able to praise a child's work, but you may be able to praise his behaviour or the effort s/he has made, or the way s/he has helped about the classroom. It is important to look out for such occasions if you are to help all the children to develop self-esteem, which is important for learning. On the other hand, false praise, given when not deserved, has a negative effect. Askew and Wiliam (1995: 28) go on to say:

If [pupils] have confidence in their ability they will expect to be successful often and, in order to gain more positive confirmation of their ability, they will seek challenges and show persistence in the face of difficulties ... However, if they lack confidence in their ability, they will try to avoid challenges and show little persistence because they believe they are likely to fail and be 'shown up'.

Barnes (1999: 10) suggests that:

If children have low academic self-esteem, the chances are that instead of involving themselves in tasks, they already rely on other strategies to feel important ... The pay off for them is probably to be stopped and for attention and peer approval to be directed their way.

There is also evidence that teachers reinforce some children more effectively than others. Kelly (1988), for example, in a study which reviewed research into gender differences, found considerable evidence that girls got less of the teacher's attention in class than boys, and this would seem to be true for all ages, ethnic groups and social classes in all subjects and for male and female teachers.

The building of self-esteem and confidence

It is very easy to think that well-behaved children have a higher academic potential than those who were less well-behaved. Research has found that there is a tendency for children for whom the teacher has high expectations to have more praise and contact with the teacher than low achievers, who received less praise and less feedback on their work, although they have more need of it. It is also very easy to be more critical of boys than of girls, and this could be one of the reasons why boys today do less well than girls in many areas of the curriculum.

Children also praise and criticise one another and this too contributes to their learning. They are building up pictures of themselves being good at this and bad at that, able to get on well with other people or having problems in making relationships and so on. By the time they leave primary school they are already confident in their ability to do some things and worried about their performance in others.

Children's self-images are also revealed in the way they relate to others. A child with a poor self-image tends to expect others to respond negatively and will often contribute to this reaction by his or her behaviour.

Parsons et al. (1976) found that girls tended to assess their abilities as being lower than they were in actuality. Girls were also more worried about failure and more sensitive to negative information than boys and this was evident from the age of about four. This may have changed in more recent times, as more women now work outside the home and receive more encouragement to fulfil their potential. This could be leading to a situation where girls may have a more positive self-image and boys perhaps a less confident one.

The development of the self-image is closely related to the effect of the expectation of others for the progress of a particular child. If the child's parents or teacher demonstrate that they have high expectations of him or her, there is more likelihood that the child will achieve and vice versa. This can work for the child if the adults show that they have high expectations which the child then fulfils and is thus reinforced by success and starts the next task with increased confidence. There is also the complementary problem that parents and teachers can pressure children with their expectations to the extent that children eventually give up trying because they do not think they can live up to such expectations. It is also the case that where parents or contemporaries tell a child that s/he is no good, the child will have correspondingly low self-image and will probably feel that it is not worth trying.

Building a negative cycle and self-image

The expectations of others can also give rise to an increasingly negative cycle in which the child fails, the teacher lowers expectation and the child's self-image is lowered correspondingly. Your professional task as teacher is to get the level of expectation high enough to challenge and encourage and yet be within each child's capacity.

Failure on a child's part may tend to be seen as the fault of the child and sometimes it is. But it can be more productive when confronted with failure to ask yourself, Where did I go wrong? If John didn't grasp the work when we were dealing with this, what might I have done differently? Of course it may be John's fault and often is, but it may have been the communicative process. What may have been needed in this situation is a more effective structuring of what is to be learned.

'Structure' implies a careful ordering of what is to be learned which matches the needs of individuals and groups of children. This also implies a good knowledge of children's learning styles.

There is a good deal of research evidence to suggest that teachers underestimate some children within the class and overestimate others. Teachers may tend to overestimate the boys compared with the girls. Bennett *et al.* (1984) describe work in infant classrooms in which the researchers checked how well the work that individual children were given matched their ability. They found that there was a tendency for teachers to underestimate high attainers. Twenty-five per cent of tasks given to the children were misdiagnosed. At the same time teachers tended to overestimate some low attainers. Teachers in other studies have been found to underestimate black children and those from working-class backgrounds.

The development of the self-image is also closely bound up with the physical, social and emotional development of the child. Part of the self-image will concern the child's physical appearance, and this may affect confidence and social development and the way in which the child learns to cope with personal feelings and reactions. There is some evidence that girls, in particular, are starting to become anorexic at the primary school stage. You need to be very sensitive to this and try to help individuals to cope with the way others treat them and at the same time encourage children to be sensitive to each other.

Some people now feel that schools are a bit biased to the feminine, which contrasts oddly with the research findings that boys get more attention than girls. On the other hand, one could argue that as girls now tend to outperform boys one can conclude that the way things are run in a school or class must be suiting girls better than boys. It is an area which needs more research.

> **Review 3.2 The development of the self-image in children**
>
> 1 Are there any children in my class who have a poor self-image and low self-esteem? Can I see any reason for this situation?
> 2 What am I doing to change this situation?
> 3 Do I look for opportunities to praise and encourage children whenever I can?
> 4 Do I pay more attention to boys than to girls? Am I more likely to over-estimate boys than girls?
> 5 Do I treat all children equally, irrespective of gender or skin colour or race or social background?

Children also develop ideas about other people. Carrington and Short (1989) describe how almost half the infants in a council estate primary school thought that it was possible for people to change colour and that black parents did not necessarily have black children and vice versa. At the very early stages very few children saw any racial problms, but from Year 4 in the junior school almost all children saw being black as a problem. Year 6 children in particular were aware of racial stereotyping.

Language development

Language development is one of the most important areas of work for the teacher and is rightly regarded as the cornerstone of each child's education. The ability to use language determines not only the nature of a person's relationships with others and the ability to co-operate but also, to some extent, the ability to think because language is the medium of a good deal of human thought. Initially children do much of their thinking out loud and this conversation with themselves gradually becomes inner speech.

Language is also the main medium by which children learn. Edwards and Mercer (1987: 164) describe the way in which teachers have to work to achieve common understanding in the language used in the classroom. They stress the importance of classroom talk as a means of learning and suggest that what is needed is 'sharing, comparing, contrasting and arguing perspectives against those of others'. They also stress the need for children to reflect on what is being learned.

The development of language skills is far from being a simple matter. A child starting school at five has often already made tremendous progress in language development. Most children, by this age, have a vocabulary of more than 2,000 words, but, more importantly, they have acquired some knowledge of the structure of the language as it is used in their home environment. They can usually form sentences which they have never heard spoken; they can speak of the past and the future as well as the present; they know the meanings which lie behind word order, that 'man bites dog' has a different meaning from 'dog bites man', which is conveyed by the way the words are put together. They have learned the language necessary to express needs, ideas and thoughts, to ask questions, to seek co-operation from others as well as many other things. Even where the language used at home is far from standard English, it will have a structure and consistency of its own and the child will have learned to apply its rules. This is equally true for children with a different home language. It seems likely that the increased opportunities for pre-school experience which is now becoming available will have a positive effect on children's language development in the future.

The intellectual achievement this represents is very considerable. No one intentionally teaches pre-school children the rules of language, and pre-school children do not know them as something to repeat but as something to apply. The acquisition of this knowledge requires reasoning power of a high order and it is interesting that one can sometimes see the process at work in the mistakes a child makes. The child who says 'mouses' instead of 'mice' or 'runned' instead of 'ran', for example, is demonstrating an ability to apply the rule correctly, but hasn't appreciated that there are exceptions.

We can conclude from this that children are capable of particular kinds of reasoning and abstraction from quite an early age if these are in context. We might go further and note that not only is there evidence of the motivation to communicate, but also that many children appear to enjoy the challenge involved. It suggests that, if we can find ways of tapping motivation of this strength, the power for learning in children is far greater than we normally see in school. It also supports the view that learning is likely to be better when children are asked to reason something through rather than just to remember or repeat it.

This learning and reasoning is all related in the first instance to particular situations. Children start acquiring vocabulary and language structure in particular contexts. By the time they are five, most of them are already using language to refer to and discuss what is not present, and they have acquired and used the language initially in particular situations and generalised from these.

Tizard and Hughes (1984) studied a group of pre-school girls from working-class and middle-class homes and found that mothers in virtually all cases talked to children of people and situations which were not present.

The fact that children acquire language in particular situations has important implications for later learning. Young children may frequently use the same words as an adult, but give them a more limited meaning. For example, the child for whom the word 'holiday' means an air journey to foreign parts will interpret the word differently from a child whose family spends holidays at home, perhaps going out for day trips. The child who lives on a remote farm has a different understanding of the word 'neighbour' from the child who lives in a block of flats or in a terrace or a council estate.

Even a teacher of older children should never assume that because a child uses particular words he or she gives them a similar meaning to that given by the teacher. Language is a way of representing the world to yourself and of talking about it to other people. Children start by talking about what is present, then develop the ability to talk about what is not present and the words gradually become the 'inner speech' of their thoughts. It seems likely that young children need to think aloud a good deal in the process of developing the ability to think silently in their minds.

Children who, in their early years, learn a different language from English, which follows different rules, will, when they start trying to learn English, probably try to apply the rules of their home language to it. It may therefore take them some time to learn that the rules of English are different. They will be discovering this in a similar way to the way they discovered the rules of their home language and as time goes on will probably be talking to themselves in a mixture of languages.

When teachers talk of extending children's language they normally think first about adding to vocabulary. There is also a case for emphasising language structure and considering those words which help to organise thinking. Prepositions, for example, represent relationships among objects or people. Comparative words are also important in representing similarities and differences in relationships, and a variety of pronouns, conjunctions and other words relate the parts of what we say and enable us to express increasingly complex ideas and relationships. Discussion about the structure of language is an important part of the literacy strategy.

Words also provide a convenient way of sorting out thinking into categories; much as in learning mathematics, children learn to sort things into sets according to their attributes. Words such as 'good', 'kind' and 'naughty' are sorting words which are learned early, but the process goes on right through schooling and we expect children to be able to classify in many areas of work. For example, in geography, we classify soil characteristics, landscape types and suchlike; in science we classify plants, animals, substances, forces, and so on; there are many other ways in which this process occurs in most aspects of the curriculum. It is the basis of the ability to generalise and to reason from one premise to the next and thus to be able to apply what is known to new situations.

The importance of spoken language

In past years so much emphasis has been placed on writing and reading in primary schools that spoken language has tended to take a second place. We are now realising how important it is that children should learn to express themselves well in speech. They need to be clear in enunciation, lucid in expressing ideas and opinions and be able to draw on a fairly wide vocabulary. Social background still has a strong influence on any child's speech, particularly at the primary stage of education, but as teacher, you still need to help children to speak with reasonable grammar and sense. Children's speech obviously depends upon the area in which they are being brought up and you need to be very sensitive in suggesting any different ways of saying things. One way into this might be in drama where you can set up situations in which children have to talk like someone from a different background.

As children move up through the school, it will be a good idea to introduce different situations which each demand appropriate language use. For example, the children might be asked to present a case for making school voluntary on some days, or for learning typing. On another occasion you might suggest that they try to formulate some new school rules. It may be an idea to introduce debates, with different children presenting the case for and against a chosen motion. Another idea is to ask children to prepare to explain something to the class and then choose one or two to do this.

In the course of this exercise you may also find group work and discussion useful.

Review 3.3 Using spoken language

1   What is the speech of my children actually like? Is there a strong local accent? Have I any children who are not able to speak clearly enough to be fully understood by others?

2   What opportunities for spoken language am I providing? Are these sufficient to enable children to develop their spoken language skills?

3   Are there particular elements in my children's spoken language that I want to change? How can I do this without implying that their current language skill is inadequate?

4   Am I using group work to provide opportunities for discussion? How effective is it?

Chapter 4

Developing the role of assistants

Most teachers now have a certain amount of support in the classroom, usually from paid classroom assistants and sometimes from volunteer parents. There may also be learning support assistants employed to help particular children with special educational needs. It is very important that these valuable resources are fully used.

School workforce development

A three-year strategy was instigated in 2006 which aimed to achieve a sustainable increase in workforce skills over the period. The strategy had three objectives:

- to support schools as they develop new ways of training and deploying their support staff;
- to develop a framework of standards and qualifications to enable schools to develop the potential of all support staff; and
- to extend training opportunities to meet the development needs of all support staff.

Teaching assistants

Teaching assistants work alongside teachers in the classroom, helping children with their learning in various ways agreed with the class teacher. Teaching assistants now have good access to training for their role and some have specialist areas in the curriculum. They work as a team in partnership with the class teacher, who does the overall planning but takes into account the particular skills the assistant has to offer.

Higher level teaching assistants

These are experienced assistants who have undertaken further training and achieved certain standards, which can be grouped under the following headings.

1   *Professional values and practice*   They have high expectations of pupils and respect their background and are committed to raising their achievement. They work well with them and are concerned with their development as learners.
2   *Knowledge and understanding*   They support, motivate and challenge pupils who are underachieving and help them overcome any barriers to learning.
3   *Teaching and learning activities*   They undertake teaching and supervision roles under the guidance of the class teacher.

The role of the classroom teacher in supporting an assistant

The advent of teaching assistants and learning support assistants should now be making a considerable difference to the role of the teacher. It will, of course, involve you in spending a good deal of time with a new assistant when she starts working with you, getting to know her and the particular skills she has to offer. She will be able to work with individual children and small groups perhaps teaching them something you have agreed with her or reinforcing the teaching you have provided for the class. She should also be able to deal with many of the minor requests which can come your way and help in keeping the materials used in the classroom in good order. She will also help children in many ways perhaps explaining work to a child who hasn't understood the work you have been doing with the class or reinforcing your teaching with individuals or groups when this seems to be needed.

All assistants, and any volunteers, will need to be briefed fully on the tasks they will be asked to undertake. Ideally they should be trained in tasks such as hearing reading, overseeing children involved in practical activities, extending the learning involved in play activities with very young children and so on. You will need to find out when an assistant first joins you, whether she has had any training for the job or plans to undertake some. There may be specific areas in which you can help in training her for specific aspects of the work she will be doing in your class.

Getting to know your assistant

When an assistant is first appointed you need to get to know each other and discover how you can best work together for the benefit of the children. You need to work as a team if you can.

In getting to know your assistant you will discover the skills and ideas she brings to the job. She may have good organisational skills, be a typist, or

> **Review 4.1 Working with a teaching assistant**
>
> 1 What skills, knowledge and experience does my assistant bring to her role?
> 2 What information will she need to be able to do the job?
> 3 What sorts of things can I ask her to do?
> 4 What training has she had in primary school practice?
> 5 What will she have to learn in order to do the job in my particular class?
> 6 How can I best help her to learn about the children?

have a lot of experience with children from bringing up her own family. The tasks you ask her to undertake will depend to some extent on the particular skills she brings to the job but they will almost certainly include some or all of those described below.

Supporting the children

One of the many advantages of having an assistant is that she will be able to provide additional support for the children, and in this way support your work. In order to provide this support she must first get to know them as individuals and establish good relationships with them so that she can help them with the tasks you have set. As she gets to know them well she will begin to recognise those who have difficulty with particular kinds of work and will be able to discuss with you the best way to help them. You may perhaps want her to hear children read, when you have had the chance to discuss this with her. You may need to help her with this in the first place, if she hasn't had any prior training, explaining the best way to correct mistakes and suggesting ways in which she can help when a child cannot read a particular word. This will all take time as she learns good ways of working with you.

Looking after equipment and materials

Your assistant can also be a real help to you in preparing, caring for and managing equipment and materials. Primary schools use a lot of different kinds of materials and equipment. There may be games designed to teach particular skills. There may be equipment to help in the teaching of reading and mathematics and perhaps other subjects. Technology may require quite a lot of preparation of materials and there will be many other areas where equipment is required.

Your assistant could also be responsible for ensuring that materials wanted for lessons are ready when the lesson starts and for helping children to use them well. It will be particularly helpful if she is knowledgeable about computers and able to help the children use them. Development in the use of ICT is going on all the time and computers grow increasingly important for all aspects of the curriculum as time goes on. You need to encourage your assistant to learn all she can about their use in the classroom.

Preparing classroom displays

Primary schools also use displays a good deal. These may be displays of children's work or displays to support a particular lesson or group of lessons. You may need to show your assistant how to mount work or other material for display and put it up, explaining how you want this done and where you want it displayed.

Providing you with information about the children

As she works with the children she will learn things about them which may be new to you, which you will find useful in planning work. She should be able to give you additional information about their reaction to particular lessons and the things that some children found difficult. You could encourage her to look out for particular things that you would like to know, such as whether certain children understood what you had told them in the course of a lesson.

Other areas of learning for assistants

You need to discuss work in the classroom regularly with your assistant and you will often be planning together. It is a good idea, if it can be fitted in, to meet for ten minutes or so at the beginning of each day to discuss what you plan to do. Similarly there is value in a brief meeting at the end of the school day to discuss how things went and what you want to do tomorrow. If you can't manage this, perhaps because one or both of you has children to collect, you could arrange a similar meeting in the lunch hour.

In doing all this you will each learn a great deal about how the other works and this provides an opportunity for a real partnership to develop. Your assistant will be learning from you all the time and the more you can find time to discuss work with her, the faster she will learn. You will also be learning from her – about individual children and what the children generally thought about particular work.

Observation of children

As a teacher you will be well aware of the need to observe children and this is a skill which your assistant, too, needs to cultivate.

Your assistant needs to observe children carefully and frequently if she is to discover what they are like as people and as learners and be able to help in linking the teaching and learning programme to their needs. Much of the observation a teacher does is automatic and you will need to give thought as to how you can help your assistant to become a capable observer, able to relate what she observes to children's learning needs. You will almost automatically note how children are reacting to the work you are asking them to do and use your knowledge of body language in observing which children are attending and which children are day-dreaming. You need to share this information with your assistant and discuss what she has seen. Encourage her to note how children are succeeding or not succeeding with the task in hand and let you know about it. She may find it helpful to observe a small number of children in some detail each day or week, perhaps following this up with a discussion with you about each child. There are always problems about fitting this into a busy day but it is well worth while. Her feedback will also be useful in helping you to match work to individual needs.

It is your responsibility to organise the learning programme but you need to share your plans with your assistant and in planning think about what her contribution will be. Sometimes this will involve a published scheme, a book or a radio or television programme or a computer program or the material you have provided or presented. If your assistant takes on the job of managing some of these resources, this should make using them easier for you both. With the advent of interactive white-boards ICT will now be an important part of the material for class teaching as well as for individual learning. Children as they grow older will need to learn how to use the internet to find things out. It will be a considerable help if your assistant is computer literate and able to help children with this.

Your assistant can help to make you aware of what you actually do in class, which children you praise and encourage, and this will give you useful information about the way you are actually using these processes. It is very easy to think that you do more encouraging than you actually do and particularly easy to encourage the able and offer little to the least able and the quiet child. It is helpful occasionally if she can check the number of encouraging comments you make in the course of a morning and note the children to whom they were addressed. It is also useful to go through the register occasionally, noting when you last said something encouraging to each child. Your assistant can also learn herself from this, noting the praise and encouraging comments you offer to individual children and the children to whom you offer them and looking at her own behaviour towards children. Suggestions for this kind of support and personal help are made in many of the chapters in this book.

Organising a learning environment

A learning environment might be described as one which is functional with regard to children's learning. We saw earlier in this chapter that this is an area where your assistant could be of considerable value in looking after materials and equipment, seeing that the environment is functional and helping the children not only to find what they want when they want it, but also to return things to the right places after use. A learning environment involves creating:

- an arrangement of furniture that provides the optimum conditions for the work to be done;
- a layout of materials that shows clearly what is available, is arranged and marked to show function, level of difficulty or progression and can be used by children without difficulty and without a great deal of attention from the teacher;
- an organisation in which it is easy to keep materials and equipment clean, tidy and in order and easy to check over to see that everything is in the right place;
- a discriminating use of display which provides standards to aim for, demonstrating what the teacher wants from children, and offers encouragement to those who need it most (the display of less good work from time to time to encourage an individual child as well as display of exemplary work); it should also provide materials of all kinds which interest, stimulate and extend knowledge and thinking.

Assessing and recording children's progress and development

Teachers have always been concerned to assess how well their children are doing so that they can decide what to teach them next. The National Curriculum has made this much more important because assessment is now formally required in primary schools. The task of assessment should inform the work selected for individuals and groups. When you and your assistant have got to know each other well and your assistant has got to know the children, she should have a good deal of information to offer you about children's learning and progress.

The importance of reflection

At all stages in teaching, reflection is an important skill to use. It is valuable to you both, if you and your assistant can find time during the day to reflect together on what has happened.

As your assistant settles into the job and observes you at work, she will not only learn from you but she too will have useful comments about what you do and the children's reactions. She could be particularly helpful if you want to find out something such as the number of children in a particular lesson who are not listening or the questions you ask in class and which children you choose to answer them.

The knowledge an assistant needs

Your assistant may start work with you without the kind of prior knowledge of schools and children that was part of your own teacher training. When she first joins you, there will be a lot of questions you need to ask about whether she has had any particular training for the job and if she has, what did she learn from it. If she has not yet had any training you will need to find out what other experience she can bring which will be useful. She may have a good deal of other useful knowledge. She may be a mother. She may have other skills from former employment. During her first weeks in the job an untrained assistant will be on a fairly steep learning curve and you will have an important training role. You will also need to encourage her to seek further training as soon as possible.

The most important piece of learning for a new teaching assistant whether trained or untrained is that of getting to know the children. While you will have lots of information about them yourself and will do all you can to help her in the process of learning about them, she may provide a fresh view for you which may be useful. Coming with a fresh eye, she may see things about them that you have missed, and you need to take advantage of this.

She will also need opportunities to learn about the National Curriculum, the school schemes of work as they apply to your class, your plans for work in different subjects, appropriate ways of helping individual children or working with a small group and many other things. There may be training for assistants arranged by your local authority or within the school and you can alert her to this; but whatever training your assistant has undertaken or intends to undertake, you will still need to train her to work with you and your particular children.

Child development

Initial training may have introduced you to ideas about the way children develop and learn, but knowledge in this area is constantly developing and you will be continually adding to this knowledge from your own observation of children as well as keeping up to date by reading and in-service education. Your assistant also needs some of this knowledge and there are likely to be occasions when you are discussing a child and knowledge of child development becomes relevant. Of course, if she is a mother, she will have first-hand knowledge of child development, but you may have to emphasise that children are all individuals and each child develops differently.

Knowledge of how children learn

Here again initial training normally introduces students to knowledge of learning, and teaching experience will add to this. Experience as a parent also gives a person a closer but perhaps more limited insight into children's learning. Good theoretical knowledge as well as experience should guide your own practice and you will be able to help your assistant find out about children's learning and recognise how children differ from one another in doing this. The following points in particular are worth considering. They should be part of the background knowledge of all teachers and assistants.

Learning depends upon motivation

A child's power to learn is considerable. It is evident from the extent of early language learning and from the knowledge that children sometimes manifest about hobbies and out-of-school interests that most children have much greater powers for learning than we can yet harness for the learning we want them to achieve. Without motivation it is difficult to get them to learn anything. They may even use their ability to avoid learning.

Motivation can be intrinsic or extrinsic. Intrinsic motivation is that which comes from within the child. He or she wants to learn because of interest in the work in hand. Extrinsic motivation is motivation from outside the child – a desire to gain good marks or the teacher's approval. Both forms of motivation have a place but intrinsic motivation is the more satisfactory form. Most people, including most children, are motivated by problems which challenge but are within their capacity. The more that learning can be presented as a series of interesting challenges, the more successfully the children will learn. Such learning is often more effective than memorising because the child makes the learning his or her own by working on it. We tend to forget that children lack experience, not intelligence. Given a problem within his or her own experience, a child may solve it more quickly than an adult. Many teachers will be aware that children have taken to computers more quickly than they have themselves.

Reward and praise are more effective than criticism and punishment

This is well known and has been frequently demonstrated in research but the knowledge tends to be used in a very limited way. As a teacher you know that you can help children who have problems or who pose problems if you use praise and reward very specifically for the behaviour you want to reinforce, doing this as soon as possible after the behaviour takes place. As far as possible the unwanted behaviour should be ignored, although this is often not possible because of the effect on other children. Brophy and Good

(1986), in one study of teacher behaviour towards children typified as able or less able, found that teachers praised those they saw as high achievers more and low achievers less and criticised low achievers more and high achievers less. While this was to some extent understandable, it tended to reinforce the original typification and gave praise to those who needed it least rather than those who needed it most. This is certainly something you should look out for.

It is necessary to use or talk about a piece of learning

Learning which has not been discussed and used may remain at a rote learning level rather than being accessible to be applied in new situations. Listening and repeating are not enough by themselves if learning is to be absorbed in a way that makes it available for use. Talking about what is being learned helps a child to structure it and so to remember it and be able to recall it. Class, small group and paired discussion may be useful if specific tasks for discussion are given. Children can learn from working together at a problem.

Language means only as much as the experience it represents

Children learn from the words of others when they can interpret them by matching them with their own experience in a way which is reasonably similar to the understanding of the person using the words. This holds true for both speech and writing. Children are also good at disguising the limited nature of their understanding, and you may think they have understood when in fact they are simply using words without adequate understanding of their meaning.

Learning needs to be made accessible and usable

The way in which learning is acquired is important in structuring it in the learner's mind. Structuring involves matching it to what the learner already knows and helping him or her to classify the new knowledge into categories so that it is easy to remember and recall. Only if the structuring process is adequate will the learning be accessible and usable. It is not sufficient for the teacher to do the structuring for the children, although the way the material is presented should have its own structure. What is needed is help with sorting out experiences so that the children create structures for themselves.

Curriculum content

The demands on a teacher at the primary stage are very considerable since he or she is expected to teach almost the whole curriculum. Your class may have some specialist teaching for a subject such as music but a primary school teacher is expected to teach most subjects and your assistant will be expected to support you across the board. She may also have areas of knowledge of her own which could be useful to you.

You need to be very honest with yourself about your strengths and limitations so far as the curriculum is concerned and all teachers need to continue learning and updating their knowledge in the areas where they are expert as well as those where they need to know more.

Parent helpers

In addition to a teaching assistant, you may have some parents who come in to help in the classroom. Here again, you need to find out what they can offer. You may, for example, have a good typist who could help in making various kinds of worksheets. Or you may have a parent with good skills in making things or playing the piano, or in cooking. Even when a parent says s/he hasn't got any useful skills like these, s/he can do many useful things about the classroom, like keeping equipment in order, or helping to mount art work for display or recording radio programmes for you for the class to hear later. It will be important to make these helpers feel valued and encouraged in what they do. Make a point of praising and thanking them quite frequently.

Review 4.2 Assessing your assistant's development

1 How is my assistant's work developing? What can she do now that she could not do when she first came?
2 In which areas does she still need to learn? Which are the most urgent areas for her learning? What provision am I making for this learning?
3 How effectively is she relating to the children? Does she have any particular difficulties in this area?
4 What particular responsibilities is she taking on in the classroom? How well is she dealing with them?
5 How effective is she in supporting my work as teacher?
6 Is she enjoying her work?

Review 4.3 Parents in the classroom

1 What tasks could a volunteer parent do in my classroom?
2 How should I brief a parent who has volunteered to help?
3 Are there any particular skills which would be valuable, which a parent may be able to offer?
4 How can I ensure that the roles of teaching assistant and volunteer parent are clearly different?

Chapter 5

Teaching style

Style is the way you do things as a teacher. While there are both good and bad ways of doing things, there are many good ways of teaching and each teacher has his or her own style.

At the beginning of your teaching career, you tend to draw on models that you have experienced as a pupil as well as the knowledge you have gained from training, but, as time goes on, you become clearer about your own strengths and limitations and your preferred way of working. It is perhaps worth noting in passing that most teachers, and especially the inexperienced, usually have too few models to draw upon. It is valuable, if you have the opportunity, to see how other teachers teach and organise, particularly at the beginning of your career.

Influences on style

Your teaching style is formed from a number of factors, of which the following are the most important.

Your personality

Your working style depends, in the first place, upon the kind of person you are. For example, a person with an open and flexible personality will show this in the way s/he works.

The Highland Council of Scotland, in a paper on Teaching Approaches (2003) notes that: 'Teachers' own preferred ways of learning affect the ways in which they teach' and suggests that 'A greater awareness of learning preferences in general, and of their own in particular, can help teachers to be more aware of their own personal teaching style'.

Experience

Experience is an important factor in determining style. In particular, experience of seeing other teachers at work gives you ideas about possible ways of working, and you may choose some of them which become part of your style. Experience also affects your style in that you gradually become more sure of yourself and more confident in what you are doing.

Philosophy and aims

Your beliefs about education and what constitutes good teaching and learning situations, and your values generally, will affect the way you work, however vague and unformed your thinking may be. Many teachers hold quite strong views which affect the way they work, without their being aware that they have a philosophy as such.

Context

Your teaching style is affected by the particular group of children you are teaching and your accommodation and resources. The same teacher will work quite differently with a reception class and with a class of juniors. You may have a class which is very responsive or conversely one in which you don't at first get much reaction from the children. Both of these reactions affect the way you work, almost without you realising it. Things which are possible in a well-resourced school may be less possible when resources are very limited and this, too, affects the way you work.

The demonstration of style

Your style is evident in what you decide to do as teacher and what you ask the children to do. This is also true of the activities you decide to delegate to your assistant. The way you present material to children is part of your style. At almost every point in the day you are making choices about how you will act and these add up to style.

The use of time

In choosing what you do, what your assistant does and what the children do you are also making choices about how to use your time, your assistant's time and how the children will use time.

Methods of tackling work

The way you set about the tasks of the classroom and the aspects of work that you choose to share with your assistant are all part of your style. You may tell the children what to do, or you may have a programme where they have some choice about the order in which they undertake particular pieces of work and when they do it. You may discuss how work will be done with them and incorporate their ideas, not only into what they do but also into how it is done, or you may insist that work is done as you wish. Many teachers will probably use a mixture of these methods, sometimes dictating what is to be done and when it is to be done and sometimes giving a certain amount of freedom.

Communication

The way you communicate with children is all part of your style. You may spend a lot of time talking about how things should be done or about the actual tasks the children are doing. You may, perhaps without realising it, talk down to children or talk at a level which is stimulating because they have to think hard to follow what you are saying. You may also talk a great deal of the time or give a lot of time to getting children to talk. Similarly the extent to which you share your thinking with your assistant is important for her learning as well as for the children's work.

Interpersonal behaviour

This is linked with communication. Teachers vary in how friendly they are with the children they teach and in how they treat children. Studies of how children view teachers suggest that they value a friendly approach and a sense of humour. Your assistant will probably take a lead from you in the relationships she tries to form with the children.

The organisation of work

Teachers differ in the way they organise work. Some teachers will choose to teach much of the National Curriculum as separate subjects whereas others will do a certain amount of integration. You may use competition or co-operative group work a good deal or very little. The extent to which teachers involve assistants and pupils in decision-making about aspects of their work also varies a good deal and some teachers do more testing than others.

Studies of teacher style

There have been a number of studies which looked at teaching style. Bennett (1976) identified a number of characteristics of traditional and progressive teachers, as they were at that time. The progressive teacher tended to integrate subject matter rather than teach in separate subjects; involve pupils in active learning, often by discovery methods; made little use of external rewards and punishments and testing; and stressed the importance of creative expression.

Traditional teachers tended to teach separate subjects, stress the importance of memory, practice and rote learning, make use of external rewards with regular testing and an accent on competition with little emphasis on creative work. There were also a number of teachers who used mixed methods. Bennett (1976) also compared the results using tests of basic skills and two essays, one on 'What I did at school yesterday' and the other on 'Invisible for the day', and found that on the basic skills tests the formal teachers and those who used mixed methods came out best.

In the essay test the formal and informal groups did equally well, and those who used mixed methods did slightly less well. However, low-achieving boys did better in the informal classes, and the best class of all was taught informally but in a highly structured way. This study is pretty old now, but a good deal of its findings would seem likely to be still applicable.

The Oracle Study (Galton and Simon 1980) looked at teaching styles in junior school classes and classified them in the following way.

Individual monitors

These teachers worked mainly on an individual basis and therefore spent much time in monitoring individual progress. This resulted in their being under pressure with a high level of interaction with individual children.

Class enquirers

This group used a good deal of class teaching and teacher-managed learning with open and closed questions in class discussion.

Group instructors

Group instructors spent a larger amount of time than others on group interaction and less on individual attention, which allowed them to engage in more questioning and making of statements.

Style changers

Fifty per cent of teachers used mixed styles to meet different demands. The group of style changers breaks down as follows:

- *infrequent changers* who gradually changed style according to the observed needs of the class group over the course of the school year;
- *rotating changers* who worked with pupils seated in groups, each working at a particular aspect of curriculum: the activities of the different groups were rotated during the course of the day or week;
- *habitual changers* who made regular changes between class and

individualised instruction; this group used questioning relatively little and had the lowest amount of time spent interacting with pupils.

Each style was considered in relation to children's performance in the basic skills. In language the children of the class enquirers were much in advance of those using other styles, with pupils of infrequent changers coming second. The children of individual monitors, rotating and habitual changers scored less well.

In reading, the children of infrequent changers did best, with those of the individual monitors coming second. In mathematics the best score came from the children of the class enquirers.

It is interesting to relate this study to the approaches being recommended for the literacy and numeracy hours which tend towards the class enquirer style.

The Oracle Study also looked at children's learning styles and related these to teaching styles. Four major learning styles were noted:

- *the attention seeker* who seeks out the teacher's attention more than the typical class member, constantly seeking feedback and reassurance;
- *the intermittent worker* who avoids the teacher's attention and only works when the teacher is watching;
- *the solitary worker* who spends most of the time working with little interaction with other children or with the teacher;
- *the quiet collaborator* who is similar to the solitary worker in that they concentrate on work; they spend more time in routine activities than other children.

When the learning styles were related to the teaching styles in this study, it was found that the group instructors had the highest proportion of quiet collaborators and the class enquirers the highest proportion of solitary workers in their classes. The individual monitors and the rotating changers had the most intermittent workers.

A rather different approach on adjusting teaching style to learning style is suggested by an American website (undated but probably about 2000). This suggests that a way of meeting children's preferred learning styles might be to group them as:

- *tactual/kinaesthetic learners* who learn by experiencing: they want to touch and feel things, smell, taste and see;
- *auditory learners* who learn by listening and recall information best by hearing it;
- *visual learners* who learn by seeing.

Cortazzi (1991), in a study of the way 123 primary teachers worked, found that almost all of them often departed from their planned work to follow up an idea which the children had put forward or an event which was in the news. They gave their reasons for doing this as 'First, flexibility, second, the need for talk and the need to follow up children's enjoyment, excitement and interest' (Cortazzi 1991: 72). The more experienced teachers did this more often than those who were new to teaching. The National Curriculum and the literacy and numeracy hours have made this more difficult to do, but there is still a place for 'playing it by ear' from time to time.

Developing your own style

Wherever you place yourself in the various classifications in these studies, you have to discover the best way to work in the classroom for you. Your best way of working depends not only upon what you see as being important in curriculum terms, but also upon your strengths, limitations and, as we have seen, upon your personality, experience, philosophy and the situation in which you find yourself. Your age may also make a difference. We grow less flexible as we grow older, but are usually more competent and confident and able to bring wider experience to the work in hand.

Review 5.1 is intended to help you to work out your personal profile as a teacher. It is closely linked to the profile given in Review 1.1 Profile of organisational preferences, but is concerned with the way you work in the classroom rather than with your philosophy of education. The items listed are all those where teachers tend to have personal preferences which it is sensible to take into account. There will, of course, be a number of items where you feel that your view is somewhere between the two extremes given. Just put a cross as suggested below if this is the case. This is only really intended as a way of helping you to think where you really stand.

Work through the list marking your views on the statements and then look at the comments which follow. You may also like to get a colleague to mark the answers he or she thinks you might give. Sometimes the gap between your view of yourself and someone else's view of you can be revealing. The list could also furnish useful discussion for a group of teachers highlighting areas of difference.

Quiet v. noise and tidiness v. mess

Quiet and clean activities and noisy and messy activities need to be kept apart. You may do this by reserving different parts of the classroom for activities which are not compatible or by keeping such activities apart by having them at different times of the day. You need to find a middle road between being too quiet and tidy and allowing children to be too noisy and messy, and this means considering your own style and its limitations. Too much emphasis on quiet tidiness may inhibit creativity, but a disorganised classroom where too much noise and mess are allowed is also inhibiting. It is

Review 5.1 Analysing your preferred teaching style

Tick the item you prefer in each case or put a cross between the sentences if you think your preference is for somewhere between them.

1   A   I like a quiet classroom for most of the time.
    B   I don't mind noise so long as I can see that the children are working.
2   A   I like a tidy and well-organised classroom.
    B   I don't mind a bit of mess so long as it results in exciting work.
3   A   I like to have everything well-planned in advance.
    B   My best work often happens when I respond spontaneously to something which has just occurred.
4   A   I like to concentrate on one thing at a time.
    B   I like to have more than one activity at a time so that some children can get on by themselves while I work with others.
5   A   I am normally even-tempered and patient.
    B   I often get excited about children's work and am sometimes irritable.
6   A   I like a regular timetable without too many diversions or interruptions.
    B   I like to create variety in what we do in the day or week.
7   A   I think children learn best when they are not given too much choice.
    B   I believe choice to be important in motivating children to learn.
8   A   I think competition in the classroom helps children to learn.
    B   I prefer to play down competition and foster co-operation.
9   A   I try to be a perfectionist, as far as I can without discouraging some children.
    B   I am normally fairly easygoing.
10 A   I prefer to have my children formally seated in rows.
    B   I like to have children seated in groups.

important for a teacher to be well organised if the children are to work in an organised way. This means making rules about how materials and equipment are used and about the times when a certain amount of noise is permissible and times when everyone should be quiet. It is helpful to discuss with children the best way to work to keep the room in good order and to use some of their ideas, reviewing their success with them after a period.

Preplanning v. spontaneity

If you are a determined preplanner, be aware that you could just miss the moment when a particular piece of teaching might be most effective because you were so busy pursuing the goals you had planned. Edwards and Mercer (1987) studying the language used in classrooms found that teachers tend to dominate what happens in the classroom by the topics they introduce, the questions they ask and the responses they give to children's answers and comments. Up to a point this is to be expected and is part of the teacher's role, but if taken too far it prevents children from having ideas. Preplanning is most valuable when mixed with a measure of flexibility.

If you are strong on spontaneity be sure that you also create situations in which children can achieve the learning necessary for the National Curriculum. You also need to make regular checks to see that all the children are getting relevant experiences and opportunities and that there are not substantial gaps in their learning or too much repetition of the things which interest you most. If you are a spontaneous teacher you need to keep good records of what actually happens.

One task v. variety of tasks

If you normally have all the children doing the same subject at the same time, remember that they take differing amounts of time to learn the same things. You may need to have some time when the slower children have a chance to catch up while the faster ones do something different. You need to provide for this variation either by giving different work to different individuals or different groups of children, or by organising so that work can be undertaken at a variety of levels. You also need plenty of interesting material for those who finish quickly. Giving them more of the same may simply teach them to work slowly! You may also need material to provide opportunities for slower children which enables them to work through the same programme as others but with more information and explanation available.

If you like to have a variety of tasks going on at the same time make sure that the children are getting enough stimulus from you and from each other.

Little choice v. much choice

Some of the studies quoted earlier suggest that there is a limit to the amount of choice which children can manage effectively.

There is no doubt that the right amount of choice is motivating to children and can also have the advantage of training them in the process of making choices. The most satisfactory use of choice comes when you provide choice of three or four possible activities which all lead to same learning. You may also choose to have a given time of day when children may work at particular interests which they have chosen in discussion with you. This takes time to set up but can be a very profitable learning situation. Choice is also possible within a given theme. In topic work, for example, there may be several ways in which children can work to acquire the learning intended by the teacher and they may have some choice of which route they pursue.

Of course, choice can be overdone, with the result that children flit from one activity to another, doing the things they enjoy and avoiding those they don't like and consequently not learning very much. Some of the choices made might be a choice of when a particular activity is undertaken rather than a choice of whether it is undertaken. Training children to choose wisely is an important part of their learning.

Competition v. co-operation

Human beings have an ancestry from a time when you needed to be competitive in order to survive and we are still naturally competitive. Even in classrooms where the teacher plays down competition, the children will create competition of their own.

Some children thrive on competition and are most likely to work well when they see themselves in a competitive situation. Others fail continually and become discouraged. The task is to get the most out of competition for those who benefit from it with the least damage for those who may fail. You might perhaps provide opportunities for competition with a group of children of similar ability or a group who have chosen to compete.

An element of competition is also useful when children are encouraged to compete with themselves or others at a similar level in simple games which create interest or give practice which might otherwise seem tedious. In any use of competition it is important to see that children do not get the idea that it is the end that matters and that the means of achieving it is unimportant, or that what is learned is important only in terms of doing better than someone else, getting marks or rewards or pleasing the teacher. One might say that if any children cheat in their learning they have gained the wrong idea of what the activity is about.

Competition may work against co-operation. There are many situations in life where co-operation is needed and school should teach children how to work effectively with other people. Researchers suggest that although many teachers give lip service to the idea of co-operative work actual examples of it are comparatively few. It is an important area of learning, and working with others is a skill which will be needed in adult life by many.

Patient v. excitable

The ability to be patient is obviously an advantage in a teacher and it can give children considerable security to know that you will nearly always treat them sympathetically and consistently. On the other hand, excitement and enthusiasm are also valuable things to offer children and when you show enthusiasm it is often infectious.

The teacher who can get children really turned on by his or her own excitement is someone whom every child needs to meet. If the other side of this valuable characteristic is that you get depressed and irritable from time to time, try to organise so that you have something to switch into when you have had enough and the children are trying you beyond endurance. For example, it is often pleasant to read them a story or get them to carry on with some activity which is quiet and interesting to them.

Perfectionist v. easygoing

All teachers should demand high standards of children in all they do, but different teachers do this in different ways. If you tend to be perfectionist, be careful not to ask more than your children can give and make sure you have your priorities right. If you were to insist that every piece of writing is done in perfect handwriting with no spelling or punctuation mistakes you may find that some children write very little in order not to expose their weaknesses. This makes it very difficult to help them and such teacher behaviour is fortunately fairly rare.

On the other hand if you are very easygoing you need to check fairly often that the work the children are offering is good enough and that they are paying enough attention to detail.

Class teaching v. group and individual teaching

The literacy and numeracy hours have brought the idea of whole-class teaching to the fore as well as providing opportunities for small group and individual work. If you are good at holding children's attention riveted when you wish to, you should make the most of it. Your children will probably remember the things they have done with you for the rest of their lives. However, you also need to vary the approach to match the situation and the needs of individuals. The important thing to bear in mind is making an efficient use of time. A number of studies suggest that teachers ask more thought-provoking questions when working with a whole class than when working with individuals. On the other hand, you may have in your class one or more very able children who need individual work for a good deal of the time. You may also have children with special educational needs who also need individual work. It is all a question of getting the right balance. It can be useful from time to time to make a note during the day of when you change organisation and the time when you do it.

Formal classroom organisation v. informal organisation

Studies of the way children are seated in classrooms suggest that when children are seated in rows rather than groups more work is done. The children themselves also said they preferred formal seating. There is also evidence that although many teachers have children seated in groups not much use is made of this for co-operative work.

Key elements of teaching approaches

The Highland Council (2003) also lists the following findings about pupil perceptions.

- Pupils appreciate teachers who value and appreciate them as individuals.
- Good discipline is important, but pupils need to understand/recognise the need for it.
- Pupils look for consistency of approach from a teacher.
- Showing genuine interest in pupils' lives is important, as is sharing your own life.
- Pupils respond to teachers who genuinely care about them and want them to succeed.
- Pupils react positively when the teacher listens and responds to their ideas rather than just assessing or judging – this will involve being prepared to deviate from the lesson plan.
- Pupils need to feel that the teacher is on the ball and aware of what is going on in the class.
- Pupils respond well to teachers who show personal enthusiasm for what they are teaching.

Review 5.2 Matching teaching and learning styles

1   Have I a usual teaching style? What do I seem to do most often?
2   How does my teaching style fit into the styles listed in this chapter?
3   How much do I know about the learning styles of the children in my class? Should I try to do more to observe them with the learning styles in this chapter in mind?
4   Which of my teaching styles would seem to fit best with the children's learning styles?
5   Do I feel that I should change my style in any way to do more to meet the children's learning styles?

Chapter 6

Children learning

We use the word 'learn' for several different activities. Sometimes we are asking children to memorise something, for example, 'Learn those spellings'. Sometimes we are describing a more complex process involving different kinds of learning, such as 'learning about conservation', and sometimes we are talking about doing something, such as 'John is learning to turn a back somersault'. These are three rather different approaches and children need to know how to tackle all three when required.

The extent to which your children are able to work independently has implications for the way you organise your work. If you want time to work with small groups and individuals, you need to do all you can to train children to work profitably without constant reference to you.

Considering learning

Early brain development

Pre-school learning has also been studied in connection with giftedness. Brain scans of children who appear to show unusually well-developed skills and knowledge at an early age, show a marked increase in synapses in the brain. There is also evidence that children who have been stimulated in any particular way in early childhood also have an increase in synapses.

Types of learning

Bennett *et al.* (1984: 24–5) suggest that there are five types of learning task:

- *incremental* which involves new learning;
- *restructuring* where the pupil is 'required to discover, invent or construct a new way of looking at problems';
- *enrichment* which 'demands the use of familiar knowledge, concepts and skills in unfamiliar contexts';
- *practice* which helps pupils to make skills automatic;

- *revision* which 'demands attention to materials or skills which have been set aside for some time'.

They found in their study of primary school children that 25 per cent of tasks were incremental, 7 per cent restructuring or enrichment, 60 per cent practice and 6 per cent revision. In planning work you need to consider carefully which of these learning approaches you plan to use. In the study they describe there were considerably more practice tasks given in language than in number work. They also found that very often the task did not demand what the teacher intended. 'Almost a quarter of tasks intended to make incremental demands in fact made practice demands' (Bennett *et al.* 1984: 33). There were also practice tasks which turned out to be incremental and there was a tendency to underestimate high attainers.

Not providing work at a high enough level for very able children is still a fairly common practice and you need to consider this group carefully and ask yourself whether you are offering them enough challenge. We tend to give more attention to the less able and as far as possible plan work for them within their capacity. We also need to plan work for the very able which will stretch them, so that they have to think hard and use all their abilities. There is quite a bit of evidence to suggest that very able children are very often given work which they find very easy.

An article in *SENCO* magazine (2007) emphasises that in future 'schools will be expected to demonstrate the effectiveness of their approach to gifted and talented pupils during school inspection and provide evidence to illustrate how their approach has had a positive effect on the children's performance'.

Personalised learning

We have for some time been moving towards making children's learning more personalised, and as help in the classroom increases and as ICT makes it more possible to provide for the needs of individuals and groups, it seems likely that classroom practice will gradually move further in this direction.

However, these moves will still need to be in the context of the National Curriculum and the skills involved in gaining Qualified Teacher Status, for example:

- professional values and practice and appropriate attitudes, leading to commitment;
- knowledge and understanding, leading to confident and authoritative understanding of children;
- teaching which involves good planning, having appropriate expectations and monitoring and assessing progress. it also involves good class management.

Both Desforges (1985) and Bennett *et al.* (1984) stress the need for teachers to spend more time in diagnosing the thinking of individual children in order to discover why errors were made and to ensure better concept development. This is still true today and the pressure on teachers' time is ever increasing. It is something with which your assistant may be able to help. With your help she can learn how to talk over errors with individuals and find out about their thinking.

These reports were written a long time ago and classrooms have changed since then although the need for individual diagnosis of thinking is still important and relevant. Computers are more available and this can often help very able children to work at a higher level, perhaps using the internet to find out for themselves about things which interest them. Whiteboards are changing the meaning of whole-class teaching and making it possible to provide work at a variety of levels in a whole-class context. Other equipment such as photocopiers and printers make it much easier to provide personalised material for children.

Most teachers now have help from an assistant and this means that you can work with individuals from time to time while your assistant also helps individuals and deals with the sort of questions that children would have asked you in the past.

Concept development

Investigatory learning needs to be part of a great deal of the work you do with children but there are some areas of work in which it is more important than others. It is particularly important for children to develop concepts. A concept is, in effect, a generalisation made from a range of different experiences. For example, children at an early age begin to acquire one aspect of the concept of conservation when they explore what happens when you pour liquid into differently shaped vessels. They need to do this a number of times before they come to appreciate that the amount of liquid doesn't change. It merely changes shape. They then need to see other examples.

One school – Kimberworth Community Primary School – won an Aspect award in 2006 for its creative approach to the education of its children. It summarised its approach and development as follows:

- Recognition that some children were not engaged in learning resulted in a complete review of the curriculum. The result has been a curriculum based on key skills. These skills are placed in a context that is exciting, stimulating, creative and has a purpose.
- All the learning is cross-curricular and the older children are encouraged to decide upon areas for their own learning to develop independence. Interest has been generated by a visual stimulus wherever possible and opportunities to apply learnt skills in an everyday context are provided.

- The effect of this new curriculum has been to observe children and staff enthused by this learning, questioning outcomes and evaluating to take the learning further.

The school described its aim as follows:

> This has been an area of development that has had an impact on children's engagement with learning. In Key Stage 2, children have been actively involved in research and are becoming effective questioners to take learning forward. They are using strategies to support their learning and are working collaboratively, feeding back factual information to each other to discuss. Teachers are more stimulated by this curriculum and, as a result, children work more positively.

Another example might be the idea of 'old'. In order to have an understanding of the past, a child needs to understand what is meant when we say that something is old. Young children use the word in several different ways: 'I am six years old'. 'My Dad has a new car. My uncle bought his old one'. 'Our church is very old'. They need to sort out these meanings through experience. In particular they need to begin to see that the term 'old' is a relative one. A boy is 'old' compared with his baby sister; his mother is 'old' compared with him; the church is 'old' compared with his grandparents, but the church in the next village is 'old' compared with our church.

Acquiring this concept of age means experiencing and noting signs of age in people and objects and buildings so that it becomes possible to make judgements about age. This means making generalisations from experience and discovering the clues about age which can be used.

There will be an element of telling in concept development, but if there is to be true understanding and consequent ability to transfer the learning to new situations children need to reach the point where they can formulate the concept for themselves.

The National Curriculum substantially consists of concepts. It will therefore be important to set up appropriate situations which lead to the development of the specific concepts listed in each of the subject areas. You may feel worried if you spend too much time on completely open-ended work, but a piece of work set up to develop a specific concept will provide many opportunities for other learning, some of which will meet other curriculum requirements.

In science, you may quite often say to your children 'Let's see if we can find out'. This kind of enquiry is not confined to science. It can be found in most subject areas. In other situations your task may be to:

- provide your children with a task or a problem but not instructions for dealing with it and give the children in small groups the opportunity to plan how to do it, working with them as they create their plan;

- discuss their plans with them before they start to carry them out;
- observe them carefully as they work at these tasks;
- give them some time at the end to talk about what they found out and what they learned from the work;
- spend some time afterwards discussing how they worked and whether it was a good way of working and whether it could be improved.

This kind of learning is often particularly effective in the context of the kind of drama described earlier (Chapter 3, p. 34) which requires certain learning because of the role the child has taken on. This needs careful preparation, so that each child understands his or her role and is able to identify what is needed to help in the particular role. It is easy to see how such learning could grow in this context. If children really get inside the role it will have tremendous motivation. There will also be a demand for information which is much more clearly defined than in the case where the children are finding out simply because the teacher tells them to.

Motivation of this kind is, of course, present when children investigate a real problem with an outcome to be judged on its use, but it is difficult to do this all the time and an imaginary but convincing framework can also do a great deal for you and the children in terms of motivation and involvement.

Whether you use drama as part of learning or work more directly to establish a concept, your task as teacher is to draw attention to what is significant in the situation and to help children to consider outcomes in such a way that your intervention leads to the discovery of answers rather than a statement of what is to be discovered. This is difficult to do because it takes time with individuals or small groups working through questions to see where they are in their thinking.

This kind of development may also come out of direct teaching, where your skill in questioning may lead to a discovery of a generalisation. This approach is far from being a soft option and it needs very careful structuring of learning if it is to succeed.

Learning strengths in children

Just as you have a teaching style which is personal to you, so children have personal learning styles or ways of learning which are most effective for them. They will be discovering these in the course of their time in the primary school. It will be helpful, if you can find the time to do it, to make a note of when any child seems to do extra well or shows extra interest in any particular way of learning. If you teach older children, it may be a good idea to discuss this with them, explaining that we all have our own best way of learning and should make the most of it. Of course, you can't always choose how you learn, but it is useful to know the best path to take when you do have a choice.

Learning by heart

Although the information explosion makes learning by heart less necessary, there is still a great deal which we all need to remember, and children need to memorise some things. They need help with this process, although it is often easier to memorise when young than it is later. Most people remember best when things make sense or can be grouped or classified in some way or associated with something else. Learning to spell correctly also depends on teaching children to group things which have to be memorised, to look for associations and write as well as say the words being learned. One may remember the feel of writing something.

Learning to structure things

Where understanding is involved, the business of grouping and seeking patterns and rearranging the material becomes essential. We understand something only when we make it our own by working with it and using it. Children need a great deal of help in learning how to structure things for themselves. Work which asks them to put things in groups or order of priority or to select things which go together or contrast with one another, all work involving sets, work which looks for patterns in numbers or spelling or involves the use of flow-charts or other forms of graphic layout all contribute to the ability to learn and understand. Structuring one's learning in this way leads to effective concept development.

Learning by doing

Doing also has an important place in understanding and learning. Physical activity is often more easily remembered than mere words. It is interesting, for example, that a hairdresser who in the course of a week may work on eighty or ninety customers, rarely forgets the way each customer's hair is done. This is quite a remarkable feat of memory and illustrates well the way in which the memory of movement helps other forms of memory.

There is a need to learn movement skills in work such as art, craft, needle-work, cookery, physical education, science, technology and handwriting. We normally teach most of the skills involved in these activities by demonstration. It seems likely that the computer will eventually be helpful here, and we should certainly teach children to work out practical tasks from written instructions since this is a very necessary skill for adult life.

Learning through play

If you teach the youngest children, you need to be aware of the way in which play can support and develop their learning. The national strategies for literacy and numeracy both stress the value of play in the early years and this is still relevant when children start school. The Department for Children, Schools and Families website 'Overviews of learning' (2006) suggests that, through play, children can:

- explore, develop and represent learning experiences that help them to make sense of the world;
- practise and build up ideas, concepts and skills;
- learn how to control impulses and understand the need for rules;
- be alone, alongside others or co-operate as they talk or rehearse their feelings;
- take risks and make mistakes;
- think creatively and imaginatively;
- communicate with others as they investigate or solve problems;
- express fears or relive anxious experiences in controlled and safe situations.

Acquiring the skills of independent learning

There is much to be said for setting out for children what has to be learned and discussing with them possible ways of learning it. Children need the skills for independent learning and these involve having some idea of how to set about the learning process in different contexts.

This stress on process makes classroom management a very complex business, and the pressure to complete what is required by the National Curriculum can make teachers feel that there is too little time to be concerned with how children learn, so long as they learn. This is a short-sighted view which in the long run works against helping children to achieve their maximum potential. Where children are involved in considering the learning process as well as the learning content, teaching can become a more exciting business because they will come up with ideas you haven't thought of and the detective work of finding out how they view things can be very challenging.

The skills involved in study are numerous and complex, but it is possible to identify some of them and to look for ways in which children can acquire and practise them. They include the following, although this list is by no means exhaustive.

Investigating

You can find out and learn from your own observation and experiment, by asking other people, by turning to books and printed material, by using a computer or perhaps using television or video. Most people use observation and questioning more than they use other sources and we need to take this source of information seriously and teach children to use it well.

Children need to learn to make observations of various kinds. This involves learning to use the tools that extend the senses, such as lenses and microscopes, and the tools that help us to measure, such as rulers, clocks, weights and so on. These are all extensions of observation. They also need to learn to use the tools of analysis, from simple graphs to databases and spreadsheets.

Asking questions to get information is also a skill to be learned. Field study work is important in providing such opportunities and this has implications for organisation since it is difficult to develop questioning skills if you don't have the opportunity for asking questions of anyone except the teacher. Children need to learn that some questions bring more information than others and that you need to ask the right person: someone likely to know the answer. Children also need to learn to ask questions in a tactful way. Practice in this kind of skill can be given as homework where children ask questions of their parents and grandparents perhaps about how they do something or what life was like when they were at school.

Sorting, classifying, ordering, generalising, making and testing hypotheses

When material has been collected, learning may involve sorting and classifying it and putting it into some sort of order for presentation or to see if there are generalisations which could be made or further questions which could be explored. It may be possible to find ways of applying what has been learned, perhaps to deal with a situation or to do or make something. As a result of sorting material, patterns may emerge which could be tested as hypotheses or problems could present themselves which could be investigated.

This again has implications for the way you teach and the way you organise. If you do not provide children with opportunities to do their own sorting and classifying with help from you, they may not acquire these skills.

Planning

You will also need to teach some planning skills. Children, as they grow older, can be encouraged to produce plans for the work they are doing, sometimes working in small groups or pairs, probably following a demonstration of how to do this, as you build up a plan on the board with them.

The plans can be written lists or topic webs with lines and arrows linking together various parts of the plan. This kind of plan will need to be turned into a list in due course and because the work has to be carried out in real time, there must be a priority order and there will need to be discussion about the order in which work might be done.

You can go on from there and encourage children to estimate how long a piece of work may take and then check to see how long it actually does take. The next step is to plan for increasing lengths of time, so that older children are eventually planning their work for some time ahead. However, you need to take into account the fact that research suggests that planning for too long a time ahead can be counter-productive.

There should be a good balance of teacher-directed and whole-class and group work and work in which children, as they grow older, have an increasing degree of choice about how they set about things and make plans for themselves.

Evaluation

A further and very important learning skill is the ability to evaluate your own and other people's work and behaviour. Young children starting school depend very much on the adults in their world for views on what is good or bad, right or wrong. Parents tell them that this is good and this is naughty and they gradually internalise these views. When they start school their teachers do much the same thing and the children internalise their teachers' views also, sometimes finding that there is a conflict between what is considered good or naughty at home and what is considered good or naughty at school.

As they grow older children learn to set their own standards and to make judgements using both the standards they have been given by adults and their own emerging judgement. The teacher can do a great deal to help this development by discussing work and trying to help children identify criteria for making judgements and then matching work and behaviour to them. It is also helpful if you make clear to children the criteria you are using to assess their work. Research suggests that children tend to regard presentation as the major criterion used by teachers for assessing work rather than the ideas expressed and how they have been used.

Problem-solving

Problem-solving, like language, is a skill which can be practised right across the curriculum and problem-solving strategies can be applied to many aspects of the daily life of the classroom. Work in mathematics, science and technology involves particular kinds of problem-solving, but nearly every subject can be approached in this way. In geography, for example, children learning to use maps could be asked to find the quickest route from A to B. In history, they could be told of a king or army commander facing a particular problem and asked how they think it could be solved. It is useful to get across the idea that there can be a process in solving problems which is widely applicable.

Review 6.1 Learning skills

1   What am I doing to help children to become aware of the skills involved in learning and develop the ability to apply them in their work?

2   What opportunities do I offer my children for investigation? Do we discuss not only what they found out, but also how they did it?

3   How can I best provide children with experience of sorting and classifying? Which subjects of the curriculum offer opportunities for this?

4   Do I give my children enough opportunities to plan some of their work? Have we discussed how best to do this?

5   Do they have real opportunities for problem-solving, not just as part of mathematics, but also in science and technology and as part of everyday life in the classroom?

6   Are they starting to develop skill in evaluation of their own work and that of others?

7   Do I give them enough opportunities to work together on different aspects of their learning? Do I train them in working together?

8   Should I talk to my children about learning styles and the value of knowing how you learn best?

Chapter 7

Effective teaching for effective learning

A new primary school review is under way at the time of writing which is due for publication in 2008. Mick Waters from the Qualifications and Curriculum Authority (QCA), commenting on the plan in 2006, stressed that curriculum is about more than subjects and and that its purpose is for all children and young people to become successful learners, confident individuals and responsible citizens. He points out that everything we do in school contributes to this end.

An article in the *Independent* by Clare Dwyer Hogg (December 2007) describes a school working with the International Primary Curriculum in which children learn not individual subjects, but subjects taught under one broad topic heading.

The Royal Society for the Arts (RSA) considers that certain skills or competences are essential for the curriculum. These include learning, managing information, relating to others and citizenship, and the RSA believes that these should be addressed through topic based learning.

Whenever you plan work in the classroom, you have a variety of possible ways of helping children to learn. The choices of teaching and learning strategies you make are influenced by five factors:

- the particular group of children;
- the subject matter to be learned and skills to be acquired;
- the environment in which you work and the materials and equipment available;
- the possible contribution of your assistant;
- your own particular teaching style and preferences.

We have already looked fairly closely at the way children learn and at children's learning styles and the effects of these for the teacher. Children's learning ability and the approaches most likely to be successful will vary within any class, but very often there are sufficient common elements to enable you to select an approach likely to match the needs of the majority, leaving you with some work to do to help individuals who differ.

Making teaching effective

Recent years have seen a good deal of concern with making teaching and learning more effective. There is now a substantial body of research into effective teaching and learning coming from studies in Britain and the USA.

Dean (2000: 4) summarises findings made by various researchers about effective teaching as follows:

- Effective teachers prepare well and have clear goals for their teaching.
- They aim to make as much teaching contact with all their children as possible.
- They have high expectations for all children.
- They make clear presentations which match the level of the children.
- They structure work well and tell children the purpose of the work they are doing and the targets they hope the children will achieve.
- They are flexible in varying teaching behaviour and activities.
- They use many higher order questions which demand thinking on the part of the children.
- They give frequent feedback to children about how they are doing and encourage them.
- They make appropriate use of praise for both achievement and behaviour.
- They keep good records of the attainment and progress of individual children and these are shared with the child and used to help in planning. Progress in learning is constantly assessed.
- Their classrooms are well organised, ordered and attractive.
- They reflect on the work they and the children have done and evaluate progress towards goals.
- Good teachers are secure in their subject knowledge at a level well above that of the demands of the children they are teaching.

Hay McBer (2000) made a study of teacher effectiveness for the Department for Education and Employment. It identified three main factors within the control of teachers which significantly influenced pupils' progress. These were teaching skills, professional characteristics and classroom climate. The professional characteristics they describe as 'ongoing patterns of behaviour that combine to determine the things that teachers typically do'. Classroom climate describes the collective perceptions of the pupils on the aspects of their environment which have a direct impact on their capacity to learn. Hay McBer (2000: 17) identified five clusters of characteristics of outstanding teachers. These are:

- *professionalism* providing challenge and support for pupils, developing confidence, creating trust and respect for others;
- *thinking* analytical and conceptual thinking;

- *planning and setting expectations*   demonstrating a drive for improvement, seeking information about how pupils are reacting, using initiative;
- *leading, demonstrating*   flexibility, holding people accountable, managing pupils, showing a passion for learning;
- *relating to others*   having impact and influence, good teamwork, other people.

Some characteristics of effective teaching

It is nearly always more productive to be positive rather than negative. Praise tends to get a more positive reaction than criticism. While criticism is of course a necessary part of the teacher role, it needs to be balanced as often as possible with a more positive comment. Rewards are more effective than punishment.

Effective teachers spend quite a lot of time talking to pupils individually about their work and this can have a positive effect on progress. They make good use of praise, often praising children for good behaviour or for trying as well as praising them when they do really well.

If you have a teaching assistant it might be useful to ask her to listen for a time to the comments you make to individual children, noting how often you give praise or encouragement and how often you make more negative comments. This can be very revealing, but it is difficult to do it for oneself. Effective teachers create a high level of industry within their classrooms and organise work so that there is always plenty for the children to do. Their lessons are stimulating and this leads to the formation of positive relationships between teacher and children.

Galton (1989) found that teachers sometimes had a perception gap between what they thought they were doing and what they were actually doing. In the Oracle Study, for example, most of the children in the primary classes they studied were sitting in groups, but there was very little work of a co-operative nature taking place and very little of the kind of extending conversation which should be one of the outcomes of group work.

It is sometimes the case that while you may be very clear about what you want to do and what you want your children to learn, as the lesson proceeds it seems that somehow what you have prepared is not effective. Perhaps the children are not very attentive, or you haven't succeeded in getting them interested. This happens to most teachers from time to time and it is important when it happens to try to think back over the lesson and why it was not a success. We can all learn from our mistakes.

Recent years have seen a move towards a greater proportion of interactive work with the whole class and generally a more structured approach to teaching and learning. This has been made more fruitful by the advent of the whiteboard which allows you to put prepared material on the screen and then use it interactively with the children, creating some very effective whole-class teaching.

Alexander *et al.* (1992: 28) note that 'whole-class teaching is associated with higher-order questioning, explanations and statements, and these in turn correlate with higher levels of pupil performance'. However, they go on to say:

> Observational studies show that pupils pay attention and remain on task when being taught as a whole class but may, in fact, slow down their rates of working to meet the teacher's norm, thus narrowing the challenge of what is taught to an extent which advocates of whole-class teaching might well find uncomfortable.

Selecting teaching methods

In selecting teaching methods you need to consider not only the ability of the group and the stage of development of the majority but also the children's experience, their interests, their language, knowledge and skill and what is likely to motivate this particular group. The younger and less able the group, the more important it becomes to start from the first-hand and the practical. First-hand experience continues to be important if a child's learning is to be carried over and applied to new situations.

The subject matter to be learned also dictates certain things in relation to teaching approaches. For example, it is difficult to teach young children very much about number in any effective way without a good deal of practical work. Geographical and historical concepts are unlikely to be fully established without some fieldwork, but you can't do much fieldwork without a lot of prior planning and arrangements, just as you can't learn to enjoy poetry without reading it and listening to it. This isn't a reason for not doing fieldwork, particularly with the older children, but it needs to be planned with care.

Edwards and Mercer (1987: 126) stress the importance of classroom discourse in children's learning. They say:

> It is largely within the teacher–pupil discourse through which the lesson is conducted that whatever understandings are eventually created, are in the first place shaped, interpreted, made salient or peripheral, reinterpreted and so on. And it is a process that remains essentially dominated by the teacher's own aims and expectations.

In today's classrooms there will also be assistant–pupil discourse and also a good deal of pupil–pupil discourse and you will need to take this into account in all your planning.

In your planning you need first to remind yourself of what the children already know, using your past experience of them, and then plan to provide new knowledge in such a way that it will interest them and thus be more likely to be remembered. We tend to remember things best when we have used them in some way so any explanation or description of what you want them to learn needs to be followed by or be part of an opportunity for action on the part of the children. Sometimes this will be done as a whole-class activity and at other times you may want different groups or pairs of children to do different things, sometimes according to their ability, sometimes according to their interests or as a free choice.

We saw in an earlier chapter that Edwards and Mercer (1987) and Bennett and Kell (1989) found that teachers tended not to tell children what it was they were supposed to be learning. This may have been because the teacher did not want to limit the lesson but to use ideas which came up as well as what had been planned. These writers make the point, however, that the lack of this information can mean that children are less able to focus their learning and that sharing with the children the purpose of what they were doing is likely to be more effective.

The environment in which you teach obviously has some effect on the way you set about things. Lack of space may limit some activities. Lack of materials or equipment may also be a limitation. If you work in a classroom which faces a main road you may find the noise affects the way you are able to talk to the class and you may need to organise things a little differently to cope with this.

Bennett *et al.* found in their study of primary school children that 25 per cent of tasks were incremental, 7 per cent restructuring or enrichment, 60 per cent practice and 6 per cent revision (see p. 57). In planning work you need to consider carefully which of these learning approaches you plan to use. In the study they describe, there were considerably more practice tasks given in language than in number work. They also found that very often the task did not demand what the teacher intended. 'Almost a quarter of tasks intended to make incremental demands in fact made practice demands' (Bennett *et al.* 1984: 33).

Although these studies are quite old, there are probably quite a lot of classrooms where these ways of working still apply.

Matching work to children's needs

The DfES Effective Provision of Pre-School Eduction (EPPE) project started off in 1980 as a study of pre-school children's experiences, but in 2003 researchers continued the study with children up to the age of eleven and looked at the effect of pre-school education on children's progress in the primary school, the characteristics of an effective primary school, the needs of resilient and vulnerable children and the contribution of out-of-school learning. The study was due for completion in 2008.

The present study has already looked at children's progress in Key Stage 2 in the primary school – looking at progress, not attainment – and so far has found that this also was something which effective schools consider, particularly for English, mathematics and science. The programme was controlled for gender, ethnic origin, the child's age, the home area of the child, which gave information about his/her social background, special educational needs and prior attainment.

They have found so far that girls made better progress in English and boys in mathematics, and that there was no substantial gender difference in other subjects, a finding which sits oddly with all that we have been hearing recently about boys' poorer performance in many aspects of the curriculum.

Where children of ethnic origin for whom English was the second language were concerned, many made better progress than the British children. They found that children who were in classes in which they were among the youngest, made better progress than other children of the same age group and this difference was substantial. As might be expected, children from poorer homes and those with special educational needs made less progress. They also found a marked difference between schools.

Other studies suggest that teachers tend to think the younger children are less able than they really are because they are behind some of the other children in their development. It was suggested in Chapter 2 that you make yourself familiar with the ages of children coming into your class at an early stage.

Matching work to children is one of the most difficult tasks for teachers. The HMI (1978) primary survey found that for high-attaining children there was a mismatch in almost half the mathematics classes observed, and in some other subjects the evidence of mismatch was even higher. Desforges (1985: 102) suggests that mismatching appears to be initiated and sustained by:

1 demanding concrete records of procedures rather than evidence of thought;
2 rewarding effort to produce rather than effort to conceptualise;
3 adopting management techniques which permit rapid responses to each child's problems but leave the teacher ignorant of the child's confusion or potential;
4 the teacher's inexperience with and lack of skill in diagnostic work and a taste for direct instruction, however informally put, rather than analysis.

Although these studies are quite old, there are probably quite a lot of classrooms where these ways of working still apply.

Personalised learning

We saw in Chapter 6 the value of aiming to personalise learning wherever possible. Desforges and Bennett (1985) stress the need to spend more time in diagnosing the thinking of individual children, which is another way of considering personalised learning.

Review 7.1 Matching work to children

1 How would the work I gave to my children last week be classified under the headings given in the research by Bennett *et al.* described above?

2 Do I normally tell children what they are going to be learning in the lesson which follows? Would there be any advantages in doing so?

3 What does the range of children in my class imply for matching work to them?

4 How many children with special educational needs have I in my class? How can I best provide for them?

5 How many very able children have I in my class? What provision should I make for them?

6 What other children have I who present a need for more individual work?

7 How far do I manage to organise so that all these needs receive attention?

8 Are there any areas of matching work to children about which I feel concern?

Children may learn and teachers may teach in the following ways. These sections should be regarded as a collection of teaching tools from which you can select according to their appropriateness for your particular children, the subject matter and the context.

Direct teaching

A high proportion of teaching at every level, but particularly with older children and adults, will still tend to consist of exposition and questioning. It will almost certainly involve a good deal of questioning designed to elicit information from the children so that you can build on what they already know and the ideas they already have.

The following would seem to be situations in which this approach is useful.

- It may be the most efficient and economical way of getting children to learn something and then checking that they know it.
- It is a valuable way of starting and ending a piece of work. At the beginning you may want to stimulate children and interest them, or direct their attention or get the work organised. At the end of a piece of work there may be a place for drawing together what has been learned, generalising, filling gaps, questioning understanding and so on. This is what the plenary sessions in literacy and number are designed to do.

- It is a good approach for giving instructions on safety or organisation where it is important that every child understands the same thing. You will still need to reinforce your points more for some children than for others.

The success of this method of teaching and the extent of its use depends to some extent on your skills and your preferred style, but recent developments such as the literacy and numeracy strategies have stressed the value of interactive whole-class teaching. This is a form of direct teaching where the children are constantly involved in answering questions, contributing ideas in discussion, explaining how to do something and so on.

Direct teaching makes the following demands on the teacher.

Good preparation

Exposition by the teacher needs to be good if it is to capture interest. Each teacher puts things over in a different way, but you need to maintain a self-critical attitude to what you do and work all the time at improving your skill. This means that some work, at least, should be prepared in considerable detail.

Making appropriate notes

This doesn't mean making copious notes which you may not be able to use in the classroom, but finding the best way of note-making for you and selecting methods of planning which enable you to file and store lesson material and perhaps reassemble it for use in other ways in the future.

Note-making may mean setting out activities in a flow diagram. You may put notes in a file or on cards which can be reshuffled on future occasions. You may also like to make material for projection. The number of pieces of work which you can prepare thoroughly is limited, but if you prepare a few things really well each week, selecting work which you may want to repeat at another time, you will gradually build up a stock of material.

Work which lends itself to this kind of preparation may include stories, where it is a good idea if you want to tell a story to try to see it in a series of scenes, thinking about what they would look like in great detail so that you can help children create pictures in their minds. Any topic which you want children to become really involved in can be prepared in this way.

Setting the scene

When you want to present material to the whole class, try to set the scene well. Make sure the children are sitting where they can see you and try to start in a way which will capture interest and will at the same time draw on their experience. It is much the same whether you are talking to five-year-olds or fifty-year-olds: getting interest is something you need to do very quickly and it is always worth preparing the beginning and the end of a piece of work extra well.

Being ready for the work to start

It is wise to look ahead to what you plan to do after introducing your topic and to make sure that books are ready, and writing materials or whatever are available. It is very disappointing to create a marvellous atmosphere with a story or account of something and get the children enthusiastic and ready to go only to be brought down to earth with a bump by minor chaos resulting from not having things ready in advance.

Exposition

Exposition involves explaining, description, linking with children's experience and is an important teacher skill. Wragg and Brown (1993: 3) describe explaining as 'giving understanding to another' and they suggest that an explanation can help someone understand:

- concepts;
- cause and effect;
- procedures;
- purposes and objectives;
- relationships;
- processes.

They stress the importance of good use of the voice.

> Correct use of the voice involves light and shade, knowing when to slow down or accelerate, which words or phrases to emphasise, when to pause, how to read an audience so that the appropriate tone of voiceis used.
>
> (Wragg and Brown 1993: 4)

It is also useful for children to explain things to each other. It can be useful to record a session when you have introduced a topic in this way and listen to it carefully and critically. It may even be a good idea occasionally to share such a recording with another teacher.

Using questioning

Questioning is a very important teaching skill. Wragg and Brown (1993: 16) note that it can have several purposes. These include:

- finding out what the pupils already know or do not know;
- shaping the line of argument by using the pupils' own ideas;
- checking how well pupils understand what is being explained;
- eliciting concrete examples of principles or concepts;
- helping children develop a desire to enquire to learn further, once the explanation is complete.

Questions are of many kinds and some are of more use than others in developing children's ability to think. The following types of questions are common in classrooms and are taken mainly from Kerry (1980). This list may be old but is still pretty valid.

Recall questions

These are probably the most common type of teaching questions. They are useful and necessary but should not be used to the exclusion of other types of questions. Recall questions can degenerate into 'guess what I'm thinking' questions in which you can see children concentrating on trying to guess what the teacher wants rather than on answering the question.

Reasoning questions

Questions which involve thinking things through using evidence are needed in most types of school work. Questions such as 'Why do you think that moss grows on this wall and not on that one?' or 'What do you think will happen next in the story and why do you think that?' can demand reasoning from children, especially if you follow up their replies so that you take them through a sequence of reasoning.

Speculative questions

Many reasoning questions will also be speculative, but one can go beyond the reasoning involved in the type of questions given above and encourage reasoned speculation about hypothetical possibilities, such in 'What would happen if school ceased to be compulsory?' or 'What difference would it make if our school was on top of a hill or by the sea?'

Personal response questions

These ask children how they feel about something, have no right answers and should help children to sort out their own thinking. Examples are 'How would you feel if someone damaged something you cared about a lot?', 'What should happen to people who damage other people's property?' or 'Why do you think they do it?'

Questioning should not be left to the spur of the moment. It is wise to prepare a good many of the questions you want to ask in advance so that you can give thought to the kind of questions you are planning to use. It may be a good idea from time to time to record a questioning session and then listen to it afterwards, perhaps with a colleague, and consider whether the questions you asked actually made the children think. You also need to consider what evidence you need to know whether you were making the children think or not and what proportion of the class this covered. Your assistant will also have useful views on this, particularly if you brief her well beforehand.

It may also be worth recording a lesson in order to listen to your responses to children. Were they such as to give children confidence to contribute? How did you deal with wrong answers? Were you able to find ways of encouraging children who gave a wrong answer and leading them towards the correct answer? Which children actually gave answers?

Holt (1984) describes how he discussed questioning with a group of children in a class with which he felt he had a good relationship. He asked how they felt when they were asked a question, and got the reply 'We gulp'. Galton (1989: 73) also describes children's views about answering questions in class:

> Older pupils described the strategy where they put their hands up to answer a question and put them down again if there was a likelihood of the teacher picking on them to answer. One pupil, referring to answering a question, said, 'It's like walking a tightrope'.

Such evidence suggests that your responses to children's contributions are very important. You also need to give some thought to how you choose children to answer questions. It is wise to pause after giving a question to give children a chance to think and then to choose someone to answer from those with their hands up. Research suggests that increasing 'wait' time for up to three seconds after asking a question can significantly improve the quality of the answers. Askew and Wiliam (1995: 16) note that 'these effects are more pronounced for understanding concepts and principles than for simple recall of facts'.

It is also a good idea on some occasions to ask children not to put up their hands because you will choose someone to answer. If they know in advance that this is what will happen, they are more likely to listen carefully because you may choose them. It can be useful in a questioning session with a class of older children to get one of them to note the initials of those children who answered questions. Your assistant could perhaps do this for you with a younger class.

This sort of record will give you a check on whether you are involving all the children over a period of time or whether you have a bias in choosing children to answer questions, perhaps towards boys or more able children. It is also relevant, when children are putting up their hands to answer, to note those children who did not do this at all.

A further consideration is how you teach children to ask appropriate questions. This is particularly important in science, where children need to learn to ask questions which lend themselves to investigation. Questioning might also be considered in relation to interviewing people and children can be asked to consider what sorts of questions get what sorts of answers. They can also be encouraged to pose questions to the class and to consider whether these were good questions for finding out what they wanted to know.

Paired questioning

It is very easy for children to get the idea that the way teachers ask questions is the norm. Most people ask questions because they want to know the answer. Teachers are unusual in that they mostly ask questions to which they already know the answer. Children need to learn to ask questions in order to understand something.

One way of giving children more opportunities to ask questions is to give pairs of children on one side of the class the task of reading something fairly thoroughly and asking the children on the other side to read something different. Both of these reading tasks should be part of something you are studying as a class. Give them a definite time for this beforehand, allowing for slow readers, and explain that when this part of the work is finished you will rearrange the pairs so that one of each pair will have read something different which they will then try to teach their partner, who will report to their teacher/ partner on how well they think they were taught. The pairs can then change over and do it the other way round. It will be both useful and interesting then to hold a class discussion on what they thought of this practice.

Using drama

Drama is another useful teaching/learning strategy. Children can learn by pretending to be in a different role and trying to act that way. For example, a group of children looking at a picture as if they were gallery owners trying to decide whether to hang a picture in their gallery will study it in order to make a decision about whether to include it. They will ask quite different questions if they are looking to see how it was done, so that they could make one like it.

Schools taking part in some work in helping children to write creatively, found that drama was a valuable way of helping children to become sufficiently involved in a writing topic before putting ideas on paper.

Review 7.2 Direct teaching

1 For which parts of the curriculum do I prefer to use direct teaching? What are my reasons for preferring this approach?
2 When I am planning such teaching, how can I best prepare for it?
3 What is the best way of capturing children's interest when I introduce new material?
4 What are my purposes in questioning? Am I using questions to find out the children's ideas or mainly to see how much they have taken in of my presentation?
5 What kinds of questions to the children seem to be most useful for different purposes?
6 What kinds of questions to the children seem to be most useful for each of the learning purposes I have in mind?
7 Do I prepare the ending of lessons adequately so that children are clear about the work that has been covered and therefore more likely to remember it?

Providing for the different ways in which your children learn

We saw in Chapter 6 that each child has his or her own best way of learning and as teacher you need to be as aware of this as you can. This is what personalising learning is really about. It means that you need to offer a variety of different learning opportunities so that each child can gradually find out the ways of learning that suit him or her best.

We all learn better the material we seek out and work on for ourselves, making our own discoveries. Primary teachers are well aware of this and work to create situations in which children experiment and discover. Sometimes a teacher will set up an open-ended learning situation in which a group of children is taken out of school and encouraged to look for things to study as well as those suggested by the teacher.

On another occasion the teacher may want to get a particular piece of learning established and may provide specific experiences and arrange for a very specific outcome. This is most easily seen when one looks at the development of mathematical concepts, where a teacher may be providing various kinds of practical work in order to develop conceptual thinking based on firm understanding. Edwards and Mercer (1987) describe teachers in this situation giving children clues about what is wanted when they don't find it out for themselves and they demonstrate how this kind of learning can degenerate into 'guess what I'm thinking'. They also show that teachers often miss useful comments by children which would have helped the learning because they are so intent on seeing that the children achieve the teacher's goals. They suggested that where this happens the learning becomes 'ritual': children go through the procedures and say the right words but do not really understand the principles underlying what they are learning. This makes the learning difficult to apply in new situations.

Providing for learning by investigation

Learning by investigation also means acquiring process skills. These skills are also needed in most other aspects of curriculum. They can be developed in the following ways.

- Provide the materials, time and physical arrangement for the children to study and interact with things in their environment. This involves children in using the evidence of their senses, finding answers by doing things, having concrete experience as a basis of their thinking and being able to check their ideas against the behaviour of real things.
- Design tasks that encourage discussion among small groups of children. This involves children in combining their ideas, listening to others, arguing about differences and refining their ideas through explaining them to others. This kind of activity is at its most valuable when the groups are of mixed ability and the more able children stimulate others.
- Discuss their work with children as individuals and in small groups. Children can be encouraged to explain how they arrived at their ideas and by listening to them you can find out about the evidence they have gathered and discover how they have interpreted it. This is also an opportunity to encourage children to check their findings and review their activities and results critically.
- Organise whole-class discussions. Children need the opportunity to explain their findings and ideas to others, to hear about others' ideas, to comment on alternative views and to defend their own. Children also need you to offer ideas and direct them to sources which will extend their ideas.
- Teach the techniques of using equipment and the conventions of using graphs, tables, charts and symbols. Children need to have available the means to increase the accuracy of their observations and to choose appropriate forms for communication of their findings.
- Provide books, displays, visits and access to other sources of information. Children can compare their ideas with those of others, have access to information that may help them to develop and extend their ideas and raise questions which may lead to further enquiry.

Much of what is suggested here not only leads to learning in science but also meets many of the demands of the National Curriculum for oral and other work in English and mathematics and has relevance in a subject such as history where children may be encouraged to look for evidence of what life was like in other times.

Computers also offer very good opportunities for investigation. The internet nearly always has some entries relevant to whatever you want to know and this offers a wonderful opportunity for personalising learning. It is also very absorbing for most children and as the provision of computers increases, you need to make good use of this facility.

Learning by investigation may also enable children to follow up interests and be stimulated by an experience and to have some choice in the way they respond. A group of children making a local study, for example, may record their findings in drawing or painting, model making, various forms of writing, music, movement, drama and so on. The study may give rise to mathematical, scientific, historical or geographical exploration. It will, of course, be important to bear in mind the demands of the National Curriculum and to use the experience to develop some of the concepts and skills involved. It will also be important when giving children a choice of response to see that individual children do not always choose the same way to work. A child who writes well and easily, for example, may choose to respond in writing every time, whereas a child who finds writing difficult will avoid it. This kind of activity requires a good deal of careful thought on the part of the teacher. It is not enough just to take children to an interesting place, even if you direct their attention to some of the things which can be seen. You need to help them to acquire the skills for studying the environment and recording their responses in a variety of ways.

This may sometimes involve looking for specific information and making straightforward statements about findings, perhaps using charts and diagrams. On other occasions it may involve suggesting that they think about how a place made them feel and write personally or poetically or draw or paint what they see. Sometimes you may suggest that they try to observe in detail and record in drawing or model making or look for things which might be investigated further, perhaps by questioning other people or by experiment. Most visits can give rise to work in all three core subjects as well as work in history and geography, art and craft and possibly other subjects as well.

Learning through play

Very young children may develop concepts and skills through play but the adult needs to see that this happens. Bennett and Kell (1989) found that teachers of infants tended to regard play as a time-filler, enabling them to hear other children read. They stress that it is not enough to provide play opportunities at the reception stage, however rich these may be. The teacher or another adult needs to interact with the children, drawing out the learning possibilities. Bruner (1985), for example, notes that adult presence

> **Review 7.3 Learning by investigation**
>
> 1 For which areas of curriculum do I provide opportunities for investigation?
> 2 How do I organise these sessions? Do I arrange for children to work together in pairs or groups? Are there any problems about this?
> 3 What skills do the children need to use this form of learning? How do I help them to acquire these skills?
> 4 Do I provide any opportunities for children to investigate ideas of their own? Do any interesting results come from such opportunities?
> 5 Do I keep a satisfactory balance between learning by direct teaching and learning by investigation?
> 6 Am I happy with the outcomes of this kind of learning?

strikingly increases the richness and length of play. Sylva *et al.* (1980) found that young children were more likely to engage in complex play if adults were interacting with them. The adult plays a fundamental part in directing the child's attention effectively. This refers to other learning as well as play.

Learning through observation

Only when children have a range of approaches and skills for making observations do they become able to use a complex environment for learning. This doesn't mean that children need training in all the skills before you encourage responses to a new environment. Skills and approaches can be built up in the course of study and during the process children will see and suggest ideas of their own, some of which you may like to help them develop. This will help them to become independent observers who are genuinely investigating for themselves.

This is one of the most important approaches to learning because it can be highly motivating and can help children to structure what they are learning and acquire concepts. It is also one of the most difficult methods to use well, and creating situations in which children can make discoveries which are within their capacity, but which extend their thinking, is a fascinating professional task.

Learning through discussion

Most of us learn a great deal through talking and we also consolidate learning in this way. One reason why this is useful is that when you want to put something into words you have to think it out. The responses and questions of others to your statement may then sharpen your thinking and enlarge it.

Teachers will also be very conscious that one way to learn something well is to have to teach it. Edwards and Mercer (1987) suggest that the whole process of teaching and learning is a matter of arriving at shared understandings, in particular of the language used, through shared activity and talk. In a conversation each speaker brings his or her own experience to the interpretation of the words of the other. If the experience is very different, misunderstanding is likely to follow. This can often be the case with children who may use the same words as the adult but give them a more limited meaning because of the limitations of their own experience.

Children therefore need to learn through discussion, and there is much that you can do to see that this kind of learning takes place. This is partly a matter of organisation but also a matter of helping children to become more skilled at being members of a discussion group.

We have already seen that questioning is an important part of the teacher's role as well as being something we should help children to do. It is also a way of stimulating discussion, and very often you ask questions to get the children to talk in order to draw from them material useful for the learning you have in mind. However, there is some research evidence which suggests that controversial statements by the teacher are often more stimulating to children than questions. Askew and Wiliam (1995: 17) note that 'when teachers make statements in order to provoke discussion rather than ask questions, pupils can display more complex thought, deeper personal involvement, wider participation, greater inter-connectedness, and richer inquiry'.

The starting point for discussion is to think out very clearly what you hope to get from it. It may, for example, provide a series of starting points for a piece of work. It may be a way to get children to reflect on experience and generalise from it. You may also be hoping to get a lot of examples to illustrate various points and ideas.

The first task in preparing discussion is to consider the function of the discussion you plan. Is it to discover what children already know or already think about a topic? Are you concerned to get their ideas about a new area of work? Are you seeking the best way into the work you had planned? There are probably many reasons for choosing discussion at this point and you need to be clear what you hope to get from it.

The next stage is to identify some key questions or statements which are likely to lead to useful conclusions. This involves thinking what experience and the language to express it your children are likely to have in relation to your key questions and statements. You can then start in areas where you know that every child will have some experience to contribute.

There are a number of important points that you need to remember when leading class discussion.

1   Look at the way you receive children's contributions. Doing this in a sympathetic and appreciative way is particularly important if you want

to get a good discussion going and it would be the same if you were working with adults instead of children.

2   Remember to scan the room looking for children who have something to say and want to get in or those who are miles away and perhaps need recalling to the present. It is easy to miss children seated at the sides of the room and those who are very near you. You need to make a deliberate attempt to look at everyone in the group every so often.

3   Every teacher becomes skilled at reading children's body language and recognising when they are telling you that they have had enough. Class discussion should generally be short, unless the children are very much absorbed.

4   Much the most important task of the discussion leader is that of summarising or pulling together the ideas and the contributions that have been made, making them into a coherent whole and then possibly pushing the discussion further or moving on to some other activity. It is a vital skill for a teacher and you need to do it consciously to begin with so that you can practise the skill and improve it. It is particularly important at the end of a discussion. Many teachers build up a summary on the board as they go along but this has the disadvantage that you lose eye contact with the children. An overhead projector or a whiteboard is slightly better for this purpose.

Discussion in small groups

Discussion can also take place in small groups and there is a considerable difference between these discussions and discussion led by the teacher. When you are leading the discussion yourself you can give it direction. If you want small groups to work on their own, you need to think carefully about the brief you are going to give them so that they can use the time really profitably.

The experience of discussion in a small group with or without the teacher is a different experience from that of discussion in a large group. In a class discussion, however good the teacher, it is possible for some children to opt out and some may have developed considerable skill in looking involved when really they are far away.

When you are in a small group, and even more so when you are talking with only one or two other people, there is some pressure on you to participate, and the smaller the group the more true this becomes. This suggests that small group discussion has a particular value, and when something new is being learned or some experience is being sorted out a small group may be the best possible way of establishing learning.

There is also a case for training older children in the skills of discussion and discussion leadership, talking with the class about what is involved in creating a good discussion and in leading it and then letting some children practise to see how well they do.

Very valuable work can be done in pairs and trios. The kind of discussion which two children might have in working out a mathematical problem together has considerable value because it requires both to put their thinking into words and the process of communication itself helps their understanding. There is also value in one child teaching another.

Review 7.4 Learning through discussion

1 What do I see as the main function of the discussion I am about to plan?
2 How shall I set it going?
3 What can I do to encourage all the children to contribute?
4 Would it be a good idea to ask my assistant to note which children put up their hand to contribute and which children rarely or never do this?
5 Can I find a way of doing something about this next time we have a class discussion? Should I perhaps tell the children not to put their hand up because I am going to just ask someone.
6 Should I also ask her to make a note of what I said in response when a child made a contribution?
7 What do I consider that the children learned from this discussion?
8 How should I set about teaching children to discuss effectively in pairs or small groups?
9 What skills do they need to do this effectively? How can I train them in these skills?

Learning from materials

All teachers make some use of books and materials in their work with children. Most frequently they use books and work cards to provide practice and reinforcement of learning, so that something is taught to a group or class and then children practise what they have learned in some way using materials. Children, particularly older children, will now be in a position to use the internet as a source of information and this will need careful introduction and management.

A rather different use of materials is for the provision of work matched to individual needs. In this situation different children may be working through some kind of structured scheme, computer program or course book, each working at the level he or she has reached. Or each child may be working more independently with work that not only matches his or her stage of development and learning but that is also related to each individual's interests.

Work cards and work sheets have been around for a long time, but we are still at a comparatively early stage of discovering how to design materials which interest children and teach them well. Computers are gradually enabling teachers to produce really good-looking materials and this development will continue.

Making materials for children's learning

Many teachers make materials to meet the particular needs of their children. In making materials you need to remember the following points.

1 *The materials must be motivating in their own right* They are most likely to be motivating if they have an element of discovery or problem-solving which is well within the child's capacity but is also challenging. For example, a child learning the various ways we spell the long 'a' sound is likely to be motivated if given a list of words and asked to work out the different ways in which the sound can be spelled and then asked to find more examples of each. This learning is more likely to be retained than a list of words to be learned because the task has demanded involvement and decision-making.

2 *Language is very important in teaching material* The language level at which a child can work independently is much less complex both in vocabulary and structure than the language level the child can manage if the material is introduced by the teacher.

3 *The layout of a work card is also important* Good spacing between lines of writing can make it more legible. The way things are arranged helps or hinders understanding. It is a good idea to study the way advertising material is set out and to apply some of the ideas to work materials.

4 *Good individualised learning material needs to be carefully structured so that a child can work through it in an appropriate way* The way it is stored should also help children to see progression through the material.

Learning with audio-visual and electronic equipment

Audio-visual equipment provides many additional opportunities for learning because it can, in some sense, duplicate the teacher. Radio and television are among the oldest forms of audio-visual learning now available to teachers and British teachers have access to programmes of very high quality. These can bring into the classroom experience which no child or teacher might otherwise encounter. The broadcasting authorities have access to the best of current thinking and do a good deal to consult teachers and to pilot and monitor their materials in the classroom. The CD and video recorder also make it possible to use just that portion of a programme which is relevant if the teacher wishes. It is also now possible to use material from non-educational programmes if your Local Education Authority (LEA) has subscribed to this use. Radio and television are a comparatively cheap resource which can be of great value and can complement teaching of the National Curriculum very helpfully. Teachers may also use digital cameras and obtain digital images from the internet and use them on the whiteboard.

The great majority of broadcast programmes are made for watching or listening with the teacher rather than as teaching materials in their own right. If you wish to use radio or television as small-group or individual teaching material, it will probably be necessary to extend the materials which go with the programme or provide other material to bridge the gap between use with the teacher and independent use by the children. This isn't true for all broadcasts but it will be true for a number.

Recording equipment is among the most-used pieces of classroom equipment, offering a considerable range of possibilities. It can be used for material created by the children and also for actual teaching and for various kinds of practice. It is also useful for recording interviews as part of environmental studies, and, as many children have access to recording equipment at home, a child can record discussion with members of the family and people in the neighbourhood and bring the recording to school to share with others.

Recording equipment is also a valuable tool for developing skill in speaking and can be helpful in teaching reading. It offers a child the opportunity to prepare reading by listening to a recording of a book or story for later reading to the teacher. It can also be used for learning phonics. Another possibility is for a child to record a story s/he has made up which can then be typed out by a volunteer parent and used for reading practice.

Video recorders and discs extend these kinds of opportunities. It is often helpful to record something at home to use in school and children who have this kind of facility at home may be able to record themselves involved in particular activities which might be of more general interest.

At a later stage there is much to be said for putting books, stories and poetry on tape so that children who are poor readers can experience the pleasure of reading, following the reading on tape or disc in their books. This makes available for slower readers some of the benefits that better readers are getting from reading. It provides models of speech and vocabulary and enables children to hear language structures which may be new to them. They will also have the opportunity to identify with people in stories and extend their experience through the text.

Such material takes time to build up, but there are often parents with an interest in drama who might help. Preparing tapes and discs could also be an activity for older children who are good readers.

In a similar way such things as spelling, mental arithmetic and word building can be recorded for children, or a child can record the words or numbers he or she needs to learn as a personal test and then return to take the test when he or she is ready. Children might also work in pairs at a similar stage and do this for each other.

Photographic transparencies are also valuable, particularly in relation to environmental studies, and it is a good idea to build a collection of slides of different buildings, landscapes and objects which can be used on a number of occasions. These can be used with a tape recorder or DVD and a hand viewer, or they can be used as material for the whole class.

It will be important to get this work into perspective and to marry it with other kinds of working which provide different sorts of learning. It would be very easy, given the availability of computers in schools and the ever increasing development of software, to forget the importance of first-hand experience.

ICT is perhaps the most important and in many ways the most versatile and valuable modern development. If offers a world of information and opportunity for teachers and for children and we need to make the most of it. Whiteboards are also a very important learning device and as they become universal, teachers will be able to provide another valuable learning opportunity for their children.

Review 7.5 Learning with audio-visual and electronic equipment

1 How competent are my children in using computers? What additional skills do they need? What is the best way of helping them to acquire these skills?
2 Am I encouraging them to use email for useful purposes?
3 How many are able to use the internet? What rules should I make about its use?
4 Am I making good use of radio and television programmes for schools?
5 What other equipment and materials do I encourage my children to use? How well do they do this?
6 To what extent are electronic and other materials contributing to children's independence in learning?
7 How well does the organisation of books and materials in my classroom contribute effectively to independent learning?
8 Is my classroom environment well organised for the work I want the children to do? Does it offer stimulation for children?

The effective school

The study of London junior schools by Mortimore *et al.* (1988: 250) looked at the factors associated with an effective school and which the school could control. They found that the following were important:

- purposeful leadership by the headteacher;
- the involvement of the deputy head;

- consistency among teachers;
- intellectually challenging teaching;
- work-centred environment;
- limited focus within sessions: not more than two subjects dealt with at one time;
- maximum communication between teacher and pupils;
- record-keeping;
- parental involvement;
- positive climate.

Although this study is fairly old what it says is still highly relevant. It also notes a number of ways in which individual teachers were effective. There was a relationship between the teacher's enthusiasm and the work provided for the children. The most effective teachers frequently involved the whole class in discussion and were skilled at doing this, which was not necessarily whole-class teaching as such. It is also possible to provide good opportunities for discussion by getting children to work in pairs and small groups with a brief to discuss a particular topic and come to some conclusions which can be reported to the whole class. Trying to personalise learning does not mean working with children as individuals for much of the time. There is evidence that this is not really effective.

Target-setting

Recent years have seen an emphasis on target-setting at all levels, for individuals and groups of children, for whole classes, for whole schools, for local authorities and nationally. Target-setting should evolve from the assessments you make of children's progress and achievement and should lead to further planning on an individual basis. Both the literacy and numeracy strategies suggest short meetings with individual children at which targets for their progress are agreed and their success in meeting them subsequently assessed. Some of these targets should be suggested by the children themselves.

Chapter 8

Teaching skills and learning strategies

Knowledge by itself is not sufficient to make an effective teacher; you also need specific and effective teaching skills. Society delegates to the teacher the task of educating children. The teacher and the children come to school each bringing with them a variety of talents, experiences and influences, which affect the way they teach and learn. Children will also have formed many ideas about the world around them before they come to school and these need to be taken into account by the teacher. In school, the teacher's task is to see that the child experiences the curriculum, develops and learns, and in the process acquires learning skills. To achieve this the teacher creates a learning environment and organises time, space and resources to enable the child to learn.

As teacher you are the most important resource in the classroom and the problem is always that of trying to meet the needs of a disparate group of children always taking into account the learning and teaching styles you analysed in Chapters 6 and 7. You need to reflect frequently on the extent to which and the way in which you are using your time to foster the children's learning and the amount of time that children are actually working at profitable tasks.

Assessment for learning

There are many ways in which you can assess children in relation to their learning and you need to be continually alert to the clues they give you about themselves, their background and their language ability.

Observing and interpreting children's behaviour

The teacher's ability to observe and interpret children's behaviour is crucial, particularly at the early stages of education when children are more dependent on the teacher and may be more limited in their ability to express their needs.

Chazan *et al.* (1987: 12) make the following points about observation:

> To provide the most fruitful experiences and to encourage children to explore and discover for themselves can only be successfully accomplished

on the basis of careful observation of the children concerned over a period of time. Teachers must therefore be observers in order to provide a structured framework for learning.

The skills and strategies involved in observation and assessment by teachers are built up gradually over the years and might be classified in the following way.

1   *General observation*   Over the years, you gradually develop skills in observing children at work, coming to know the signs of underfunctioning and of learning problems of various kinds and what may reasonably be expected from any individual or group.

2   *Systematic observation*   General observation is largely a matter of observing things as they happen. Children's performance should also be reviewed more systematically on a regular basis, working through the list of children every so often and considering each in turn and perhaps discussing their progress and setting targets with them. It might be a good idea to observe and talk individually to a small number of different children about their work each week as part of your overall assessment procedure. Part of this review might be to make an opportunity to work diagnostically with the children, using such opportunities as hearing them read or discussing work with them to identify particular problems and difficulties. It is wise to keep a record of such observations so that you can refer back to it when you want to remind yourself of what happened earlier.

3   *The use of tests and check-lists*   Systematic observation may include the use of teacher-made or standardised tests and check-lists. These require skill and knowledge in their interpretation. The National Standard Assessment Tasks (SATs) should add to the observations of the teacher as well as providing information about the stage each child has reached and it seems likely that you will soon be able to decide when a particular child takes the test. This will have all sorts of implications for your organisation and the way you work. It should certainly have an effect on the time you spend preparing children for the SATs because they will become ready for them a few at a time.

In addition you need to have material and practices which help you to identify particular problems such as inadequate phonic skills or lack of knowledge of particular mathematical operations.

In observing any individual child a teacher might look at the following four areas.

1   *Personality and learning style*   There are many differences in children and the way they learn. This was discussed in more detail in the previous

two chapters. You need to find the 'best fit' learning approaches for the particular group of children and the individuals within it.

2 *Experience and interests* Communication depends upon experience shared between you and your children and the language needed to express a response to it. Any new work needs to be planned in the light of observation, discussion and conjecture about the relevant experiences that children already have and those they may need for new learning and understanding.

3 *Stage of development* A child's stage of development will to some extent determine his or her thought processes and specific development within subject areas. It is therefore necessary to discover how children are thinking and what their ideas are in developing any area of work. Research suggests that this is particularly important in science, in which children come to the subject with their own ideas about why things happen that are often at odds with the scientific knowledge you want them to acquire. It will also be necessary to assess specific skills as part of your assessment procedure.

4 *Abilities* You need to match work to individual ability on many occasions and ensure that the most able are not marking time or underachieving and that the least able or least interested are not doing less than they might because you are showing them that your expectations of them are low. There is evidence to suggest that both these groups underperform.

Review 8.1 Observation skills

1 How good were the assessments of children that I made when they first came to me? Have I changed my views much as I have come to know the children?

2 Am I being sufficiently systematic about assessing each of my children and keeping good records of my findings?

3 Do my records of the academic progress of each child give me the information that I need to help them to learn?

4 Do my records of each child's behaviour and development give me the information I need to help them to develop socially?

5 Does my use of tests and check-lists contribute satisfactorily to the knowledge I need to help children to learn and develop?

6 Do I observe individual children to find starting points for their learning?

7 Do I look for the right moment to intervene to help individuals to learn?

8 Do I discuss progress with individual children, helping them to set targets for their improvement in a regular and systematic way?

9 Do I observe in order to identify individual children's problems and deal with them?

10 Do I study children who are exceptionally able as well as those who have learning difficulties in order to help them learn at a suitable level?

The organisation of the learning programme

The learning programme needs to be organised to meet the needs identified from observation, relating each day's work broadly to a plan for the week, the term, the year or the school life of the children, using interests and experiences to provide learning opportunities and checking that the necessary ground is covered. You need to be opportunistic but systematic.

The work you do with your class is part of a programme for the whole school, and you need to work closely with subject leaders so that your work fits with what other teachers have done in the past and will do in the future.

The developing use of ICT is likely to make a difference to your role as teacher and should eventually enable you to match the learning needs of individuals very closely and personalise their learning more fully. It seems likely that technology will enhance the role of the teacher rather than usurp it, freeing the teacher for tasks that only a person can do, such as helping individual children to identify their strengths and weaknesses and find ways of working which are really effective for them as individuals. However, it also means that you need to do all you can to keep up to date with the technology involved. This may not be easy with all the other tasks you have, but you need to bear in mind that it may eventually save time for you.

ICT

The most important and in many ways the most versatile and valuable modern development is the computer. ICT offers a world of information and opportunity for teachers and for children and we need to make the most of it. One school, Longwell Green Primary, set out its rationale for ICT (May 2007) as follows:

> We are proudest of the achievements we have made so far at Longwell Green in ICT and have great hopes for the future. We now live in a society that is heavily dependent on the understanding and use of technology and therefore strive to provide our children with the best possible education in ICT. We also appreciate how ICT can be a valuable tool for both teaching and learning and therefore believe it can be implemented through many other subject areas. ICT has become an exciting aspect of life at Longwell Green and we hope that it will continue to grow and develop as it has done so far.

The selection of learning material

Being a teacher at the primary school level is very demanding in terms of subject knowledge. You need to have a good understanding of all the subjects of the National Curriculum if you are to be in a position to select learning material which will enable individuals and groups to learn that part of the curriculum appropriate for their age and ability. This task involves not only considering how to teach the different aspects of the National Curriculum but also looking at how they can be combined so that learning in one area complements and enhances learning in another. You also need to be aware of the way in which children's interests and experiences can be used for their learning. Quite often children's current enthusiasms can be used as an inspiration for writing or reading or exploring something.

The presentation of learning material

Children need constant interaction between first-hand experience and other learning materials if they are to be able to transfer what they have learned from one situation to another. The provision of first-hand experience through visits, exploration of the school environment or of material brought into the classroom is basic to effective learning. The whiteboard should also make a real difference to working with the whole class, because of the possibilities for interactive work. Your task then will be to help children to become aware of and focus on aspects important for learning and help them to structure what they are learning so that it fits into a developing pattern in their minds.

You will also need to provide materials within the classroom that are designed to foster learning. Sometimes this will involve a published scheme, a book or a radio or television programme or a computer program or the material you have provided or presented. Presentation by the teacher requires skill in talking about the topic under consideration. It requires the ability to describe something in a way that captures children's interest and to give explanations which are clear and understandable. It also requires the ability to question in a way which stimulates thinking.

ICT will now be an important part of the material for learning. Children as they grow older must learn how to use the internet to find things out. It will be a considerable help if your assistant as well as you is computer literate and able to help children with this.

The structuring of children's learning

Chapter 6 suggested some ways in which you could help your children to structure their learning and develop concepts. In Chapter 7 we looked in some detail at the need to match work to children's needs both as individuals and as a class. Learning is easiest where the material to be learned is part of an overall structure and the learner can see where the new piece of learning fits in. Children in the primary school are all the time developing structures and forming new concepts in their minds and these will form the basis of some of their future learning. The way they organise their thinking at the primary school stage may govern their ability to learn in the future. They are sometimes helped by being given a structure, but it is also wise to help them to form structures of their own.

For example, at one time, tables were taught mainly by rote, using one particular structure. One effect of this was that children sometimes found difficulty in using the information, because they felt that they had to go through the whole table each time they wanted to know the answer to multiplying two numbers together, and this was a slow process. We now tend to lead children to work out a number of different structures for tables including the standard one.

Another example is seen in the development of classifying skills. Children learn about sets in mathematics at quite an early age, but very often this knowledge is not applied when, for example, children go out and come back with a collection of varied objects. These could be sorted into sets according to their attributes, which is what has happened when biologists, botanists and geologists have classified the material they have found.

It is your responsibility as teacher to help your children to create the mental structures which are essential for thinking about the work in hand. The way you present material, summarise, point out links, encourage classifying and ordering and so on helps children to create appropriate mental structures and concepts which enable them both to understand the work they are doing and to remember it.

Vygotsky (1978) suggested that there is something which he calls the 'zone of proximal development': the gap between what a child can learn by him or herself and what is possible with the aid of an adult. The adult provides a scaffolding or structure which enables the child to learn. The way material is presented and the discussion that goes with it are all part of these structures.

Training learning behaviour

The ability to work independently and in groups does not come automatically. A good deal of work needs to go into training these abilities throughout the primary school. With a new class you need to start with very little independent work and gradually increase the amount you expect. A study by Mortimore et al. (1988) found that junior school children worked independently in a satisfactory way for short periods, possibly no more than a morning. This report also suggested that choice should be limited. What is not clear from this study is whether the teachers concerned trained their children in independent learning and whether training produced increased ability to work in this way. The teacher's attitude towards making children independent is also important.

Group work was discussed in Chapter 7 and it is important to see that children are fully aware of the kind of behaviour which is needed if group work is to be effective.

Providing inspiration and encouragement

An important part of the teacher's role is to stimulate and interest children in whatever is to be learned. This is a valuable part of working with the whole class and is one reason why you should often work with the whole class or with groups of children. You can only inspire a few children if you do this individually but you may inspire many more if you do it with everyone at once or with a group. However, individual encouragement is also needed and should be regarded as a teaching tool because children tend to repeat what is praised and encouraged. There is some evidence that teachers praise and encourage differentially.

It is very easy to think that you do more encouraging than you actually do and particularly easy to encourage the able and offer little to the least able and the quiet child. It is helpful occasionally to try to check the number of encouraging comments you make in the course of a morning or afternoon, perhaps with the help of your assistant.

Skills of organisation and control

The actual process of organisation in the classroom involves selecting things to fit your particular style, your children and the situation as well as the topic under discussion. You need to be able to anticipate likely problems and avoid them by careful planning, particularly at points of change of activity. You also need to train children to work as you think best, using the resources of time and space to full advantage. In addition you need to be able to control children as a class, in groups and individually. Very few teachers escape altogether from problems of managing the classroom and almost all beginners need to work to achieve control. Although it is certainly true that some people achieve control very easily right from the start, most people have to develop this ability over a period of time.

Factors involved in classroom organisation and control

There are many factors involved in good classroom organisation and control and some of these, such as grouping and the use of time and space, are dealt with in detail later in this book. The control of children is very much bound up with the organisation that a teacher sets up. The following points need to be considered.

- *The quality of the classroom as a learning environment* Children learn from the environment as well as from the teacher and each other, and the way the classroom is set up for learning is important. It should be attractive and welcoming but also have much available which encourages learning. Display should be either encouraging children by showing their work attractively or it should be stimulating material which invites questions and exploration. There should be a good deal in the classroom which supports independent learning. It is useful to ask oneself whether children left to their own devices in the classroom would be able to go on learning because of the way the room is organised.

- *The use of space and resources* The way space is organised in the classroom has a considerable effect on the way children work. If resources are easily to hand and are organised so that it is clear which materials a child should use next, it is likely that there will be better concentration on the work in hand and fewer interruptions for the teacher. It is also important to try to use resources as effectively and fully as possible. For example, are any computers in your classroom out of use for much of the time? If so, it is worth considering whether some slight changes in organisation would give more children a chance to use them.

- *Grouping for learning* A good deal of primary school learning takes place in groups, although this is sometimes a matter of children working individually within the group at work given to the group as a whole. There should also be some co-operative work in groups and some work where the grouping is according to ability.

- *The use of time* Time is the one resource which cannot be increased. You can only look for better ways of using the time that you have. There are suggestions in Chapter 18 for checking how you are using time with a view to seeing whether you are making the best possible use of it.

- *School support for teachers having difficulties with behaviour* Teachers need to feel supported both by colleagues with whom they can discuss problems and also by school management. A teacher should know what s/he will be able to do with a child who seems to be beyond his or her ability to control. This will be particularly important for newly qualified teachers.

Classroom control

It can be frightening to find yourself not in control, and inexperienced teachers need to remind themselves not only that they can learn to control children but that the ability to do this, while a prerequisite for good teaching, does not itself guarantee it. That depends on how you use the opportunities which the control you achieve offers. There are teachers who have excellent control, but offer little of quality to children. There are also outstanding teachers who have had to work hard in their early days to achieve control.

Principles of classroom control

There are a number of principles for classroom control which it is useful to remember.

Children misbehave when they don't know what to do

Think out the organisation of your work in detail beforehand, especially when you will be changing activities. You also need to think carefully about how you are going to instruct children about the work you want them to do. This is just as important when you are working with a group of children you know well as when you are working with a new group and establishing ways of doing things.

Always get attention before giving instructions

It is a good idea to get children to look at you so that their attention is alerted and you can make eye contact with them. You may also need to find a way of attracting attention when children are doing noisy work or are absorbed in what they are doing, especially if you have a quiet voice. Establish the idea that when you clap your hands or signal in some way you want everyone's attention. Learn to give instructions so that each important point is reinforced and is clear to everyone. Be careful not to give too much information at once. It is often a good idea to ask particular children what the instruction was to make sure that they have grasped the message.

Be ready when children come into the classroom

The way you start work is important. It can be a recipe for trouble, and a waste of time, to insist that children wait quietly without anything to do for too long. It is generally better to establish a pattern in which everyone is expected to come in and start working at something. This may be a preplanned activity which is self-explanatory or work from instructions written on the board or it may be a daily pattern of quiet work or any other regular activity. The important thing is not to leave children with nothing to do but misbehave.

This isn't nearly as easy as it seems when you see a capable and experienced teacher at work. As with so much else in teaching, you have to work to establish the behaviour you want.

It may be useful to get the children to discuss this in groups as a problem and see if they can suggest a solution. This has the advantage that they will feel ownership of what they decide.

Be individual in calling children to order

It is generally more effective to pick out individuals by name when you are trying to get attention than to speak to the class generally. You can single out children doing the right things: 'I can see that Karen is ready', or you can comment on those who are not doing what you want: 'Peter, I'm waiting for you'. By and large, the first is more effective and you may find it useful to check from time to time what you are actually doing, so that you are not being too negative to particular children without realising it.

Learn to scan the class

Good teachers are said to have eyes in the back of their heads. Beginners often get absorbed with individuals or small groups and ignore the rest of the class. You need to look round very frequently so that you anticipate misbehaviour. This also keeps children aware that you are watching them and so helps to prevent deviant behaviour.

The Oracle Study (Galton and Simon 1980), described one group of children as intermittent workers and noted that these children only worked when the teacher's eye was on them. If you scan the class regularly, very often a child about to waste time or do something unacceptable will catch your eye and settle to work again. If catching the child's eye doesn't work, try moving towards him or her in a determined way.

Set rules of behaviour from the beginning

Wragg (1984) describes how experienced teachers in his study used the first lesson with a new class. Almost without exception, they said they would use the first few lessons to establish the rules they wanted the class to follow. They varied in the extent to which they intended to dictate the rules or discuss them or work them out with the pupils, but the areas covered tended to be fairly similar. They included rules for entering and leaving the classroom, rules about work, a rule that there should be no talking when the teacher was talking and rules about property and safety.

These were teachers in a secondary school. In a primary classroom you will still want some similar rules, and you may also want to make rules about the degree of movement around the classroom that you will allow, the numbers of children who can undertake a particular activity at the same time, occasions when choice will be allowed and so on. It may be a good idea with older children to have these rules displayed somewhere.

You need to be consistent in dealing with children, making sure that you treat them in fairly similar ways and that you enforce the rules that you have made or agreed with the children without too many changes.

Review 8.2 Skills of organisation and control

1 Is my classroom attractive and welcoming to children?
2 Is the furniture in my classroom arranged to provide the most suitable pattern for the work being undertaken?
3 Is my classroom a learning environment in which children can sometimes learn independently?
4 Are the resources of equipment, materials and books arranged so that they can be fully used by the children as well as the teacher?
5 Are they organised so that they are easy to keep tidy and in order?
6 Do my plans include provision for children of different levels of ability and stages of development?
7 Is each child in an appropriate group for learning?
8 Am I using my own and the children's time to the best advantage?
9 Do children discuss work together in pairs and small groups when this is appropriate?
10 Have I adequate control of the whole group, even when I am working with individuals?
11 Have I agreed rules of classroom behaviour with my children?
12 Am I using my assistant as effectively as possible? Am I doing enough to help her learn?

Work out changes in activity in careful detail

Most of the things which go wrong in the classroom do so in the process of changing from one activity to another. You can avoid problems by thinking out how to make the change and how to get from the first activity to the second, asking yourself what different materials the second activity will need and what each child will be doing and listing the steps which will be needed.

It is wise to think out the organisation of your work in some detail beforehand, especially when you are changing activities. You also need to think carefully about how you are going to instruct children about the work you want them to do. This is just as important when you are working with a group of children you know well as when you are working with a new group and establishing ways of doing things.

Able and experienced teachers often give the impression that all you need to do when you change activities is to say 'It's time now for you to go to your number groups' for there to be a well-organised move round which leaves everyone in the right place in the least possible time. The ability to do this has been built up with the children and through experience over a long period. It takes time and effort to get children to work and move as you wish.

A good deal of the ability to control a class is in the confidence in your voice and manner which implies that children will do as you wish. The trouble is that it is difficult to have confidence when you don't know whether what you are asking for will actually happen. It is possible, however, to learn to behave as if you are confident. Confident people are relaxed and speak confidently and you can learn to do this. Good teachers not only use their voices when they give an explanation of what they want but they also reinforce their words with gestures, facial expression and general body language as well as tone of voice. Smiling conveys confidence. Fumbling and self-grooming convey a lack of confidence, and walking to and fro is distracting.

Assessing the effectiveness of the learning programme

You also need to observe in order to assess the learning programme you are providing, the effects of your classroom environment and organisation and your own contribution. Much of this will be your own observation, but it can be helpful to ask a colleague to observe something you are doing and give you feedback. Your teaching assistant will be in a very good position to give you feedback, both on your own performance and also on its reception by the children. This will enable you to see your work from a rather different viewpoint.

We have already noted that children can give you useful feedback if you discuss with the class their reactions to the various things you and they are doing.

If you ask someone else to observe you, such as your assistant, you have to define what you are trying to do and what you want to know about it, and this is a helpful activity in its own right, particularly for a teaching assistant. She will need to be very clear about the particular things you want her to observe. You might be asking for information about the kinds of comments you make to individual children and to whom you make them. She might look at which children put up their hand to answer questions and which children had questions of their own to ask. It can be valuable also to talk over with her how she felt a particular lesson went and whether she felt there were any children who hadn't understood. You might also think about the clues which will tell you how successful you have been and ask her to observe these too. This kind of involvement will not only be useful to you but can also be part of your assistant's training and development. Asking her to look for something when you are teaching the class as a whole will be helpful to you both and will also help her to concentrate on what is happening which she will find useful subsequently in working with the children to follow up what you have been doing with them.

Children too, particularly older children, can give you useful information about the effectiveness of your work. Take an opportunity at the end of a piece of work to ask what they found interesting, what they enjoyed, what they found easy or difficult and anything they would like to hear more about. Children are often very honest in giving you feedback and their opinions are often very helpful in planning future work.

Communication skills

The ability to form good relationships with children is a prerequisite of clear communication and effective teaching. It is difficult to communicate or teach well if you are not on good terms with your children. The ability to form sound relationships depends a great deal on your personality and is also partly a matter of attitudes which help you to demonstrate to the children that you care about them and have confidence in their ability to learn.

Communication takes place as a result of people attending to each other. It is not simply a matter of the meaning of the words you use, but is implicit in your choice of words and language structure to match the listeners and the situation. (Think how you would say the same thing to your class and to your headteacher.) It is also implicit in your tone of voice, the inflections you use, what you say and how you say it. In addition, you convey messages by your body language and facial expression as well as by words and you automatically modify your message in the light of the response you get. Your view of your listeners is demonstrated in your choice of content, vocabulary and sentence structure and in the use of pitch and pace and the use of pauses.

Movement as communication

The children, in their turn, will respond not only verbally when you ask questions but also in terms of body language and as you grow more experienced you will read this and respond to it automatically. There will be children who are looking at you intently and apparently taking in every word. There will be others who may be looking out of the window or at something which seems to be more interesting to them than what you are saying. There will be those who appear to be bursting to say something and others who avoid catching your eye in case you ask them something. If there are too many who are not reacting to what you are saying you will, almost without noticing it, say the same thing in a different and perhaps a simpler way.

Your task is to get the message over as clearly as possible in ways which draw an appropriate response from the children and help them to match what you are saying to what they know already. Try to record yourself in the classroom from time to time and listen to the recording critically later on.

Movement is the most basic form of communication, operating from birth or perhaps even earlier. Because it is so basic and automatic, the movement message goes over even if you actually say something different. Movement and facial expression are all the time sending messages to others. Your observation of the children involves interpreting the movement messages that they are sending. Their observation of you does likewise. Very young or disabled children often also communicate with their teachers by touch.

It is often through non-verbal communication of this kind that people get across the message that they are warm and sympathetic, brisk and business-like, tired or bad-tempered, pleased or sorry and so on. Children learn to interpret these messages very early because it is important for them to recognise when mother or teacher is pleased or angry.

Eye contact is also an important aspect of communication in this context. We use eye contact to signal the beginnings and endings of pieces of communication as well as to send messages to control children's behaviour. By making eye contact with individual children you can imply that they are being noticed and had better behave or that they are important and being cared for.

Communication through the environment

This is an extension of communication through movement. An experienced observer quickly takes in the messages which a teacher's classroom is putting over. It will tell the observer something about you as teacher, by observing how the classroom looks: does it look well organised and cared for or untidy? Is there display that both reflects the children's work and also what they are learning? How are the children seated: in rows or in groups? You also send messages by the way you dress and care for your appearance. These all reflect philosophy and teaching style.

Spoken communication

Your voice and those of the children and your assistant are likely to be the most frequently used forms of communication in the classroom. The way you use it affects children in different ways.

For example, any teacher who has tried to work with a barely audible 'lost voice' will be aware that it is possible quite quickly to have the children whispering too. You provide an important speech model for your children and your patterns of speech will affect theirs. You need to remember, however, that children learn to use spoken language by speaking and it is not easy to orchestrate opportunities for talking for a whole class. Paired and small-group discussion provides opportunities for children to talk through ideas with others, but you also want opportunities for them to experience speaking in a whole-class situation. Good spoken language skills will be important for children in their future lives and they need to acquire this ability as early as possible.

Communication is a two-way process. The warm and trusting relationship necessary for good communication is something built up over time, but when you start work with a new class it is particularly important to be as responsive as you can to children's ideas and confidences. Your response at this stage to something a child volunteers may determine whether this particular child will risk suggesting something again, and also, if other children are listening, they too will be influenced by your reactions. A teacher who says 'My children never have any ideas' needs to look at the way s/he is reacting to the ideas they offer. It is not unusual to see a group of children silent and unresponsive with one teacher but full of ideas with another.

Trust in the teacher – once established – brings a necessary degree of security to children. As we have seen, security depends a good deal on knowing what to do, knowing the boundaries and what is expected and knowing how the other person will react to different kinds of behaviour. Security often stems from predictability.

What are the communication skills the teacher needs? The following need consideration.

Presentation skills

Every teacher needs to be able to present material to children in ways which capture attention and help them to focus on what is important. This means making good preparation and good use of voice and gesture. It also means continually scanning the class to see how they are responding and being aware of how long you can talk before children cease to listen.

Questioning skills

Questioning is one of the most important teaching skills. You need to think out very carefully in advance the different types of question you want to use so that you challenge the thinking of all the children in the class. Questions can be classified in a number of ways. One common classification is into open and closed questions. Another is into questions requiring recall and questions requiring thinking. Research suggests that teachers tend to ask more closed and recall questions and not enough open and thought-provoking questions. It is also very easy for teachers to ask 'guess what I'm thinking' type of questions and, in responding to children's answers, turn aside all answers but the one which gives the correct guess.

Leading discussion

Leading a class discussion is a more difficult skill than it seems in the hands of an expert, partly because most classes are rather large for satisfactory discussion. It therefore requires a good deal of effort on the part of the teacher to include the whole group. A very important part of leading discussion is the ability to draw together the points that have been made and to reinforce those that are important for the children's learning. It is also

Review 8.3 Communication skills

1 How well do I present material to the whole class?
2 How good am I at explaining things?
3 Do my questions achieve the results I intended?
4 Do I use a sufficient variety of questions demanding enough to get children thinking?
5 Which children rarely put up their hand to answer a question? What can I do to change this?
6 How competent am I at stimulating and leading discussion?
7 Is it always the same children who contribute?
8 Do I get more contributions from boys than girls or conversely?
9 Do children from other cultures and those whose home language is not English make any contribution in class discussions? How can I help them to become more involved?
10 How good am I at drawing the children's contributions together to help them all to learn?
11 How skilled am I at discovering what individual children are thinking?

important to respond positively to the children's contributions. Even when a child gives a wrong answer it may be possible to say something which is encouraging. Positive reactions to contributions encourage children to be more ready to respond the next time and negative reactions inhibit them.

Helping individuals

Whatever the organisation of the class, you will always need skill in helping individual children to move on from their present understanding. You therefore need to be good at analysing a child's thinking so that you can suggest ways forward. You also need to have the class well organised so that you are free to deal with individuals from time to time.

Problem-solving skills

Human beings develop and learn by solving the problems which face them. This is true whether one looks at problems in one's everyday life or at problems in one's place of work.

Unfortunately there is also a human tendency to regard difficult problems as someone else's fault or someone else's problem or as something about which nothing can be done. While it is true that there are always aspects of problems which cannot be solved, the fact that there is an obstacle does not mean that it cannot be overcome.

The process of teaching and organising a class is very much a problem-solving activity for both teacher and children. For the teacher the basic problem is that of how to reconcile the heterogeneous collection of children who make up the class with what they need to learn in such a way that the optimum amount of learning takes place. The solution to this set of problems is the main subject of this book.

The development of work in design and technology has brought the idea of problem-solving to the fore for work with children but the teacher must also be a problem-solver. The skills involved in problem-solving which are evident in design and technology are also applicable to the teacher's problems. Both teacher and children need to acquire problem-solving skills and positive attitudes to problems, and they acquire both skills and attitudes by working to solve problems.

For example, if you are looking at the problem of how to provide for a wide range of abilities in your class, you need to start by defining the problem and then look at what you want the outcome of any action to be. There are probably a number of ways in which you could continue from this point. Two which seem particularly interesting are described below.

Force field analysis was devised by Kurt Lewin (1951) and involves considering the forces which are acting for and against you in solving your problem. Supporting forces in the situation described above might include good accommodation, a head who is prepared to let you try things and will support you financially and a class that is easy to handle. Restraining forces might be the fact that the teacher who had your class last year did nothing to encourage independent working, pressure from parents to work in traditional ways with the most able children, a lack of materials for the most able and a lack of knowledge on your part of the best way to deal with the least able children. You can then consider how you deal with each of these, looking at how you make the most of the supporting forces and at what you can do to minimise the effect of the restraining forces.

Another approach, part of which fits well with force field analysis, is described by Jackson (1975) in *The Art of Solving Problems*. He speaks of considering the obstacles to solving a problem, which is a little like looking at the restraining forces. He suggests working through some possible ways of tackling each obstacle. You might overcome an obstacle, go round it, remove it, demolish it, neutralise it, prove it to be illusory, turn it to advantage, buy it off, alter it, find its weakest point or wait for it to go away.

If you take the restraining forces listed above as the obstacles in your situation, you might remove one of the obstacles by instituting a careful programme of training your children to work more independently. The pressure from parents might be partly demolished by parents' meetings at which you explain what you are doing and why. It might also help to involve parents in the work you are doing in various ways so that they see for themselves what can be effective.

If your head is supportive, it might be possible to meet the obstacles about materials by buying more. However, you would be wise first to analyse the kind of material you need to meet the full range of abilities that your children represent and gradually build up materials which fit into a framework, coding new material as you add it so that you are aware of what you have available. In practice, many teachers spend a lot of time making material but don't take enough time to sort out a structure so that new pieces of material fit in. If you can find time to make a structure, everything you do by way of making or buying material will fit into an overall plan.

Another possibility is to get out all the materials you have which might be relevant and look to see whether any of them could be made more self-contained and usable by children without help from you. You might like to make some bridging materials to go with some other material so that a child who is less able can use it.

When you address yourself directly to an obstacle you find there are frequently possible ways forward. A useful strategy is to ask a series of questions such as 'Can I overcome the problem by looking at it in a different way, by using materials differently, by looking for time to do some basic thinking and sorting out of ideas in order to move forward, by working with colleagues, by involving parents and others, by getting children to work differently or getting their views about how to solve the problem, by reorganising the situation or use of materials, and so on?' This kind of thinking is often most profitable when undertaken with others. It is certainly a good idea to talk over such problems with your assistant. She knows the actual situation in a way that other colleagues can only guess at. She may also have suggestions and ideas which have not yet occurred to you. It is sometimes a useful activity for a class of children as well as for interested staff.

List possible solutions

You will already have a number of solutions as a result of your examination of forces and obstacles and you can add to these. Write down as many ideas as you can think of, however unlikely some of them seem. Don't stop when you think of an idea which seems good but go on generating further ideas until you have quite a number. Letting your mind range over ideas in this way influences the idea you finally choose, which may be a mixture of several ideas. It can sometimes be useful to aim for a particular number of ideas; to set out, for example, ten ways of achieving the objective you have in mind. It can also be useful to do this with someone else, perhaps with a colleague or your assistant.

If you are working with a group of colleagues, one way of working would be to pass round a piece of paper for each objective, on which each person writes an idea which could be used to achieve that objective. It is better still to do this on the whiteboard where you can display the ideas listed for discussion.

Examine solutions

The next stage is to look at the solutions you have listed. It may help to draw up a page with four columns headed 'Idea; Advantages; Disadvantages; Points to note'. Talk over your lists with your assistant who may have further ideas. Then take each idea and sort it out under those headings. This will lead to making a choice of possible solutions. You may want to use several of the ideas you have listed in any particular case.

Make an action plan

Include the following steps.

- Select what seems to you to be a realistic date by which you want to have achieved your objectives.
- Set down in detail the steps you need to take. It may be a good idea to do this in the form of a flow-chart, but it depends upon the problem.
- Consider who else is involved, including the children, and note what you need to do about informing or consulting others.

Plan evaluation

It is very easy to try out some new idea and do nothing about evaluating its success except in a very casual way. When you are planning, it is much better to decide in some detail what you will consider as success and how you will know whether you have achieved your goals.

This is a very detailed way of tackling a problem. There will be many occasions when you have ideas and put them into action more casually. The point about suggesting a programme is to stress that there is always some step you can take to deal with a problem and that having some strategies for generating ideas and solutions can help. This is also a useful set of strategies for a group of teachers working together to solve a problem.

Make a point of periodically reflecting on what you have done, perhaps using some of the reviews provided in this book. This is especially useful at the end of the school year, to make sure that you have learned all you can from the way you tackled particular problems.

A report of research into teacher effectiveness by Hay McBer (2000) reported in the *Times Educational Supplement* lists the descriptions overleaf made by children about a good teacher. How well would you do if evaluated by the same group of children? What do you think your own class would put in such a list?

A good teacher:

- is kind and tells you how you are doing;
- is generous and allows you to have your say;
- listens to you and doesn't give up on you;
- encourages you and cares for your opinion;
- has faith in you and makes you feel clever;
- keeps confidences and treats people equally;
- likes teaching children and stands up for you;
- likes teaching their subject and makes allowances;
- takes time to explain things and tells the truth;
- helps you when you're stuck and is forgiving.

Chapter 9

Planning for learning

A good teacher is always searching for the best way of using the time, space and other resources available for the children's learning. The National Curriculum places a certain amount of pressure on teachers to cover the ground and this makes it even more important to use resources well, which makes planning especially important.

In recent years there has been a good deal of government interest in education and schools. The National Curriculum has been developed and a good deal more testing than most teachers and schools think necessary. Many articles in the press give the impression that education is going rapidly downhill and this makes very depressing reading for a very hard-working and conscientious profession. It was therefore a joy to read a statement by Charles Clarke (in the foreword to a 2005 DfES report) which starts: 'Our primary schools are a success story. The best are the best in the world. They are a joy to visit and a credit to our nation.' He goes on to stress the idea that 'Excellent teaching gives children the life chances they deserve' and 'Enjoyment is the birthright of every child'.

Statements like these encourage teachers to continue to give children all they can and to contribute to their children's life chances by good planning and good teaching.

Planning for learning

Planning skills

Every school and every teacher needs an underlying structure and plan of work which is clear and which allows scope for flexibility but which also has enough system behind what is done to ensure that children make progress. To some extent the National Curriculum and the associated assessment provides something of a structure but it mustn't be allowed to become a straitjacket. The school will also have schemes of work to guide you.

Planning ahead does not mean a loss of spontaneity or flexibility. It is simply that you must be clear where you are going if you want to make the most of the opportunities that arise. You also need to share your planning with the children quite frequently, telling them about what you are planning to do next with them.

Forward planning

Your planning as classroom teacher must be set in a wider context. You are normally responsible for planning the work of your class. Your planning is part of the planning needed for the whole year group if your school has more than one class in each year and this, in turn, is part of the planning for the whole school and eventually for the whole school career of your children. It is helpful to see what you are doing in these wider contexts and to know where your work fits in to the overall pattern. The National Curriculum makes this in some ways rather easier to do than in the past, though perhaps more limiting as well.

In planning you need to be sure that some common ground is covered by all children. This will be partly ensured by the National Curriculum. It is important to remember that objectives can be met in a variety of ways and that one activity can meet more than one objective. There is a case with older children for a formal programme of fairly specific teaching, such as that required by the literacy and numeracy hours, which needs to be complemented by an informal programme which uses opportunities as they occur.

Planning the learning programme

The learning programme needs to involve both long- and short-term planning and also some consideration of teaching your children to plan.

Long-term planning

Long-term planning should involve the following in some form:

1 identifying aims and objectives;
2 making general long-term plans to meet the aims and objectives which evolve from assessing the needs of children and making systematic reviews of their progress;
3 making broad outlines of curriculum plans;
4 setting dates or periods of time for completing different aspects of the work;
5 considering how you wish the children to work and if necessary planning a training programme for them;
6 planning appropriate tasks for your assistant and discussing them with her;
7 considering the books, equipment and materials you will need at each stage and taking any necessary action to provide them;

8 considering the first-hand experience which will be needed and planning the action needed to provide it;
9 making plans for evaluation, including the criteria by which you will judge success and deciding on the records to be kept;
10 considering your own development and planning any necessary action to develop your own skills and knowledge.

It may also be helpful to consider what use might be made of the computer for planning and for recording. It may be helpful to store outline plans on the computer so that you can come back to them and update them when you are working with a new group.

Finally, in long-term planning it is important to consider your objectives for training children to work in the organisation you have in mind. What do you need to do to train them to become independent learners? How are they going to acquire learning skills? These can all be acquired as part of the learning which is in hand, but you need to be conscious of what is involved and how you can help them to develop the necessary skills.

Short-term planning

You will also need to make short-term plans for day-to-day work which:

- will provide for children of all abilities;
- are flexible enough to include interests which may arise;
- pay attention to details or organisation and enable work to run smoothly;
- decide on the role your assistant will play and consider how best to prepare her for this;
- enable you to achieve your long-term aims and objectives.

Your teaching plan for a piece of work

Whether you are planning work within a particular subject or as a topic it is a good idea to start by setting down your objectives which will be based on the National Curriculum requirements. These may be from one subject or more than one subject and may include objectives for training children as independent learners as well as subject knowledge. They should be stated in a form that enables you to see easily whether they have been achieved.

In the past there have been many occasions when teachers have taken advantage of something topical or something which interests the children and used this as a stimulus to help them to learn. Local events such as the fiftieth birthday of the school, new school buildings, national and international events and annual events can all be used for learning within the National Curriculum. While this should not be the main way of working, partly because of the time element, such opportunities should be looked for and used.

However, it is difficult to ensure progression and coverage of the National Curriculum if work is too opportunist. The development of scientific understanding, for example, requires progression in the ability to identify questions which could be investigated and ability to apply scientific thinking to the investigation, and there is a similar need for progression on most subjects. If progression is to be achieved, it must be planned.

Topic work

Although the National Curriculum is set out in the form of subjects, teachers are free to introduce work in the form of topics or projects provided that the required subject-related skills and concepts are developed. Cross-curricular work can be an efficient and effective way of working in that the same experience may provide material for learning in more than one subject. It also shows how subjects are related to one another. Young children tend to learn from everything that happens to them and project work seems a natural way of learning, but as they grow older the work can become more subject specific.

It is perhaps worth considering at this stage what topic work offers as a learning medium. In the first instance, a topic helps to place learning in a context. Children learn about a number of related things at the same time and this makes it more likely that the learning will be retained. A good topic should involve a strong element of first-hand experience as well providing the opportunity for a variety of different approaches to learning. Children will observe, question, use first-hand experience, use computers and use books to find out; they will write, draw, paint and make models. You will give them information and help them to add to it, leading them to form appropriate concepts. They will also develop and practise skills of various kinds. They may also learn to work together if group work is part of the activity. All these approaches can help to reinforce learning.

There are also some problems about topic work. Different children may undertake different tasks and it is then difficult to be sure of who has learned what. A child may get a biased view of a particular topic because he or she has chosen particular aspects of it to work on. Topic work tends to make continuity difficult because of the different tasks children have undertaken and it is more difficult to ensure progression in the context of a topic. You have to allow for each of these difficulties, mainly by the care with which you record what each child has done. Nevertheless, topic work offers some excellent opportunities for children to get really involved and learn a lot and it is well worth while. With older children you can ask them to record the ground they have covered on a particular topic for your records.

Aspects of planning

Whether you are using a topic as the basis of your teaching in a particular area or are dealing with a specific subject directly, the following need consideration in planning.

- *Children's existing experience* What have the children already experienced on which I can build?
- *First-hand experiences needed* What experiences should I provide for the children so that they understand the work we shall be doing?
- *Language* What words and phrases will children need to understand the work we shall be doing? What new language will they learn as a result of this work? What varieties of language can be practised? (Formal/informal modes, transactional language, expressive language, poetic language?)
- *Knowledge* What do I hope children will know at the end of this piece of work?
- *Concepts* What concepts do I want the children to have understood by the end of this piece of work?
- *Skills* What skills should my children be able to use as a result of this piece of work?
- *Creative work* What creative work might grow out of this work?
- *Outcomes* How will the children's learning be demonstrated?
- *How will I evaluate what has been learned?*

In working out your plan it will always be important to think carefully about what you will want your assistant to do at each stage.

This pattern of planning can be used for whole topics or a series of lessons on a particular subject. The plans given at the end of this chapter set out a form which could be adapted for use with other topics.

This type of plan gives you a clear picture of what the outcomes of your work might be but does not limit the possibilities which may emerge. With a new group you might plan the broad areas in which they might be working. For example, you might plan the fieldwork involved in the living things project described below and discuss with the children what they might see and what they might collect. You then feed in ideas such as the quadrat as a means of helping observation.

Gradually, you build up a list with the children and you can then add to these ideas from the lists you have prepared yourself. Although the outline is given here in detail, in practice quite a lot of the items might be those suggested by children.

From there, you go on to plan which children should undertake which tasks. Some of the organisation here will be a matter of children choosing tasks which interest them and some tasks you may want to allocate taking children's abilities and interests into account.

Bennett and Kell (1989) found that teachers do not always judge what has been achieved in terms of their original intentions. The same study also suggests that teachers often do not make it clear to children what is the object of a given piece of work. If children are to be partners in their own learning, it is essential that they know the purpose of any work they do. The National Curriculum also makes it important to judge work in terms of intended learning.

The conclusion of any piece of work is important for establishing the intended learning. Both the literacy and numeracy strategies suggest ending the lesson with a plenary session which draws together what has been learned and looks forward to the next lesson. HMI (1999a, b) found that this was the least well-used part of the lesson. Teachers did not always have a clear understanding of the purpose of the plenary session and sometimes they did not leave enough time for it.

The conclusion of any piece of work should therefore demonstrate what has been learned in a way that enables you to assess whether you achieved your intentions. In planning, you need to decide how the work will be concluded. Will there be an exhibition or talks or presentations by groups of children? How will you draw things to a close and what important points do you need to bring out in doing this?

Review 9.1 Planning skills

1   To what extent do I identify clear aims and objectives in my planning?
2   Do I make broad long-term plans for curriculum?
3   Do I also plan evaluation and record-keeping?
4   Do I work out in advance the books, equipment and materials that will be needed and see that they will be available?
5   Do I plan adequately for the first-hand experiences my children may need?
6   Do I share my plans with my children and also help them to become planners in their turn?
7   Do I think out in advance how I want the children to work and the training they may need?
8   Do I make allowance in my short-term planning for interests which may arise?
9   Does my planning include provision for the whole range of children? Do I make adequate provision for the most and least able?
10   Do I plan my organisation in sufficient detail so that things run smoothly?
11   Do I plan how my assistant and I will work together?
12   Do I plan for my own professional development?

The children and planning

So far we have been thinking about planning from the teacher's point of view. We also need to think about helping the children learn to plan so that they can eventually become fairly independent learners. As teacher you have to find the right path between making the decisions yourself and leaving too much to the children. If you decide exactly what is to be done and how it is to be carried out, the children may learn some things extremely well, but they will not become independent learners. You may also miss the inspiration which children can bring to work when they have a measure of freedom about their ideas and how best to carry them out. If, on the other hand, you leave too much to them, they will lose the inspiration which you can bring to them as teacher and they may not learn what you intend. You need to plan flexibly yourself so that your planning can be adapted to children's current interests and changing circumstances.

Different pieces of work provide differing opportunities for children to contribute ideas about learning. In some situations you need to dictate fairly fully what is to be done and what is to be learned and how the learning is to be carried out. In other situations there can be much more freedom and the opportunity for children to choose and develop ideas of their own. Both approaches are needed and both are important.

Helping children learn to plan

When you first start work in which you want to give the children a good deal of freedom to make their own choices and plans from a range of ideas, they will need help in the planning process if they are going to do any of the planning for themselves. It will, of course, depend on the age and stage of development of your children how much you get them to do, but even with quite young children you can start to discuss planning.

At the first stage of planning you might suggest an idea, such as 'this term we are going to do a study of the school field – how do you think we might set about it?' This may bring some useful ideas and suggestions. It might then be sensible to arrange for some discussion of this idea in small groups. When they have discussed it for a short while you could get each group in turn to write their main ideas on the whiteboard for everyone to see. There could then be a bit more discussion looking at where the different plans overlapped or were very similar and you could then ask the children in their groups to make a plan for the work they have chosen. You might organise this by discussing with the class what the plans should contain and putting this on the board too.

There will always need to be a good deal of work for which you do the planning and for which you plan in more detail, but planning should often be shared with the children, when the idea lends itself to this with you adding in ideas and suggestions. This mixed approach should both help children to become independent learners and also ensure that planned programmes of work which are part of school schemes are covered.

Short-term planning

In addition to planning long-term and planning major pieces of work, you will need to make plans for day-to-day teaching. The more experienced you are, the less detailed these plans need to be, but the need for planning remains, however long you have been teaching. The following need to be prepared in advance.

- *The range of activities and objectives you intend to pursue during the day* It is essential to think clearly about these since some will need careful preparation of the classroom.
- *The provision you intend to make for the range of pupils* Some activities will be for the whole class; others will be for different groups and individuals.
- *Questions to ask in relation to the activities planned* It is important to plan questioning. Higher order questions, in particular, need to be considered in advance because it is often difficult to think of such questions on the spur of the moment.
- *The role that your assistant will play* She will need briefing beforehand if she is to make a useful contribution.
- *The resources you will need* Your assistant could be very helpful here in preparing resources, if you brief her well in advance.
- *How you plan to undertake starting, changing activity and clearing up* If you are experienced and your class is well trained this needs no preparation. Inexperienced teachers would be well advised to plan starting, changing and clearing up very carefully because these are times when things can go wrong.
- *The children for whom individual help may be needed* You will have identified some children from previous work who will need extra help or perhaps different materials from the others. You may also need to consider the needs of the more able children. Will they need more challenging work or work to extend their thinking or work to go on to if they finish before the other children? Your assistant could also be very useful in working with particular individual children.
- *The children whose work you plan to check yourself* It is a good idea to have a systematic plan for checking the work and understanding of a few children in detail each day.
- *How you will assess the effectiveness of the work you have done* It is a good idea to identify some success criteria for your day's work. Select some areas of work in advance and go over them carefully at the end of

the day, looking for things which worked well and those which were more doubtful and consider the implications of your findings for future planning.

Theme outlines

Figures 9.1–9.6 give outline plans for work on three themes which arise from National Curriculum requirements. The themes are communication, materials and living things.

Review 9.2 The learning programme

1 How do I plan long-term? What do I find difficult about long-term planning? How much do I change my plans in the light of children's reactions? Am I happy about this?

2 How do I plan short-term, for next week and tomorrow? Am I satisfied with the kinds of plans that I make?

3 Do I plan effectively for progression?

4 How do I plan for first-hand experience for the children? How much freedom shall I give them in the ways in which they might follow up the experience?

5 Am I teaching the children to plan their work? How successful is this?

6 Am I teaching them how to evaluate their work? Should I encourage them to do this in pairs or small groups? How well does this work?

Existing experience	Tv and radio; observation of forms of communication; use of telephone; signs and symbols in environment; possible experience of other written language symbols; sounds of musical instruments
First-hand experience	Opportunity to handle musical instruments; experimental work making sounds; visit to printer; observation of signs and signals
Language	Names of forms of communication e.g. books; graphs; newspapers, maps etc.; words connected with sounds and the way they are made e.g. vibration; names of types of communication. e.g. signs, braille, language of the deaf etc.; know something about musical notation; know something about how to match speaking or writing to an audience or readership
Knowledge	Know how musical sounds are produced and the types of instrument making them; know how advertisers capture our interest; know the ways in which we communicate over long distances
Concepts	Sound is produced by vibration; vibration is caused in a variety of ways; we use many forms of communcation which are not dependent on language , e.g. road signs; we speak and write in a different way according to the audience or readership
Skills	Work with a group on a communication task; collect information about types of communication and organise it as a block graph; write about findings using full stops and capital letters correctly; prepare and give a talk to a specific audience (e.g. children from another class), matching the talk to the audience
Creative work	Invent a language; invent signs; create a newspaper; devise musical instruments; devise advertisements
Outcomes	Exhibition and presentation to another class; class newspaper

Figure 9.1 Analysis of thematic material for topic on communication

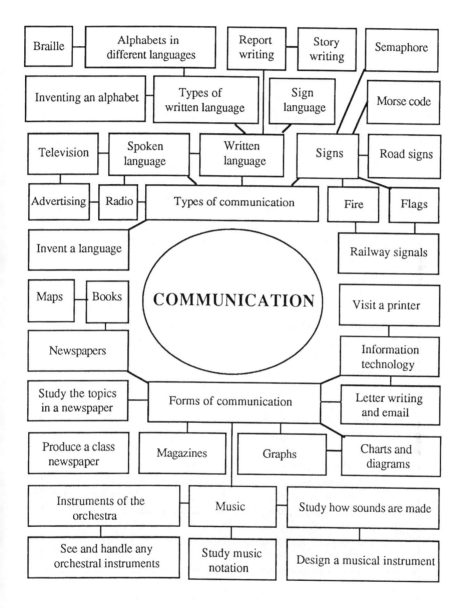

Figure 9.2 Communication web

Existing experience	Observation of plants, birds and animals in environment; plants grown in classroom; keeping of pets; observation in gardens and parks; television wildlife programmes
First-hand experience	Visits to field, woodland, pond; growing plants in the classroom; keeping small animals in the classroom; observation in school environment and home areas
Language	Names of plants and animals; names of their parts; words describing plants e.g. deciduous, evergreen. Words describing what animals do e.g. hibernation; descriptions of animal movement; words describing animals homes and their young; explain work being done; relate events in the life of a plant or animal to other children
Knowledge	Plant and animal life cycles; some of the habitats of different plants and animals; some of the food chains of different animals; the effects of season and weather
Concepts	Basic life processes are common to all living things; living things grow and change over time; different living things require different habitats; a habitat must have appropriate conditions for the plants and creatures that live there; plants and animals can be classified in various ways
Skills	Making classes and sorting; devising questions for research; making and using a database; speaking to the class; using lenses; making tables/bar charts; recording over a period; making and using a quadrat; drawing and naming parts of animals and plants
Creative work	Making pictures of the areas studied and of plants and animals using different media; writing poems about the areas studied and setting them to music; drawing plants and animals as they grow; writing stories about animals which include knowledge of their life style; making leaf prints; making lino blocks from drawings of plants and animals; printing fabrics with them
Outcomes	Exhibition of what has been discovered; talks by individuals and groups about their findings; making of books; sharing of creative work; class discussion about what has been learned

Figure 9.3 Analysis of thematic material for topic on living things

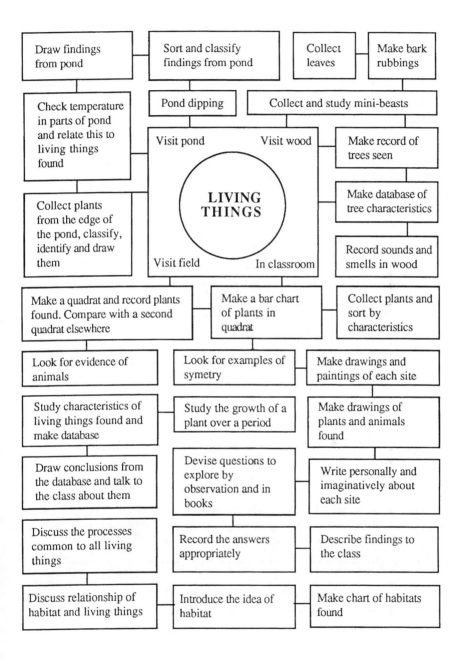

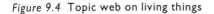

Figure 9.4 Topic web on living things

Existing experience	Experience of a variety of materials in everyday life – fabric, food, furniture, materials, building materials, use of yarn in clothing, knitting, woodwork, experience with clay
First-hand experience	Visit local street and small manufacturing unit e.g. a pottery; bring in fabrics, dig clay, collect sheep's wool, collect similar sized twigs of different woods, survey buildings, visit building site
Language	Names of different fabrics, dye plants, stones, woods etc. Transparent, opaque, porous, inflammable, saturated, flexible, rigid, man-made, natural material Discussion of how to test materials; presentation to others of findings; use of books and computers to find out; writing of reports on findings
Knowledge	Sources of different materials; their characteristics; uses of different materials
Concepts	Some materials are natural and some are man-made; different materials have different characteristics which determine their use
Skills	Testing materials for different characteristics, e.g. hardness/softness, flexibility etc.; making bricks and pots, making dyes; spinning; weaving
Creative work	Making a picture with stones; making bricks and pottery; making dyes and using them; making a fabric collage; spinning and weaving; writing about how different materials make you feel
Outcomes	Exhibition of work; discussion of experiments and findings; planning for presentation to parents

Figure 9.5 Analysis for topic on the theme of materials

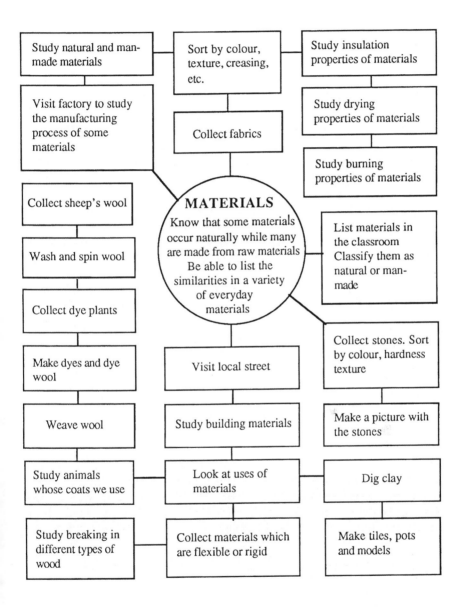

Figure 9.6 Topic on materials

Chapter 10

The curriculum

A main concern of this book is classroom organisation, but we need to consider what we want to organise before we can consider how to do it. Many studies suggest that how children learn is probably as important as what they learn. The way work is organised affects the extent of each child's contact with the teacher, the opportunities and resources available and the actual learning which takes place, both by conscious intent on the part of the teacher and also as a hidden curriculum with its own values and assumptions.

There are many definitions of the word curriculum. The National Curriculum and the National Primary Strategy, for example, might be defined as the intended content of children's learning. However, children learn a great deal in school which is not intended directly or even not intended at all. The definition of curriculum used in this chapter includes all the learning which a child does in any aspect of his or her school life. This might be seen to include at least three kinds of activity: the taught, the institutional and the hidden curriculum.

The taught curriculum

This is the usual meaning of the word curriculum. It covers all the teaching and learning which goes on intentionally and deliberately within the classroom and elsewhere during the school day. It is the work which those outside the school recognise as what the school is in business to do and is largely covered by the National Curriculum.

The institutional curriculum

Any organisation involves and teaches those within it – teachers, other staff and children – about its way of life, its culture, its values and codes of behaviour: 'the way we do things here'. Sometimes this is done explicitly, as when a teacher tells children how to behave in particular circumstances or talks about school and classroom rules, or perhaps involves them in making some of the rules. Sometimes this learning is implicit, as when children are praised for behaviour which accords with the views and values of the head and staff and the rules they have laid down, or scolded for behaviour which is not in accord with them.

Primary schools are usually very clear about the patterns of behaviour required from teachers and children, partly because the immaturity of the majority of the school population requires the support that this offers. The patterns of behaviour demanded of children teach them many things and should often be discussed by teachers and children so that shared values are reinforced and differences recognised. This learning is sometimes less effective than it might be because of inconsistencies in what is demanded by different teachers. Children may also find themselves unwittingly behaving in ways which teachers dislike, but which may be acceptable at home. For some children, school life can be fraught with problems in working out the demands of the institutional curriculum.

The institutional curriculum also includes opportunities for both children and teachers to take responsibility and for leadership and for working with others. It includes the social learning that goes on in the playground and in the classroom, the learning which takes place at lunch and in assembly and all the attitudes developed as a result of the way a child is treated in school by teachers and by peers.

The hidden curriculum

Some parts of the curriculum are hidden, not only from the children but also from the teachers. Much of what we would now list under the institutional curriculum was once part of the hidden curriculum. As soon as we become conscious of it, it is no longer part of the hidden curriculum, which is, by definition, hidden. Since it is hidden, a school cannot control it, although by sometimes discussing what is possibly hidden, it may be brought into the light of day.

It is therefore possible, indeed probable, that there is learning going on which you don't know about. Is the child who is able, for example, learning to work slowly because finishing first brings more of the same or because other children accuse him or her of being a swot? Are children learning to give you the answers they think you want rather than seeking a thought-out answer? Do some children get the impression that they are unimportant because they are, for example, not good at mathematics or games or writing? Do some children get the impression that reading, writing, mathematics and possibly science are the only things that matter? Do girls feel inferior to boys or conversely? Do children get the impression that it is better to be white than black?

Factors affecting the curriculum

The curriculum that a school offers is determined by government by means of the National Curriculum and the Primary Strategy. However, it is also affected by the views of the LEA, the school governors, the headteacher and the teaching staff. Thus, although the National Curriculum and the Primary Strategy are laid down in some detail, they are very far from dictating all that an individual teacher or school does. Some schools have made considerable strides in their children's progress by studying the National Curriculum and the Primary Strategy critically, looking at where it fits with the school's philosophy and where it is at odds with it. This is by no means to suggest that schools should ignore aspects of the strategy and the National Curriculum which they perhaps don't much like, but to look instead for possible alternative ways of working which will meet the school's own ideas and principles as well as what is laid down for them. It would be difficult to provide a National Curriculum which met the particular needs and interests of every school.

What influences the taught curriculum within a school?

The National Primary Strategy as well as the National Curriculum affects the curriculum and provides a framework for literacy and numeracy. The headteacher will have particular views about what goes on in the school and what s/he encourages teachers and children to do. Individual teachers too affect the curriculum because each teacher has a particular personality and teaching style and a particular set of skills and knowledge to offer. As teacher you are also free to select material to teach the National Curriculum, use the literacy and numeracy strategies as you wish and do anything else which you think will be appropriate for your particular group of children. As teacher you work with three sets of variables.

Variables which are predetermined

- Current educational thinking
- Current national policies, strategies and needs
- The National Curriculum
- Your particular class of children and their parents
  - their social and educational background
  - their ability levels
- Your particular school building and facilities
- Your headteacher and colleagues
  - their backgrounds, skills and experience
  - their ability
  - the staffing ratio in your school

Variables which you can influence but not determine

- Parental expectations of the school and the child
- Support from parents
- Support from governors
- Support from LEA
- The behaviour and background of your children
- Attitudes and views of your head and colleagues
- Your school organisation
- Your interpretation of the National Curriculum
- The literacy and numeracy strategies
- Your school schemes of work
- Use of buildings, facilities and resources
- Money available

Areas of self-determination by teachers

- Vehicles for curriculum: choice of books, materials, approaches, some subject matter
- Use of time within the classroom
- Use of learning space
- Use of resources
- Teaching style
- Teaching skills and knowledge
- Teaching methods and approaches
- Children's learning

These areas are not separated very clearly, but you are most likely to be using time effectively if you concentrate on the last section.

The whole curriculum

The National Curriculum specifies: equal opportunities regarding race, gender and disability. The National Curriculum also includes statements about the values to be inculcated regarding self, relationships, society and the environment.

In addition to the requirements of the National Curriculum, all schools must teach religious education according to the local Agreed Syllabus or the Diocesan syllabus, although parents who wish may withdraw their children from work in this subject.

Personal and social development and health education are not compulsory in the primary school, nor is citizenship, but schools are encouraged to include them. They are, in any case, part of classroom management and of helping children to live happily together.

Language

Each subject discipline has its own language, its linguistic register, and even when subjects use the same words they may not be using them with the same meaning. For example, at an early stage, children discover that, when they paint, the primary colours are red, blue and yellow and they learn how to mix these colours together in pairs to make another colour. At a later stage in science, however, they learn about the colour of light, where the primary colours are different and they have to adjust to the difference in meaning.

Children's language problems

We tend not to think very much about this kind of problem and yet it is relevant from the earliest stages. A child at home learns that the postman brings a letter. At school the same child has to learn that a letter is something different.

There are many such linguistic traps for children and it is often valuable to list the words and language you want to use for a given piece of work and ask yourself what experience the children will need to understand them fully. This would be a useful thing to do with each part of the National Curriculum and the Primary Strategy.

If you teach very young children you are more likely to be aware of this than if you teach older children because young children force you to recognise the inadequacies in their understanding. They often give you clues to their thinking in the mistakes they make or in what seem to be amusing sayings. For example, the child who defined 'less' as 'downer' partly understood the word, but one could not be certain that her understanding would be sufficient for understanding a phrase such as 'less space' or a more abstract phrase such as 'less hope'.

If you teach older children, the problem is still with you and is possibly increased by the fact that older children sometimes learn to disguise their lack of understanding. It is important to ask questions to see whether language is really understood.

Thought about language as part of the framework in major areas of knowledge must also include thought about the use of symbols in mathematics and science, the language of movement in dance and drama, the language of shapes and forms in art, sounds in music and so on. Each subject area not only has its own linguistic register or way of using language but also has its own forms of expression which need to be studied and understood so that they can be used.

Cross-curricular learning

Schools also need to be concerned with skills which go across the curriculum – communication, numeracy, study, problem-solving, personal and social skills, health education, information and communication technology, economic and industrial understanding, citizenship, environmental education – and with those subjects which are clearly cross-curricular.

Concepts, knowledge, language and skills

One breakdown which can be applied to most subjects is a division into underlying ideas or concepts, knowledge or information, subject-specific language and skills.

Each subject discipline has a set of techniques and skills required for its study, and these too can be listed although they are best acquired in the context of their use. If the emphasis is placed on concepts, the skills often come naturally. For example, children acquiring the concept of area by counting the squares that are covered by a leaf are not only practising counting in whole numbers but are also likely to find ways of adding fractions to account for the parts of squares covered. In writing, children are most likely to persist in practising if they want to express something on paper, and this motivation has to be reconciled with the need for appropriate teaching and practice of letter formation.

One primary school, Paddox Primary in Rugby, set out a curriculum statement for its programme in 2007, as follows:

At Paddox Primary School we endeavour to provide high quality teaching and learning in a stimulating environment, using a variety of methods appropriate to the age of the child. We provide a well-planned curriculum which:

- Is broad and balanced, based on the requirements of the National Curriculum and the local syllabus for Religious Education.
- Is stimulating and challenging, seeking to extend pupils' knowledge, skills and creativity in order to develop enquiring minds.
- Is firmly committed to the principle of equality for all pupils and is relevant to the needs of all pupils.
- Provides pupils with the means to develop their intellectual, physical and emotional potential.
- Enables pupils to question, acquire self-knowledge and develop independence.
- Helps pupils to develop self-esteem.

Communication

Communication is also a cross-curricular study, which we looked at in Chapter 9 where a project on communication was suggested. Communication skills are clearly an important part of the National Curriculum, running through all the Core and Foundation and the Cross-Curricular subjects.

Communication is part of the general life of the school, the classroom and the playground. A child should learn to communicate and receive communication using movement, spoken and written language, mathematics and graphics, adequately and appropriately for use with different people, situations, purposes and topics. The development of communication is highly relevant when one looks at organisation, since children cannot learn unless they and the teacher can communicate well with each other.

Children's overall happiness might also be said to depend on their ability to communicate with each other as well as with teachers and assistants. All aspects of living involve communication and the teacher who is clear about what the children might learn incidentally will find opportunities at all times of the day for using the ordinary work of the classroom to foster learning in this area. We saw in an earlier chapter that spoken language is a very important basic skill for today's children and we need to see that this is well developed in the primary years.

The word 'communication' is often used in schools in relation to language. It can be looked at much more widely, however, as we saw in the last chapter. It comes in different forms in every subject of the curriculum. In technology, for example, communication is often through drawings and diagrams. In physical education and games, it comes through movement, in music through sound and so on.

All the higher forms of animal life have sophisticated forms of communication and human beings are no exception. We differ from other animals, however, in the primacy afforded to language, particularly as a way of representing experience to ourselves and others, and we use language as an important and integral part of our thinking. It also enables us to co-operate and achieve collectively more than any individual can achieve alone.

This stress on language tends to make us less aware of other kinds of communication, particularly that transmitted by movement. Movement communication is present before language and it continues to be an essential part of the way we relate to other people and communicate with them. Teachers of young children, in particular, need to be aware of the importance of body language for communication because they both read this kind of communication made by their children and themselves use it to help children understand what they are saying. Facial expression, gesture, movement of the body and extensions of this, such as the way you dress and organise your environment, all communicate something about the kind of person you are, the mood you are in, the kind of relationship you see yourself having with the children and so on.

Children explore a great deal of this in play, and school can take this further as children grow older in work in drama and in talking about how people behave in different situations.

Children are also discovering how other people react to them and part of the response will be demonstrated by movement and facial expression which the children gradually learn how to read.

Teachers of children from ethnic minorities may find that their children have a different body language from that of the indigenous population. This can sometimes lead to misunderstanding when a child shows in his or her movement something which has a different meaning at home from that expected at school. This is particularly true of children with Afro-Caribbean ancestry, whose body language is often misinterpreted.

A further extension of this is graphic communication. One might argue that the way people dress and organise their environment is a form of graphic communication in that other people draw conclusions from appearances. Teachers of younger children will be aware that children not infrequently use drawing, painting and modelling to express their feelings and reactions.

At the other end of the range of graphic communication is the use of maps, graphs, diagrams, tables, charts, and so on. It is particularly relevant to work in technology, where drawing is often needed to explain ideas. These are all part of the communication process, complementing language and sometimes communicating more effectively than language since graphic communication can show more easily than words how things relate to one another. For example, a map shows more than a verbal account of how to get somewhere. It can also be seen all at once, whereas verbal instructions have to be heard or read in sequence.

Certain kinds of organisation within the school will give children better opportunities for practising this kind of learning than others. For example, if children are expected to work collaboratively on something, a good deal will be learned about communication within the group and this will be complementary to the language learning taking place.

Numeracy

Being numerate requires us to have the skills which are widely needed in everyday life. The basis of those skills is acquired at the primary stage of education. The skills will be learned in mathematics lessons but may be practised across the curriculum. Technology and science will involve measurement and calculation. Geography will involve map-reading skills; history the use of a time line. Calculation may be involved in art from time to time as in block printing where children will need to work out how many prints can be fitted into a sheet of paper.

In recent years calculators and computers have changed our needs. Many jobs that require calculation now involve the use of calculators or computers. Neither can be used intelligently without understanding, however, and it is important that children develop understanding and skill in using these aids as well as the ability to calculate without them.

The calculator and the computer enable a child to perform many calculations quickly so that patterns can be seen which might not be evident if all the calculations had to be carried out manually. This enables children to reach a level of understanding which was difficult to achieve before calculators were available. Calculators also make it possible to use more real-life problems in which the numbers involved would be too difficult for them to manage if the calculation had to be carried out manually.

Review 10.1 My class and the curriculum

1   What is there that could be described as the institutional curriculum in my school and my class?
2   What ideas do I have about the children's hidden curriculum?
3   What particular factors in my school affect what I teach and how I teach it? Do I find any of them difficult limitations? If so, can I do anything about them?
4   In what areas of work do I feel that I have a real personal choice? Am I using this to the best advantage?

Chapter 11

The Primary Framework – language and literacy

Over the past thirty years or so, some important developments have taken place in our knowledge of language. In particular the use of audio recording systems has made it possible to study language as people actually use it, giving us valuable insights which have implications for teachers. We have become aware that we use language in different ways according to our background, the particular situation, the persons to whom we are speaking, the subject matter and so on.

Many schools now have the problem that some of their children come to school with very little knowledge of the English language. Various arrangements have been made nationally and locally to help schools with this problem and it is much to the credit of teachers and the education service that such children appear to learn English quite rapidly.

We each use language in ways which are personal to us. Your language initially developed from your background, upbringing and education and many of us retain traces of the speech of the area in which we grew up, sometimes as accent, sometimes in the tunes of our speech and the words and language structures we employ. Children starting school may find that their teachers and other children speak in much the same way as their parents or they may find that language is used in a different way in school from the way it is used at home – so different in some cases that children have difficulty in coming to terms with it.

The Primary Framework for literacy

The Primary Framework for literacy is a central part of the Primary Strategy, providing a focus for this subject. It recommends various approaches to support teaching, learning and assessment across the whole curriculum.

There have been many changes in education since the launch of the original Framework for teaching literacy and mathematics. The Foundation Stage was developed to become the first stage of the National Curriculum. ICT and its use in teaching and learning has been continuously and significantly developing right across the curriculum.

We have also learned a good deal from more recent research into children's learning, and there have been some significant studies into the lasting effects of early education (such as the Rose Report). There have also been developments within the National Curriculum and a move towards more personalised approaches to children's learning. The Every Child Matters (2004) agenda focused on the following five outcomes for children, supporting the drive towards improved standards of learning.

1 Be healthy: enjoying good physical and mental health and living a healthy lifestyle.
2 Stay safe: being protected from harm and abuse.
3 Enjoy and achieve: getting the most out of life and developing the skills for adulthood.
4 Make a positive contribution: being involved with the community and society and not engaging in anti-social behaviour or offending the law.
5 Achieve economic well-being: not being prevented by economic disadvantage from achieving their full potential in life.

There have also been developments in our knowledge about early reading following research and the publication of the Rose Report (2006), the *Independent Report of the Teaching of Early Reading*. All these developments have encouraged schools and teachers to take stock and to look afresh at children's learning. A new statutory framework for children's learning and development from birth to five: the Early Years Foundation Stage (EYFS) is now being developed.

All these developments have pointed to the need to look again at the original frameworks in order to include the developments that have taken place over the last eight years.

A clearer structure for literacy

To simplify the structure of the objectives and to incorporate speaking and listening, twelve strands of literacy learning have been identified (see below). These give a broad overview of the curriculum for English in the primary phase. The objectives are aligned to the twelve strands to demonstrate progression in each strand. Strand 5, word recognition: decoding (reading) and encoding (spelling), reflects the recommendations of the Rose Report in that the teaching of phonics is time-limited and seen as the principal strategy in word recognition, and also reflects the reversibility of blending (decoding) and segmenting (encoding) to support reading and spelling.

Learning objectives

A clearer structure for teaching literacy has been provided by simplifying the structure of the objectives, with the identification of twelve different strands of learning, giving a broad overview of the literacy curriculum in the primary phase.

These strands link directly to the Early Learning Goals and aspects of English in the National Curriculum. The organisation of the objectives into these strands also supports alignment with the assessment focuses for reading and writing used in National Curriculum assessments. Covering these objectives will allow children to reach the Early Learning Goals for Communication, Language and Literacy and the appropriate National Curriculum levels for Key Stages 1 and 2.

Language is an integral part of most learning and oral language in particular has a key role in classroom teaching and learning. Children's creativity, understanding and imagination can also be engaged and fostered by discussion and interaction. In their daily lives, children use speaking and listening to solve problems, speculate, share ideas, make decisions and reflect on what is important. Most social relationships depend on talk and in the classroom children's confidence and attitudes to learning are greatly affected by friendships and interaction with others.

The learning strands for language and literacy

1 *Speaking* The ability to describe incidents or tell stories from their own experience, in an audible voice.

2 *Listening and responding* The ability to listen with sustained concentration to what other people say and take note of the important points.

3 *Group discussion, interaction* The ability to ask and answer questions, make relevant contributions, offer suggestions and take turns in speaking and perhaps group planning for future work.

4 *Drama* The ability to take part in improvisation and role-play and be able to take part in improvising a short play based on a story a group has been reading. The ability to discuss why they like a performance and talk about effective features of dramatic performance such as voice, gesture, movement.

5 *Word recognition, reading* The ability to decode (reading) and encode (spelling) to retell stories, order events using story language and use different techniques to recall and invent well-structured stories

6 *Word structure and spelling* The ability to spell words in common use and know how to form related words from one another. Know how to build new words from their phonic components.

7 *Understanding and interpreting texts* The ability to retrieve and use information and use context to understand word meaning and explain

and comment on writers' use of language, including vocabulary, grammatical and literary features.

8   *Engaging with and responding to texts*   The ability to enjoy fiction and become competent at using texts to find out information of interest or relevant to the work in hand.

9   *Creating and shaping texts*   The ability to write for a variety of purposes and in a variety of different styles, matching style to purpose.

10   *Text structure and organisation*   The ability to organise written work in a way and in a style suitable for its purpose.

11   *Sentence structure and organisation*   The ability to write using a variety of sentence formation according to the purpose of the writing.

12   *Presentation*   The ability to write clearly and legibly, setting out work well.

The importance of speaking and listening

Speaking and listening are a very important part of children's education and one that was rather neglected in the more distant past. Whatever you do in life, your ability to speak clearly and confidently affects what happens to you. You make friends by talking to other people. You may get employment as a result of an interview. If you want to get something done for you, you need the ability to ask in a way that brings a willing response. Your happiness in life can depend on the ability to talk well.

You also need good listening skills: really attending to others when they talk to you, knowing what to say in response because you have understood what the other person was saying to you. Taking in instructions at work or elsewhere is also important. Listening also involves concentrating on what the other person is saying and not letting your mind wander off to something more urgent or interesting. This is not always easy!

This would seem to point to the conclusion that we need to teach speaking and listening explicitly and also seek to find opportunities to reinforce and extend children's spoken language skills. Learning to speak well and to listen well might be thought of as something for work in English, but it is really part of every aspect of the curriculum and the school day.

Changes to the original framework

The revised Primary Framework for literacy and mathematics reflects national policy developments and takes account of relevant research and evaluation undertaken since the late 1990s. The revised framework suggests the following changes.

- Support improved leadership and management of literacy and mathematics to stimulate and improve standards further. Extend it to the beginning of funded education, to create greater coherence and continuity within and between stages of care and education.

- Create a clearer set of outcomes to support teachers and practitioners in planning for progression in literacy and mathematics, to help raise the attainment of all children, personalise learning and secure intervention for those children who need it.
- Bring an increased sense of drive and momentum to literacy and mathematics through the primary phase, involving some scaling up of expectations and a greater focus upon planning for progression through a teaching sequence over an extended unit of work covering two or three weeks.
- Support schools and settings in implementing the recommendations of the Rose Report (2006) through the provision of high-quality teaching of phonics and early reading.
- Reduce workload and foster professional dialogue on how to use the Framework flexibly to meet the needs of children through focused CPD.
- Introduce a new, electronic format which allows for customised planning, teaching and assessment, with the ability to link quickly to a wide range of teaching and learning resources available through the Primary National Strategy.

The Rose Report (2006) looked at early literacy learning and found the following:

> Despite uncertainties in other research findings, the practice seen by the review shows that the systematic approach, which is generally understood as 'synthetic' phonics, offers the vast majority of young children the best and most direct route to becoming skilled readers and writers.

Phonic work is also essential for the development of writing, especially spelling. The teaching of beginners must lead them to understand how reading and writing are related.

It is widely agreed that reading involves far more than decoding words on the page. Nevertheless, words must be decoded if readers are to make sense of the text. Phonic work is therefore a necessary but not sufficient part of the wider knowledge, skills and understanding which children need to become skilled readers and writers, capable of comprehending and composing text.

For beginner readers, learning the core principles of phonic work in discrete daily sessions reduces the risk of paying too little attention to securing word recognition skills. The Rose Report has been influential in creating the new Primary Framework.

The new framework

The new framework quoted below provides more help for teachers with planning, teaching and assessment.

It helps to:

- Provide direct links to a wealth of useful materials which will help in planning teaching and children's learning.
- Provide a clearer picture of progression in core aspects of literacy and mathematics, including the development of early reading within the EYFS and supporting whole-school curriculum targets which identify key steps in learning that children need to secure if they are to make progress and achieve appropriately high standards throughout the primary phase.
- Improve access to guidance that will support the teaching of specific ideas that children may find difficult, with greater control on how much or how little of this guidance to use, depending on the context and needs facing teachers and practitioners.
- Clarify and support the significant development in the teaching of early reading, in the teaching of phonics, and in the implementation of the 'simple view of reading'.
- Support assessment and its effective use.
- Support the development of longer-term planning of teaching sequences that build learning over time.
- Integrate provision for speaking and listening strands to promote children's learning in literacy and mathematics.
- Offer significant support on how the key aspects of learning in the teaching of literacy and mathematics can be applied across the curriculum.
- Place greater emphasis on the use of ICT to support learning and teaching in literacy and mathematics.

What communication, language and literacy means for children

The Primary Strategy states:

> The development and use of communication and language are at the heart of young children's learning. Learning to listen and speak emerges out of non-verbal communication, which includes body language such as facial expression, eye contact, bending the head to listen, hand gesture and taking turns. These skills develop as babies and young children express their needs and feelings, interact with others and establish their own identities and personalities.

Children's ability to communicate with others creates in them a capacity to participate more fully and feel that they belong. Babies and young children need to be with people who have meaning for them, such as their parents or siblings and experience warm and loving relationships. This helps them to develop other social relationships, such as friendship, empathy and the opportunity to share emotions.

Parents are usually very good at interpreting their children's communications and can often help by interpreting them for others. Even as babies children respond differently to some sounds than others and are soon able to distinguish different sound patterns. They use their voices from a very early stage to try to let others know what they need and how they feel. Music and dance also play a key role in language development for young children and they enjoy rhymes and songs. In the beginning learning children need physical action and experience and they learn best when activities engage several senses. They start by trying to communicate non-verbally. Then as language develops and they learn about conversation, their thought becomes less dependent on action, although non-verbal messages continue to remain important throughout life.

As children gradually develop speaking and listening skills, they build the foundations for reading and writing. They need lots of opportunities to interact and talk with others as they develop these skills, and are helped if there is a wide range of resources for early work in reading and writing.

The environment in which learning takes place

If children are to have the best opportunities for effective development and learning in communication, language and literacy, you need as their teacher to give particular attention to:

- providing opportunities for them to communicate thoughts, ideas and feelings, and build up relationships with adults and each other;
- giving them opportunities to share and enjoy a wide range of rhymes, music, songs, poetry, stories and non-fiction books;
- giving opportunities for linking language with physical movement in action songs and rhymes, role-play and practical experiences such as cookery and gardening;
- planning an environment that reflects the importance of language through signs, notices and books;
- providing opportunities for them to see adults writing and for them to experiment with writing for themselves through making marks, personal writing symbols and conventional script;
- providing time and opportunities to develop spoken language through conversations between children and adults, both one-to-one and in small groups, with particular awareness of, and sensitivity to, the needs of

children learning English as an additional language, using their home language when appropriate;

- providing time and opportunities for them to develop their phonological awareness through small-group and individual teaching when appropriate;
- planning opportunities for all children to become aware of languages and writing systems other than English and communication systems such as signing and Braille;
- early identification of, and response to, any particular difficulties in children's language development;
- close teamwork between bilingual workers, speech therapists and practitioners where appropriate;
- providing opportunities for children who use alternative communication systems to develop ways of recording and accessing texts to develop their skills in these methods.

Developing literacy skills

As well as reading and writing, literacy involves the development of speaking and listening skills. The framework encourages teachers to use a variety of approaches to teaching literacy. It recommends regular, dedicated literacy lessons, but recognises that pupils can also develop literacy skills while they learn about other subjects in the curriculum.

The framework encourages teachers to put a greater emphasis on using 'phonics' (teaching your children to recognise the sounds of parts of words). It also stresses the part which can be played by parents in helping their child to develop literacy skills.

Over the past thirty years or so, some important developments have taken place in our knowledge of language. In particular, the use of recording systems has made it possible to study language as people actually use it, giving us valuable insights which have implications for teachers. We have become aware that we use language in different ways according to our background, the particular situation, the persons to whom we are speaking, the subject matter and so on.

Each group of people – the family, the friendship group, the social class, the professional work group, the nation – has uses of language which are peculiar to it, that is, the language register. We also use language differently in different social classes, and in Britain this is still very marked, although the use of 'upper-class' language has diminished: even the young royal princes don't use it! The use of language in this way is a mark of membership and a way of excluding those outside the group – which is why it can be very difficult to persuade children from a working-class background to use language in a middle-class way; their use of language identifies them with the home and their peer group and pressure to change language may be seen as a threat to personal identity.

The importance of standard English

The National Curriculum for English makes it very clear that teachers should work towards all children acquiring standard English, not with the idea that there is something wrong with whatever variety of English a child may use at home but because this is the most widely used and widely understood form of the language. Using standard English does not necessarily mean acquiring a middle-class accent. It refers to a standard use of grammatical constructions and use of words, which enables you to be understood in places other than your home and home area.

We need to stress in school that adopting standard forms of English is necessary and appropriate for some purposes, but does not mean abandoning other ways of talking at home or with friends. The individuals who can do this, and are in this sense bilingual and able to use language in different ways, have an advantage. They can feel at home and be accepted by a much wider variety of social groups than would be the case if they were unwilling to extend their use of language in this way.

Appropriateness of language use

Appropriateness of language use is a very useful concept for teachers. If we want to help children to use language in ways which match situations and purposes, we must not appear threatening or apparently condemning of the language they already possess if we ask them to extend their language knowledge and skill and learn to select the language behaviour they need for a particular situation.

In this context it is helpful to seek out opportunities to match language to real circumstances. The teacher is a very particular kind of audience or readership because it is his or her task to read what children write and listen to what they say, whatever it may be and in whatever way it is said. Teachers usually read or listen in the classroom not because they want to know, in the sense that the reader of a book may want to know about its content, but in order to assess a child's ability or progress, to see what help is needed or what has been learned. The child reading or writing for the teacher is thus in a different position from the adult speaking or writing with a particular purpose which affects the nature of the communication.

When we speak or write, we try to match the language we use to our purpose, situation and to its recipient. We use language differently in speaking to children as distinct from speaking to adults and try to find language they will understand. We use written language differently in writing to apply for a job from the way we use it in writing to a friend. Talking to a group is different from talking to an individual. Giving instructions is different from persuading and so on.

These variations are reflected in our choice of content, vocabulary, language structure and form, in the way we speak, in our body language of gesture and facial expression. In writing we have fewer variables but still match language to likely readership. It can be useful to look at language work in the classroom with these variations in mind and consider whether children have enough opportunities to practise the variety of language this suggests.

This is more difficult to do than it seems at first. It is easy to feel that the need is being met by writing letters for practice or writing as if one were someone else. This kind of work is necessary and has a valuable place, but children really need the incentive and the discipline of working from time to time for a real audience or readership, who will read or listen only if the material is right. Many opportunities for this may be found as part of other aspects of curriculum. For example, children may plan to interview adults in connection with a local study and may need to write letters to arrange this and also to plan and undertake the interviews. Inviting a visitor who has valuable information to give into the classroom offers similar opportunities, plus a need to think about how to make a visitor welcome and the questions which might be asked. Some topic work can be planned with another group of children, perhaps much younger, whose understanding of language will need to be taken into account. Making books for younger or less able children is also a useful task for older children. Email offers many opportunities to write for a different readership. Correspondence with children in another school, by letter or email can give children some good opportunities for writing 'for real'.

HMI (1996–7), the *Standards in the Primary Curriculum* survey, looked at standards in English in primary schools. They found that good or satisfactory progress had been made in 90 per cent of schools, with work weakest in Years 3 and 4 and strongest in Year 6. There was a 10 per cent gap between the performance of boys and girls at Key Stage 1 and this widened to leave boys even further behind at Key Stage 2.

The effects of the National Literacy Strategy

In 1999, HMI made an interim survey of the effects of the National Literacy Strategy (HMI 1999a) followed by a further survey to evaluate the first year of the strategy (HMI 1999b).

They found the following strengths.

- All the schools in the sample were implementing the policy in all age groups and teachers were positive about it. Workloads for teachers were high.
- Teaching was satisfactory or better in 80 per cent of lessons.
- The best teaching was in Years 5 and 6, where whole-class teaching of text and sentence-level work was good in two-thirds of lessons.
- Reception class teachers were implementing the literacy hour as soon as possible and the children were responding positively.

- The teaching by literacy co-ordinators was much better than that of the rest of the staff.
- Teaching of shared reading was the most successful part of the hour and was well taught in almost 90 per cent of lessons.
- The headteacher's leadership was satisfactory or better in 85 per cent of the schools receiving intensive support from their LEAs.
- Training by LEAs had been well received.

Weaknesses were as follows:

- Word- and sentence-level work was the weakest part of the hour. The teaching of phonics was omitted in some lessons and was unsatisfactory in others. It was improving at Key Stage 1, but was only taught well in about half the classes.
- Insufficient attention was being given to word-level work in Years 3 and 4. There was no phonics teaching in one-third of the Year 3 lessons observed in the interim survey.
- Insufficient attention was being given to shared and guided writing.
- Independent group activities were weak in one-fifth of the lessons and good in only two-fifths.
- Too few teachers used the plenary session to reinforce teaching points and review the lesson's objectives.
- The performance of boys, of whom in 1999 only 46 per cent achieved Level 4 in writing as compared with 61 per cent of girls, is worryingly low.

Further development needed

HMI (1999b) reports that 'The framework for teaching has raised teachers' expectations, increased the pace of their teaching – particularly of reading – and brought about a substantial improvement in teachers' subject knowledge' (HMI 1999b: 8). They note that teachers have moved from the practice of attempting to hear children read individually as often as possible to one in which pupils are more often taught to read more directly as a group. They suggest that the following developments were needed:

- more training for teachers in how to teach writing effectively, particularly the teaching of grammatical awareness and sentence construction;
- more emphasis on the teaching of shared and guided writing;
- training in the teaching of phonics at Key Stage 1 and more systematic attention to phonics in Years 3 and 4;
- consideration by teachers of how pupils can apply and develop in other subjects the skills they are learning in the literacy hour;
- consideration by schools of the best way to use assistance by other adults in the classroom.

This research also suggests that it is important for children to understand the purposes of reading and writing and that a teacher's understanding of a child's errors was important.

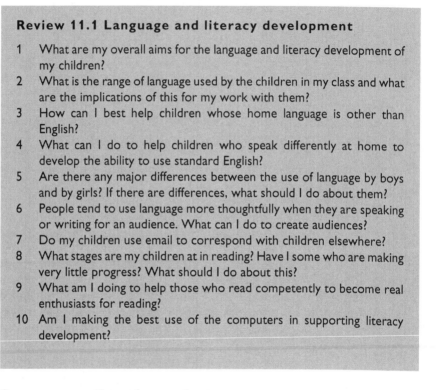

Review 11.1 Language and literacy development

1   What are my overall aims for the language and literacy development of my children?

2   What is the range of language used by the children in my class and what are the implications of this for my work with them?

3   How can I best help children whose home language is other than English?

4   What can I do to help children who speak differently at home to develop the ability to use standard English?

5   Are there any major differences between the use of language by boys and by girls? If there are differences, what should I do about them?

6   People tend to use language more thoughtfully when they are speaking or writing for an audience. What can I do to create audiences?

7   Do my children use email to correspond with children elsewhere?

8   What stages are my children at in reading? Have I some who are making very little progress? What should I do about this?

9   What am I doing to help those who read competently to become real enthusiasts for reading?

10 Am I making the best use of the computers in supporting literacy development?

Some suggestions for projects

Each of the following topics could be used in some way by children at any stage of primary education. The suggested activities can be adapted to meet the needs of different age groups. In each case you need to start your preparation by considering what experience the children already have of the area you plan to explore and the relevant language. This should give you some useful starting points.

The suggested projects should all provide good opportunities for talking and writing both factual accounts and more imaginative ones and perhaps some poetry. They all offer good ideas for drawing, painting and for modelling.

Project on communication

All animals communicate with each other in some way. As human beings we have a very wide range of ways of communicating with other people. A study on this topic might have as its purpose: *Helping children to become more aware of the ways in which we can communicate and enabling them to use their communication skills effectively.* The project might involve the following activities.

Start by considering the different forms of communication that we use

Ask the children how many ways of communicating they know, listing these on the board as they suggest them. They should be able to suggest a good many such as movement and gesture, facial expression, posture, speech, print and writing, email, pictures and diagrams, signs and notices, plans, maps, graphs and charts, musical sound and notation, radio, television, telephone and possibly others. Then select those most relevant for your particular children, taking them one at a time, and discuss them, drawing out from the children what is important in each case and considering what use they make of them.

Then take each form of communication in turn.

Communicating by movement, gesture and facial expression

Discuss with the children how they read the way that you, as teacher, use these forms of expression and how they know what you are thinking and want them to do without you saying anything to them. Then go on to ask them how they read each other's movements and those within their families and those they encounter in shops and in the street. This theme lends itself well to work in drama. Children can work in pairs or small groups aiming to communicate by gesture and movement. They may also like to consider how animals use this kind of communication with other animals and with human beings.

Communicating and receiving communication through sound

All sorts of sounds have meaning for us. We recognise sounds about the home and school and in the street outside. We know whether a machine is working by the sound it makes. We can hear music which is made up of loud and soft sounds arranged in different patterns for different occasions: how does the music differ for sad and happy occasions?

Communicating through speech

Speech is characteristic of human beings and we use it from a very early age. We use and receive various messages through speech. We take in both what is said and what is implied by the tone of voice and the way it is said. We also recognise overtones in speech as when a person is irritated but is trying not to show it, but you know that s/he is angry by the tone of voice s/he is using. Consider with your children, what can be learned from listening to someone else, not only in factual terms of what is actually said, but what you can learn about the speaker and how s/he feels about what s/he is saying.

You may also like to explore some of the problems about speech: differences in the language spoken and in the way it is spoken, the problems of the deaf and hearing impaired, what can be done for them. Most communication by speech is direct and we can see the speaker and learn from gestures, and so on, but we also listen to radio and use the telephone. It is interesting to consider how we interpret speech when we cannot see the speaker.

Visual communication

We are surrounded with visual communication. There are many street signs; some are provided to help us, perhaps in finding the way or a particular place, but many are advertisements persuading us to buy particular things. We may look at pictures in a book or magazine or visit an exhibition to look at paintings and other exhibits. We not only gain information from looking, but also pleasure, perhaps by looking at a beautiful view or beautiful flowers. You can discuss what they feel they gain from visual communication and how they learn from it.

Communication through written and printed language

Consider with the children what they can gain from this form of communication. You can learn from reading letters and books about things you want or need to know which are communicated by the writer of a letter or the author of a book. You can learn from a computer by using the internet to find out about something which interests you and you can ask questions of other people by email. You can enjoy stories by reading a book and learn about things that are happening in the world by reading a newspaper. You can cook or make something by reading instructions. Reading maps and street signs and directions can help you find your way somewhere. You can do the right thing by reading rules which apply in particular places (such as the school and classroom). Some languages, such as Japanese and Chinese use a different form of writing from us and it may be interesting to the children if they can see some examples. Music also has a written language which children can learn.

Communication for people with visual or hearing impairment

People who are unable to hear or see have special ways to communicate. Deaf people have for many years used a sign language. There is less need for this now because modern hearing aids are very effective, but for many signing is either useful or essential. Blind people have traditionally used a special form of writing called Braille, which enables them to read and write messages, books and even music.

Discussion of all these aspects of communication offers interesting opportunities for group work, with each group exploring a different area and reporting back to the class. All these forms of communication also lend themselves to different forms of creativity.

Of course, the level to which you can take the discussion and exploration will differ according to the age of your children. If you teach in a school with many children from ethnic minorities, this sort of exploration provides good opportunities for looking at the different things such children may be concerned about in communication. Movements may have a different meaning for some of them from the meaning understood by others. Some may come from a background which not only involves a different spoken language but also a different way of writing. This can all be interesting material to explore with your class.

Project on living things

Children's experience and knowledge about plants and animals will vary widely with the location of your school. If you serve a country area, the children will be aware of the effects of the changing seasons and be familiar with the more common birds, animals and plants in their environment. If they come from a farming family, they will already know quite a lot and you will need to start from this knowledge.

If your school is in an urban area, children are less likely to have good knowledge of living things and you start from a different angle. In this case you will need to provide opportunities, perhaps to visit a more rural environment or a park or open space where some living things can be seen in context. It will also be a good idea to keep some small animals in the classroom and to grow some plants from seed. You may also find it useful to take some photographs of plants and animals which you can project in the classroom. You may also be able to find some film which you can show.

Starting points

A good place to start would be a discussion with the children about the plants and animals they know about, putting special emphasis on those they have actually seen as well as those they have seen on television. Many of them will have dogs or cats as pets at home and will be able to talk about them. Some will have gardens which they can talk about. Assess carefully the experience of living things possessed by your particular children, aiming to identify what they already know and what they need to know. The experiences you then plan can be relevant to your particular group of children.

Whatever the children's background, there is considerable scope for drawing and painting as a means of recording and for different forms of writing in poetry and prose.

Provide some first-hand experience of plants and animals

You may do this by visiting a country area or a park or zoo which gives the children a chance to look carefully at the plants and animals there. In discussion before this visit, consider with them what they might see and introduce any new words you want to use, like 'evergreen', 'deciduous', 'hibernation', names for animal homes like 'burrows' and so on. Decide with them what they are going to look for, perhaps providing them with drawing or writing materials if this seems appropriate.

Discuss life processes with the children

All living things go through a life process. Start by thinking about human development, perhaps asking them to remember the stages they have gone through in the growing up process. How you do this will differ a good deal according to the age of the children, but if it is appropriate, you may want to discuss the way new life comes into being both in human and in animals. You can then go on to discuss the ways plants reproduce and grow, using plants in the classroom to observe these stages.

This leads to further discussion about the later stages of life in plants and animals, including human beings.

Chapter 12

Information and communication technology (ICT)

It could be argued that ICT is creating the biggest change in education since schooling was made compulsory. We are only on the fringe of this development at present. Already there are computer programs which allow printed documents to be produced from spoken input and this development is likely to create a rather different situation for children and schools. These programs are not very well developed as yet but will probably affect the children now in primary schools during their secondary education. Whiteboards are also transforming the way that teachers can work with their whole class and there are an increasing number of programs designed to be used with whiteboards.

DfES e-strategy

The DfES published an e-strategy in 2005: *Harnessing Technology – Transforming Learning and Children's Services*. This had four objectives:

- *Transform* teaching, learning and child development to enable everyone to meet their highest expectations;
- *Connect* with 'hard-to-reach' groups in new ways;
- *Open up education* to partnerships with other organisations;
- *Move* to a new level of efficiency and effectiveness in delivery.

The strategy saw ICT embedded into everything. The paper acknowledged that it was an ambitious plan which should lead to a transformation in education.

Tomorrow's computers

Computers are developing at an astonishing rate. The latest information (2007) suggests that the computer as we now know it will disappear and many of the other things that we use frequently, such as watches and microwaves, will fill the role of the present computer. There will be access to them from almost anywhere in a building where there is a monitor and they will control TV, telephone, DVD player, stereo, and so on. Other studies suggest that the future will see a miniaturising of computers. There are already computers which can deal with voice recognition and it seems likely that this will develop further over the coming years.

In schools, interactive whiteboards are already having a considerable effect in classrooms, making interactive whole-class teaching much easier, and opening up new possibilities for ways of teaching.

Ofsted findings

Ofsted, reporting recently on pupils' achievements in ICT, found that there had been a steady increase in primary schools in children's levels of achievement. They found that 'Pupils respond very positively to the use of ICT, they engage well with lessons, their behaviour is good and their attitudes to learning are very good.' They were developing the skills of using the medium and children at Key Stage 1 could use word-processing, save, print, retrieve and rearrange sentences. They had also learned to create pictures with ICT. At Key Stage 2 most were competent and keen to develop their skills further. They could check their spelling and use the internet, evaluating what they found and incorporate some of it into their work. They displayed high levels of interest and concentration and talked enthusiastically about ICT. They also found that teachers had increased confidence and competence in the use of this medium.

They found good teaching with ICT in 60 per cent of lessons which was a rise of 6 per cent from the previous survey. They rated the impact of ICT on teaching as good or better in 53 per cent of schools.

BECTA report on provision for ICT

In 2005, BECTA (the British Educational Communications and Technology Agency) produced a review of the current situation regarding ICT and schools. They found that there had been significant progress in learner access to ICT. There had been a growth in teacher confidence in using this medium and an increase in computer provision. The UK was now a leading nation in the development and use of ICT in schools. There had also been a considerable development in the provision of whiteboards in schools. However, the provision was still better in secondary than in primary schools, where a small but significant minority had poor access to ICT.

BECTA also looked at the provision and use of interactive whiteboards in primary school classrooms as part of this study, and concluded that it was likely that by now every primary school child would have some experience of them. Some other researchers, in a paper presented to a conference in San Francisco, noted that whiteboards had been introduced into British schools at a faster rate than anywhere else in the world.

BECTA also found some evidence that support and advice improved the ability of schools to implement ICT sustainably. There had also been a trend towards improved supply of content across the curriculum. The ratio of computers to pupils had improved considerably and in primary schools it was now 7.5 to one compared with 12.6 to one in the year 2000. This included broadband provision. There had also been a move towards laptops. However, a significant number of primary schools had worse ratios. It found that 68 per cent of primary schools now felt that the funding available for ICT was about right.

The purposes and uses of ICT in primary schools

ICT can support children's learning across the curriculum. The DfES paper (2005) sets out ways in which ICT can support reading and mathematics from the early stages. It suggests that:

> ICT can provide opportunities to:
>
> * use the Interactive Whiteboard and on-screen interactive reading materials
> * teach phonic knowledge, teach the application of the skill of blending phonemes to read words, broaden children's reading.

It goes on to suggest that at later stages, children may be helped by reading on screen:

> This strand will develop children's experience of interactive, non-linear and/or multimodal texts and explore how such texts can be used particularly effectively to support and encourage the development of comprehension and reader response. In the learning and teaching of reading comprehension skills, interactive materials may be used to develop reading comprehension skills, engender reader engagement, enjoyment and response, develop awareness of how texts are written, structured and presented for particular purposes and effects.

Small group work with ICT

Wegerif and Dawes (2004) write of the value of ICT for small-group work in which children work in pairs or trios with a computer, talking together about what they are trying to find out. This involves learning dialogues about the contribution of what they are finding on the computer to what the whole class or the particular group is trying to do. It will also involve, at an early stage, instructions about how to use the internet to gain information. They suggest that the best kind of learning happens when children find things out for themselves.

They found it necessary to arrange 'talk lessons' to prepare children to work in this way. These lessons focused on how to ask each other questions and respond with reasons, asking questions such as 'What do you think?', 'Why do you think that?' and then considering how to respond, perhaps with a statement such as: 'I think ... because'. The teacher's aim was to encourage children to listen to each other actively, respecting the thoughts and ideas of other people, giving reasons for their opinions and giving everyone the chance to participate. These are important life skills which have to be learned. This work should not replace work on paper but provide opportunities to explore ideas and effects which would be much more difficult to produce in traditional ways.

Wegerif and Dawes suggest that talking effectively with one another implies values such as respect for other people's views, empathy, a sense of fairness, tolerance for differences and a rejection of coercive pressure in favour of persuasion. These are important life skills which ICT learning can support.

The use of whiteboards

The majority of schools will probably now have at least some whiteboards and many are now gradually moving to a situation where the whiteboard has replaced the blackboard in almost all classrooms. A report by BESA (2001) suggested that at that time approximately 20 per cent of schools in the UK had an interactive whiteboard. Ofsted (2002) reported that:

> There is an increasing use of data projectors with presentation software to present information to pupils for discussion. Teachers are thus able to produce resources that exactly match their objectives and use them in a way that encourages interaction with pupils. Such resources also enable pupils to be given clear instructions and demonstrations, which are crucial to successful teaching.

The whiteboard now offers teachers many new opportunities for working with the class. Cogill (2003) describes how teachers can use the whiteboard in many ways to enhance children's learning. It can:

- provide an initial structure for their teaching;
- save time scribing;
- provide a large display that children could see and read easily;
- demonstrate skills for children;
- attract and retain children's attention;
- provide images or text that children could not easily have had access to in other ways;

- allow children to engage in quizzes or tests within the whole-class environment;
- increase class participation by children writing their solutions on the board;
- save work so that the teacher and class could access their joint contribution at a later stage;
- provide a tool for children to create their own multimedia screens for class presentations;
- enable collaborative work;
- provide images that could later be adjusted by children to display their own work;
- foster independent thinking skills in children and improve their cognitive skills.

In this strand there are video examples of children using ICT to support synthesising information from different sources and building comprehension skills to engender reader engagement, enjoyment and response, develop awareness of how texts are written, structured and presented for particular purposes and effects.

ICT has something to offer for every aspect of the curriculum and for almost every possible teaching and learning approach. Teachers and children will be able to find something on the web for whatever they want to study. Whiteboards offer the opportunity for a really effective kind of whole-class teaching. It can make personalised learning a reality.

Skill in using ICT is now essential for future employment, although at the present rate of change the current learning of primary school children may be out of date by the time they seek employment.

Somekh and Davis (2002), quoted in a research report by Cogill (2007), note that early research suggests that ICT has the potential to transform learning. Cogill suggests that the presence of ICT in the classroom has the potential to change the culture and relationship between teachers and children. She notes the use of a teacher and children working round a large screen enabling collaborative tasks and the opportunity for the teacher to provide scaffolding:

- It is important that teachers conceive the role of technology in a new way, as a cognitive tool that can be used by students in many ways.
- Teachers need to recognise the potential of computers to take some of the labour out of learning and use it for higher level tasks.
- Teachers should integrate ICT into classroom practice through framing tasks rather than as an add-on extra.

> **Review 12.1 The use of ICT in my classroom**
>
> 1 The DfES strategy suggests that ICT should eventually be embedded in everything that happens in the classroom. How far does this apply in my classroom?
> 2 What are my aims for work in this area?
> 3 How am I using the whiteboard? Am I really making the work with it fully interactive? What can I do as a result of having it that I couldn't do before?
> 4 What ICT skills have my children developed since they came into my class? What am I aiming for next?
> 5 Is ICT doing anything to help me personalise children's learning? Is this a possibility with the number of computers I have available?
> 6 Have I enough suitable software for the work I would like the children to do?
> 7 Am I making full use of ICT for my own work?

Using the internet

Computers are gradually providing more and more learning opportunities. Already the broadband service and the internet provide an extensive source of information which children can learn to use. It will be important that they gradually learn to be discriminating in what they find. It is all too easy to spend a lot of time sifting through information without really learning anything useful. This is another activity in which it is valuable for children to work in pairs and talk to each other about what they are finding and its relevance to the work in hand.

Teachers of older children in the secondary school have for a long time been concerned about young people who spend their time accessing unsuitable sites. It is likely that there are also some children in Year 6 doing the same.

Using email

Email offers opportunities for children to write for a real audience, perhaps to children in another school or another country, particularly if the school is teaching a foreign language. It offers an opportunity for children to ask questions about another town or village and gives very real opportunities for learning geography and history from those who can actually give first-hand information. It is also useful to do this the other way round, perhaps liaising with a teacher friend in another area and asking him or her to ask children in his or her class to email your children. This could be done on a class or one-to-one level and it offers a considerable incentive to write well and correctly.

Review 12.2 Are we making as much use as possible of ICT?

1 Do my children sometimes work together at computers? Does this help their learning? How can I help them to do this most effectively?
2 How competent are they in using the internet? How can I best ensure that they do this profitably? Have we a school policy about this?
3 What uses are we making of email? Are we using it as an incentive to write? Is it providing opportunities for children to find out about other people and other places? Am I making sufficient checks on their use of email?
4 Are we making good use of the graphic opportunities offered by ICT?
5 Could I make more use of ICT for record-keeping?
6 Are there any ways in which we should be doing more in this area?

In 2008, Schools Minister Jim Knight made a statement that the government envisaged a future in which every child would have a computer at home to help them with their education, regardless of family circumstances. He went on to say that the government was in talks with IT firms about this and was planning a pilot project with two of them. This could make a real difference to a child's ability to use a computer in school.

The needs of teachers and assistants

Studies of the work with ICT in primary schools suggests that the ICT skills of the teacher are crucial. It will therefore be important to see that teachers and assistants have every opportunity to become fully computer literate and able not only to guide their children in the profitable use of ICT, but also to be well aware of its possibilities for their own learning. This is something which the headteacher and governors should look for in appointing teachers, and those involved in appointing assistants should also look for this knowledge. Where a candidate appears to have much else to offer but is not strong in this area, it should be made clear when they are appointed that they will be expected to undertake training in the use of ICT. This may be provided by the school or by an external course.

The leadership of ICT work

It will be very important in all but very small schools to have someone leading the work in this field, someone to whom colleagues can turn for help and advice and with whom they can discuss ways forward. The headteacher may also need advice on computer provision and the new purchases which may become necessary.

The ICT leader will also need to work with colleagues to provide a scheme of work for each year group in the school and to keep these up to date – which may mean revising quite frequently as new materials and equipment come on the market. S/he is also likely to have a training role as new teachers and assistants join the staff with very varying abilities in this field.

Review 12.3 My ICT needs and those of my assistant

1   Are there any areas of work with ICT in which I feel ignorant or incompetent? What can I do about them?
2   Am I using the whiteboard to the best advantage?
3   Am I making as much use of the internet as I might as a source of information for my teaching?
4   Could I make more use of the computer for record-keeping?
5   How competent is my assistant with ICT? Are there areas in which she needs to learn more?

Chapter 13

Mathematics and science

The National Numeracy Project, which was introduced in the late 1990s, stated that numerate pupils should:

- have a sense of the size of a number and where it fits into the number system;
- know basic number facts and recall them quickly;
- use what they know to figure out an answer mentally;
- calculate accurately, both mentally and with pencil and paper, drawing on a range of strategies;
- use a calculator sensibly;
- recognise which operation is needed to solve a problem;
- be able to solve a problem involving more than one single-step operation;
- know for themselves that their answers are reasonable;
- explain their methods and their reasoning using correct terminology;
- suggest suitable units for making measurements, and make sensible estimates of measurement;
- explain and make sensible predictions from the numerical data in a graph, chart or table.

The starting points for children's mathematical learning

If you teach a reception class you need to discover each child's starting point for mathematical learning. Some teachers have found that a number of their children starting school had quite a lot of mathematical knowledge in practical situations. It might be a good idea at an early stage to talk to the parents about this and ask them to tell you what their children seemed to know and could do.

Sometimes children have a problem in moving between their everyday language and mathematical language and this difficulty can persist for quite a long time.

The trouble is that for children the phrasing of mathematical problems can be ambiguous. Hughes (1986) gives an example of the kind of difficulty which some children encounter. A child was asked 'What is the difference between 6 and 11?' and gave as the answer '11 has two numbers'. When she was told that this was wrong, she answered that 6 was curly and 11 was straight. This exemplifies the kind of difficulty which children meet over language. The child in question was giving everyday meanings to the mathematical question when what was wanted was a mathematical interpretation.

Hughes goes on to suggest that many difficulties arise from the use of the mathematical symbols +, −, × and ÷. Children come across numerals in many contexts outside school, but the mathematical symbols are, for children, peculiar to the classroom and they may take a long time to link them with their experience. This suggests that it might be a good idea to look for ways in which these symbols could be used in as many practical contexts as possible.

Askew and Wiliam (1995) write of the importance of finding out how pupils are thinking, perhaps by asking them to write about what they have learned. Many children have misconceptions or intuitive methods which seem to them to make sense, believing, for example, that subtracting a larger from a smaller number gives the answer nought. You need to find out how children arrived at incorrect answers whenever you can, if you are to help them to overcome their difficulties. Askew and Wiliam (1995: 20) go on to say:

> Knowledgeable teachers questioned pupils about problem-solving processes and listened to their responses while less knowledgeable teachers tended to explain problem-solving processes to pupils or observe their pupils' solutions.

Concept development

The ability to use calculating skills in a practical setting depends to some extent on the acquisition of concepts. A concept is acquired when a child has met a range of examples and non-examples and can use and apply the underlying idea. Discussion can be helpful in developing concepts, with children being asked to find examples and non-examples. Practical work is also important.

Using a computer

Askew and Wiliam also found that using a computer to teach particular topics resulted in more rapid learning and higher achievement. They make the following comment about this:

The crucial feature in evaluating educational software appears to be the tension between the extent to which the software supports and constrains the activity of the pupil. Using computers allows the teacher to create an environment for the pupil where the options open to the pupil are limited, so that the pupil is pushed into thinking about using a particular aspect of mathematics (constraint). At the same time the software allows the pupil to do things that would be difficult without the computer (support).

(Askew and Wiliam 1995: 34–5)

They also note that co-operative group work has a positive effect provided there is a shared goal for the group and individual accountability for the attainment of the goal. They suggest that near-mixed-ability groups containing perhaps high and middle attainers or middle and low attainers are the most effective. There should also be a balance of boys and girls in the group.

Effective teachers of numeracy

Askew *et al.* (1997) studied the work of effective teachers of numeracy and categorised teachers into three orientations: the connectionist orientation, the transmission orientation and the discovery orientation.

They found that the connectionist teachers emphasised the links between different aspects of mathematics. The transmissionist teachers demonstrated a belief in the importance of routines and procedures and stressed the importance of pencil and paper methods for each type of calculation. The discovery-oriented teachers tended to treat all methods of calculation as equally acceptable and valued pupils' creation of their own ways of doing things, basing work on practical approaches. Overall, they tended to find the connectionist teachers to be the most effective. They listed the characteristics of effective teachers of mathematics. These included the following:

- a coherent set of beliefs and understandings which underpinned their teaching of numeracy;
- a belief that being numerate requires a rich network of connections between different mathematical ideas;
- a belief that almost all pupils could become numerate;
- a view that discussion of concepts was important, particularly in revealing the pupils' thinking processes;
- attention to careful monitoring of pupils' progress and the keeping of detailed records.

The National Numeracy Strategy Framework (Department for Education and Employment, 1999) also lists the characteristics of teaching which leads to better numeracy standards.

These come about when teachers:

- structure their mathematics lessons and maintain a good pace;
- provide daily oral and mental work to develop and secure pupils' calculation strategies and rapid recall skills;
- devote a high proportion of lesson time to direct teaching of whole classes and groups, making judicious use of textbooks, worksheets and information and communication technology (ICT) resources to support teaching, not to replace it;
- demonstrate, explain and illustrate mathematical ideas, making links between different topics in mathematics and between mathematics and other subjects;
- use and give pupils access to number lines and other resources, including ICT, to model mathematical ideas and methods;
- use and expect pupils to use correct mathematical vocabulary and notation;
- question pupils effectively, including as many of them as possible, giving them time to think before answering, targeting individuals to take account of their attainment and needs, asking them to demonstrate and explain their methods and reasoning, and exploring reasons for any wrong answers;
- involve pupils and maintain their interest through appropriately demanding work, including some non-routine problems that require them to think for themselves;
- ensure that differentiation is manageable and centred around work common to all the pupils in a class, with targeted, positive support to help those who have difficulties with mathematics to keep up with their peers.

A survey by HMI (1996–7) suggested that at that time there was a need for more direct and whole-class teaching, more frequent oral and mental work, clear targets with suitably demanding expectations and more monitoring and review of progress analysing performance against benchmarks. To some extent these issues have been addressed by the National Numeracy Strategy (HMI 2000).

Anita Straker, Director of the National Numeracy Strategy, talking to a task group from the NUT in 1999, stressed that the structure should not be treated as a straitjacket. Teachers should use their professional judgement to determine the activities, timing and organisation of the lesson. She thought that at Key Stage 1, forty-five minutes was long enough for a lesson. While there should be some direct teaching and a high proportion of work with the whole class, there was also a place for different groups working at different levels and different tasks. She also suggested that towards the end of the lesson, the teacher might ask such questions as:

- What was the most exciting thing about this lesson?
- What was the hardest thing in the lesson?
- What have you enjoyed most during this lesson?
- What do you think is the most important thing you have learned today?

These would seem to be questions which might be asked, perhaps in a slightly different form, after almost any lesson.

The interim evaluation of the National Numeracy Strategy by HMI (2000) found that schools had made a good start with the strategy with the quality of teaching good in about half the lessons seen. There were weaknesses in the progression from mental to written mathematics and work with fractions, decimals and percentages. Teachers also found it difficult to achieve an appropriate level of differentiation, particularly where the range of ability was wide. The plenary session was the weakest part of the lessons seen, with only four out of ten lessons satisfactory. Teachers did not always leave enough time for it and often did not use it to identify and correct errors and misconceptions and reinforce teaching points.

Review 13.1 Mathematics

1 How well do I fit the characteristics of effective teaching listed by the National Numeracy Strategy? Are there any areas listed with which I disagree?

2 Does the list suggest to me any areas in which I would like to develop my work further?

3 Am I aware of areas in which my children appear to be confused between language use in mathematics and language use in everyday life?

4 Are any of my children having difficulty with mathematical symbols? If so, what should I do about it?

5 How much co-operative work takes place in my mathematics lessons? How successful is it?

6 How many of my children can calculate accurately at their present level of mathematical knowledge?

Science

A number of writers stress the importance of taking children's initial ideas into account when working with them in science. Children develop their own ideas of why things are as they are from a very young age, and if they do not have opportunities to investigate these ideas some errors may persist and may be very difficult to overcome later. It is important that they understand from an early stage that scientific knowledge is continually subject to modification as more becomes known through investigation. The question 'Will it always happen like that?' following an investigation should gradually lead children to the idea that there can never be a certain answer to this question.

Ways of thinking about evidence

Science requires a way of thinking about evidence which is relevant in other areas as well. For example, evidence is very important in learning history; the idea that something may be the case increases as more evidence is gained applies here as well as in science. Work in geography on the nature of the earth has very strong links with science – in fact the boundary between science and geography is not a clear one. Technology is perhaps more involved with science than any other subject and much work within it will be the practical outcomes of the applications of science. Food technology is also related to science and provides the opportunity for considering why foods behave as they do, what happens when we cook food, what happens when food decays, what our bodies need for nourishment and growth, and so on.

The making and testing of hypotheses is also a way of working which can be applied to any area of curriculum. Considering and predicting what happens if you take particular actions and then checking to see if the prediction was right is relevant in many aspects of daily life and is something which might often be the subject of classroom discussion.

Science and children's development

Harlen (1985) gives some useful summaries of what may be expected by way of scientific work from children of different ages. This review of development has application in other parts of the curriculum. The following is an abbreviated version of these statements.

Five- to seven-year-olds

1   They cannot think through actions but have to carry them out in practice.
2   They can only see from their own point of view. They need to move physically to see from another's point of view.
3   They focus on one aspect of an object or situation at a time; for example, their judgement of the amount of water in a container will take into account only one dimension, often the height the liquid reaches, not the combination of the height and width of the container.
4   They tend not to relate one event to another when they encounter an unfamiliar sequence of events. They are likely to remember the first and

last items in a sequence but not the ones in between.

5   The results of actions not yet carried out cannot be anticipated.

Seven- to nine-year-olds

1   They begin to see a simple process as a whole, relating the individual parts to each other so that a process of change can be grasped and events put in sequence.
2   They can think through a simple process in reverse, which brings awareness of the conservation of some physical quantities during changes in which there appears to be some increase or decrease.
3   They may realise that two effects have to be taken into account in deciding the result of an action; for example, if a ball of Plasticine is squashed flat so that it gets thinner as well as wider, it is not any bigger overall than before.
4   There is some progress towards being able to see things from someone else's viewpoint.
5   They can relate a physical effect to its cause.

Nine- to eleven-year-olds

1   They can to some extent handle problems which involve more than one variable.
2   They can use a wider range of logical relations and so mentally manipulate more things.
3   They show less tendency to jump to conclusions and a greater appreciation that ideas should be checked against evidence.
4   They can use measurement and recording as part of a more systematic and accurate approach to problems.
5   They can go through the possible steps of an investigation and produce a possible plan of action.

The teacher's role in concept development

Edwards and Knight (1994: 60) write of the teacher's role in helping children to develop concepts in science. The teacher's task is:

- to have an idea of which concepts are to be improved;
- to know which alternative concepts children are likely to hold;
- to provide situations in which children may be encouraged to notice discrepancies;
- to use that observation to get children to suggest an explanation;
- to get them to play with the explanation, making fair tests of it;
- to get them to apply and consolidate their conclusions.

They go on to suggest that the teacher needs to help children to see and understand:

> sometimes by drawing attention to what children have done, sometimes by asking for ideas, sometimes by asking if there are alternatives that might have advantages and sometimes by getting children to compare and evaluate what they are doing.
>
> (Edwards and Knight 1994: 61)

Science and mathematics both require substantial time to be devoted to them, but there will be opportunities for practising both in many other aspects of the curriculum.

Opportunities for scientific investigation will arise as part of other work on many occasions. An environmental study will provide many opportunities for studying plants and animals and perhaps looking at soil and rocks. A study of a historical building could lead to an investigation of how people raised stone before modern equipment was there to help them or it could offer the opportunity to study the effect of weathering on materials.

HMI (1996–7), studying science in primary schools, found that standards had improved and compared favourably with standards achieved by children in other countries. Four-fifths of pupils achieved or exceeded the expected national standard at Key Stage 1 and more than two-thirds at Key Stage 2. Attainment was similar to that in English and better than that in mathematics. Teaching was good in 40 per cent of schools and at least satisfactory in 90 per cent. The least satisfactory area of science teaching was the use of information technology to collect, store, retrieve and present information. They also found that assessment procedures were often inconsistently applied and not incorporated into planning.

Review 13.2 Science

1   What initial ideas do my children have about why particular things happen? Could I use some of these ideas as a starting point for investigation?

2   The understanding suggested at different ages in the text above is also a matter of stage of development. At what stages of development are my children and what are the implications of this for their work in science?

3   Do I give my children opportunities to predict outcomes of actions as part of their work in science?

4   Are there opportunities in other areas of curriculum to explore scientific ideas as part of the subject learning?

Chapter 14

The foundation subjects

Art

Drawing is a very natural form of expression for young children which they enjoy using from a very young age. Drawing and other forms of art also have much to contribute to the teaching of other subjects and in topic work but it is important that it is explored as a subject in its own right. Four areas need exploration:

1   Children need first-hand experience of drawing and this can usefully be part of other work, although encouragement to draw anything and everything is also needed.
2   They need to explore what different media will do, in both two and three dimensions.
3   They need the opportunity to think about putting these skills together to make compositions of one sort or another in both two and three dimensions.
4   They need, perhaps at a later stage, to study the works of artists and to explore some of the ideas and techniques they see used.

The teacher's basic role in the exploration of media is to provide opportunities. It is then to set problems which encourage exploration. For example, you might ask children to make a picture or pattern using as many different reds as possible, making the colours by mixing red with every other colour in differing amounts. You might ask for a pattern or picture using as many different textures as possible or get children to explore ways of representing the texture of things around them. With clay you might ask children to move in particular ways and then make figures doing exactly the same thing. Or you might ask children to explore surface textures in clay, perhaps making them by impressing the clay with different objects.

You can also encourage children to look at the relationships of the things they put into their pictures or creations. You can encourage them to make first-hand observations of the objects they draw or make, or experience how a person might look when moving in a certain way by moving themselves in a similar way or by watching someone else moving like that.

In looking at pictures with children you can draw their attention to the way in which the artist has used texture or arranged the shapes in the picture. They can then go on to try to use similar techniques in their own work.

HMI (1996–7), looking at art in primary schools, found attainment and progress good in 30 per cent of schools, with the best teaching in Year 6. They note that where standards were high, pupils explored a wide range of materials in two and three dimensions, such as paint, clay, pastel, collage and modelling materials. In such classes pupils began to develop observational drawing skills from an early age. They found that assessment in this subject was weak compared with that in most other subjects.

Design and technology

Bennett *et al.* (1992) and Webb and Vulliamy (1996) found that technology was the subject in which teachers felt least competent. HMI (1996–7) found that, while work in this subject continued to improve, the standards achieved were lower compared with most other subjects, mainly because teachers lacked subject expertise and often failed to provide a programme which built successfully on earlier knowledge. There was also a dip in attainment in Years 3 and 4. On the other hand, pupils' attitudes were generally positive.

These findings are perhaps not very surprising, given that this subject still seems rather recent. Nevertheless it is now quite a time since it was introduced but some teachers still need to develop the knowledge and skill needed and some schools still need to acquire and develop more resources.

Technology has a very close relationship with science, but whereas science is concerned with the pursuit of knowledge through investigation, technology is concerned with meeting human needs and with making things and it requires pupils to apply their knowledge and skill to solving practical problems. It is also frequently concerned with working with others as a team, which is a useful life skill.

The basic concern of technology is problem-solving and the processes used can be applied to other areas of work and to teaching. Problem-solving was discussed in Chapter 8. Problem-solving in technology requires similar steps, which are as follows.

1 Define the problem

This is a necessary starting point for all problems. It might be a problem such as how to make a bird-table which the squirrels cannot reach, or a problem in the classroom such as difficulty in keeping some areas tidy or everyone wanting the same things at the same time. You need to work with children to help them to make statements about what the problem really is. We saw in Chapter 6 that it is often helpful at this stage to consider what you wish the outcome to be.

2 Examine the problem further

This is a matter of discussing the nature of the problem and the needs which it must be designed to fit. It might be a matter of defining the social setting of a problem or discussing the range of materials which might be used or discussion of why the problem arises. In some cases a good deal of research will be needed to find out about the needs and the situation which the design must meet. If we take the problem of the bird-table, children will need to find out what squirrels can do and what would make the bird-table inaccessible to them while meeting the needs of birds.

3 Define your objectives

It is very helpful in problem-solving to know exactly what it is you are trying to do in as much detail as possible. If we take the problem of keeping an area of the classroom tidy, it may help to discuss what should be available in that area and in what sort of order and try to define what is meant by 'tidy'.

These three items provide the design specification. There are several more steps.

4 Consider possible solutions

Here, children need to be encouraged to find a number of alternative solutions before settling on one. It may be a good idea for them to work in groups, each group trying to make as many suggestions as possible. This may be the stage with some problems for sketching ideas.

5 Examine possible solutions

The next stage is to examine the possibilities and problems of each solution. Children need to look at such things as practicality, ease of making or doing, the cost in terms of materials and the extent to which each solution meets the criteria set out in the design specification.

6 Select a solution

If this is a group decision it will need a good deal of discussion; the final decision might be made by voting or by discussing to the point of consensus. Whether it is an individual or a group decision, it will involve careful weighing of the points arising out of the consideration of possible solutions.

7 Make an action plan

It is valuable to get children into the habit of making action plans for work in hand and this is particularly relevant where problem-solving is involved.

8 Make an evaluation plan

Evaluation should be part of the planning with any problem-solving activity and should take into account the criteria which were part of the design specification.

9 Carry out the project

It will be important to think out the organisation for this well in advance. Much will depend on the nature of the problem and the types of solution suggested.

10 Evaluate the result against the criteria defined

Children should be encouraged to consider their work and look to see whether anything could have been done differently or improved.

Part of the work in technology will involve evaluating one's own work and that of other people. Different artefacts may be discussed, looking at what they were designed to do and considering how effectively they do it. Children may also be involved in finding out how things work. They need to learn how to use tools and devise mechanisms that make things move.

The teacher's role in technology will be to define the parameters within which work takes place. In many cases it will be the teacher who identifies the problems to be tackled, although children should be encouraged to identify problems as well. It is important to define tasks in such a way that there is ample scope for children to solve them in their own way, selecting materials and tools as seems best to them.

Geography and history

Over the years there has been a good deal of discussion about how far schools should be concerned with knowledge in these subjects and how far with the interpretation of evidence and empathy with people who live in other places or lived at other times. There would seem to be a need for some emphasis on both.

Both history and geography require an act of the imagination to understand the way different people have lived or do live in the world today. Children easily get the impression that people who live differently from them are in some way odd and a variation from the norm. People who lived in days gone by and people who live in other places, may be influenced or have been influenced by different things from present British people, but they all knew in the past and know now what it is like to be hungry or thirsty, tired, happy or unhappy, to love and to hate, to have ideas and hopes and so on.

Since children's experience is limited, it is important to provide as much first-hand experience as possible and to complement this with video material, film and television programmes. If you have children of different nationalities in your class and they have enough English to talk about their background, this will be very valuable from many points of view: not least in helping the children of British background to realise that people who live in other countries are like them in many ways but also, like them, have their own ways of doing things which are different from ours but equally important and valuable.

Fieldwork

Fieldwork can be a useful part of both these subjects. Many children will go to other countries for holidays and if you know about this before they go, they could be encouraged to find out what they can about the native people who live there. Parents may like to help with this, if you tell them about it early enough and make some suggestions about what they and their children might do and find out. You also need to do some local fieldwork, discussing in advance what to look for and sometimes doing a study of the countryside in your own area. You might also visit places of historical interest and look at some very old buildings such as churches, or places where there are lots of old buildings. With older children you might go further afield and explore some new areas, where possible choosing an area very different from that surrounding your school.

Other learning about foreign places

Geography must also involve learning how to use globes and maps and the characteristics of places and the effects of different places on the people who live in them, and also the effect of people on the places in which they live, perhaps looking at the effect people have had on your area over the years. Children can also share information about their own environment with children in other locations in other schools through email.

HMI (1996–7) looked at the teaching of geography in primary schools and found well-organised and managed field studies and good practical work in the school grounds and elsewhere. There was good development of investigatory and mapping skills, particularly in Years 5 and 6, and children enjoyed their work. They found weaknesses in some schools where geography was only taught infrequently and skills were not well developed and there was a lack of use of information technology. There was also a dip in attainment in most schools in Years 3 and 4.

Drama may help in enabling children to imagine what life was like at another time or in another place. A visit to one of the museums where children are incorporated into a drama about a particular period in history will be immensely valuable.

History involves learning how to find out about the past from various sources and children should learn to place events in chronological sequence.

HMI found that history teaching compared favourably with that in most other subjects and they felt that this was mainly owing to the fact that teachers' subject knowledge was good. This led to good progress and a high degree of enjoyment of the subject in many schools.

Planning for progression was weak in a number of schools in both these subjects, as was assessment.

History and geography may be incorporated into topic work, but it will be important to have a clear idea of the historical or geographical learning which is intended.

Music

Music teaching has changed radically in recent years, partly as a result of electronic music-making. There is now also a much greater emphasis on composition. Singing is still important and children need to sing a wide variety of music and learn to play different tuned and untuned instruments and compose rhythms and tunes for them. There should be good opportunities for playing with and to others and discussing critically both performance and composition. Children need eventually to learn to read music but this is probably best approached by asking children to invent methods of writing down the music they make up and then gradually introducing more formal ways of writing.

It is also important for children to listen to a wide range of music and discuss their reactions to it and to the music they compose.

Physical education

Physical education should serve two important purposes in school. It is concerned with achieving and maintaining fitness and it is also concerned with helping children to move in a controlled way. There is a good deal of concern at the present time about the fact that children are taking less exercise than in the past and the long-term effects of this for their health, and particularly about obesity which is now fairly widespread among primary school children. This makes the subject of particular importance. Physical education also aims to teach the beginnings of games skills which may form the foundation for activity in adult life, in a society where much work is sedentary. There should be opportunities both to create dance and to perform dances from other times and places. Swimming is also an important element in the physical education programme. Children should be encouraged to look critically at their work in all aspects of physical education and consider ways in which their movement could be improved and to think about the need for exercise and the disadvantages of being overweight.

HMI (1996–7) found that in most schools pupils made good progress in games, gymnastics and dance, although there was a tendency to repeat known skills rather than seek to improve them. Teaching was good in nearly half the schools and at least satisfactory in 90 per cent. The least satisfactory aspects of the subject were assessment and recording, which was not well done, with records of children's progress rarely kept. It might be a good idea with older children to get them to keep some sort of diary record of their physical activity both in and out of school. This could serve other purposes as well.

HMI also found that athletics and outdoor and adventurous activities tended to be neglected and this is almost certainly due to teachers' concern about safety and the possible consequences of accidents for the teachers involved. A common failing also was the lack of attention to involvement of pupils in a cycle of improvement and skill development. The diary idea would be useful in improving this too. HMI noted that good physical education teaching was characterised by clear task-setting, challenge and a focus on skill learning.

There is a tendency to regard physical education lessons as separate from the rest of the curriculum. There is a need to make links in many ways. In physical activity, a teacher can see whether children are understanding the language he or she is using in a way which is more difficult elsewhere because in physical education they have to respond physically to instructions. Many mathematical words come into physical education: fast, slow, circle, line, shape and so on. It is also valuable to observe children's movement in the classroom and about the school and to consider the implications of the way children move at other times than in PE lessons.

Religious education

Religious education is not an easy subject to teach in a pluralist society. On the other hand, the presence of children of different faiths in a school gives the study of religion a reality which is more difficult to achieve when all the children are at least nominally of Christian background or of no faith at all.

Religious teaching in schools other than church schools is teaching about religion and the part it plays in human history. An understanding of Christianity is essential for an understanding of British history and customs. An understanding of Judaism, Islam, Sikhism, Buddhism and Hinduism is necessary to understand present-day British society and also to understand what is happening in different parts of the world, as well as for understanding world history.

Religious education in schools other than voluntary schools is governed by Agreed Syllabuses devised by local Standing Committees for Religious Education (SACRES).

Religious education is also concerned with moral education, although this needs to be pursued in many other contexts as well. Children need to know the moral basis of Christianity because it is the moral basis of much in our society. At a later stage in education they may learn about the moral ideas of other religions.

HMI (1996–7) found that religious education was taught to a satisfactory or better standard in 90 per cent of schools but was good in only about 20 per cent. Years 5 and 6 made better progress than Years 3 and 4 and teaching was slightly better at Key Stage 2 than Key Stage 1. The quality of teaching was inconsistent. Teachers generally had the necessary knowledge but lacked the confidence and expertise to teach religious education effectively. There was a tendency to emphasise the facts about religion rather than beliefs and values. Assessment of performance was also weak and rarely related to specific objectives. There were fewer good standards of attainment and progress than in other subjects and the teachers tended to have low expectations of pupils. The teaching of religious education was rarely monitored although subject leadership was improving. Pupils' attitudes were mainly positive.

Review 14.1 Thinking across the curriculum

1   Which curriculum subjects provide opportunities for cross-curricular experience and work in which children can learn about different subjects through the same work?
2   Which subjects involve practical work and creativity of various kinds?
3   In which subjects is first-hand experience or fieldwork of some kind needed? What sorts of experiences would have cross-curricular possibilities?
4   In which areas of curriculum could I use television or other recorded material? How should I use it?
5   How should I use the whiteboard so that children share in what we do with it?
6   In which areas might I use other forms of ICT? Are my children developing the ICT skills to use this resource profitably? Do they need to learn any further ICT skills for future work?
7   What sorts of records should I keep of work in different areas of curriculum? What purposes will my records serve?

Chapter 15

Creativity

What is creativity?

Creativity is not altogether easy to define. It is the ability to have ideas, to invent, to see new avenues, to explore. It can be expressed in a multitude of ways and is not just concerned with the arts. It is needed in all areas of our lives and in all areas of education. It is a way of thinking and expressing, of behaving, of working and a way of teaching and learning.

The National Advisory Committee on Creative and Cultural Education (1999) in their report on creativity made the following statements.

- By creative education we mean education that develops young people's capacity for original ideas and action (p. 6).
- Serious creative achievement relies on knowledge, control of materials and ideas. Creative education involves a balance between teaching knowledge and skills, and encouraging innovation (p. 7).
- Creativity is possible in all areas of human activity and all young people and adults have creative capacities. ... The roles of teachers are to recognise young people's creative capacities, and to provide the particular conditions in which they can be realised. Developing young people's creativity involves, among other things, deepening young people's knowledge and understanding (p. 10).

Schools might well be asking why creativity has recently come to the fore. Experienced teachers might say 'We've always given children opportunities for drawing and painting and making things, for drama, for writing stories and poems; what more are we supposed to do?'

Creativity is much more than work in the so-called 'creative' subjects. It is a way of thinking which applies right across the curriculum. You can be creative in finding ways of solving a mathematical or scientific problem, in exploring in the mind what life would be like if you lived in a different place or at a different time, or thinking of a new way of doing something or a new approach to learning. It is a way of thinking which it is easy to discourage because sometimes children will come up with ideas which are completely impractical or lead to blind alleys or are inconvenient. Yet creativity is important because it brings with it enormous enthusiasm and interest which you can often harness for some aspect of a child's learning. It is also a valuable life skill. Whatever you do in life, it can be enhanced if you have good ideas and can see possibilities in all sorts of places and situations and perhaps also have the ability to carry them out.

The importance of creative work in many aspects of the curriculum

Primary schools in recent years have felt the pressure to achieve in the core subjects and perhaps less time has been devoted to creative activities of various kinds than was once the case. Creative work in whatever medium is important in its own right as a form of expression. It is also a medium for learning other things. Opportunities for both are needed. It is important as a teaching approach because children need to understand some things with their emotions and imaginations as well as in cognitive terms. Creating a picture or model or a piece of drama may help a child to understand what it was like to be alive at a different time or to live in a different part of the world. The experience of using implements or wearing clothes from a different period or place may bring a new understanding of people who used such implements or wore such clothes. A story may make more sense when children make a picture of it. Taking a role may make it possible for a child to enter imaginatively into learning.

It is not easy to provide for this kind of learning in such a way that all children get this kind of understanding. You need to be on the lookout for opportunities in other work to complement it with creative work. In science, for example, children could be encouraged to think creatively about how best to tackle a particular science problem. You might trawl for ideas about how to find out why the leaves on a plant you have on the classroom windowsill are turning brown. Mathematics may be made more real by asking children to undertake such activities as taking on the role of someone who needed to measure something but had no measuring tools, or an architect who wanted to copy some features of your school building but was unable to borrow the plans. You can think creatively about almost anything and this is an ability which needs to be encouraged and developed in all children.

You also need to be aware, as the report from the advisory committee quoted above suggests, that in every subject there is a chance to be creative by thinking of new ideas and ways of doing things. Subjects such as English, technology, art, drama, music and dance offer particular opportunities, but there are also opportunities to think creatively in pretty well all the curriculum. Craft (2005) writes of the growing assumption 'that the creative individual is a fulfilled one'. As teachers, we need to appreciate that every child has creative abilities which can be applied in many different ways. You need to do all you can to help your children to be confident in their creative ability.

Creativity is important for future employment

In 2006, the Department for Education and Skills and the Department for Culture and Sport made the following response to the report *Nurturing Creativity in Young People*.

> We know that if Britain is to retain its competitive edge in the future, then it will need to ensure that our education system continues to do all it can to give children and young people the creative skills they need ... We know that if Britain is to retain its creative edge in the future, then it will need a creative work force ... so we need to ensure that our education system continues to do all it can to give children and young people the creative skills they need.

The development of creativity in schools has government backing.

The creative possibilities of computer technology

Computer technology is also providing excellent opportunities for creativity and these are likely to increase with time. Computers not only provide access to a vast range of information and material, but also offer scope for exploring creative ideas of many kinds. Exploring language by using it in stories, poems, letters and accounts of various kinds is much easier with a computer, which offers you the opportunity to correct mistakes as you go along, to change your mind and rewrite something differently, to try out ways of expressing yourself and much else. The computer also offers scope for drawing and painting, again with the possibility that you can change and develop work as you go along. The possibilities are endless.

Creative thinking can be fostered in many ways. It can involve trying to think of new ideas or new ways of doing something or trying something new – perhaps using new materials in art and craft or writing a story from a new point of view. How about telling the story of Cinderella as it might have been seen by the ugly sisters?

The environment needed for creativity to flourish

If your children are to be prepared to take the risk of being creative, you will need to create an atmosphere in which children feel safe in trying new ideas, one in which you are encouraging even when what is suggested is rather impractical and not very useful for the task in hand. You need to look for anything which suggests a way forward in this kind of situation. You need to encourage lateral thinking, which children can often do more easily than adults because their minds are usually more open to new things. The way you praise and encourage will also be important. Just saying that something is good is not enough by itself. You need to select out particular aspects of whatever contribution a child has made, and either praise these or make suggestions about how they could be still better. Your assistant also needs to be aware of what you are trying to do and the need both to encourage unusual ideas and suggestions and also to be prepared to look for ways in which they could be further extended.

Craft (2005) suggests that creativity occurs in environments which foster innovation, control, relevance and ownership for both teachers and learners. She goes on to say:

> In creative classrooms innovation was demonstrated by:
>
> - opportunities for pupils to suggest, invent and propose ideas;
> - encouragement of pupils in making connections;
> - provision of an atmosphere of fun, enjoyment, exploration and possibility;
> - the use of humour in encouraging invention.

In such classrooms children's work was celebrated and their ideas taken seriously. The outcomes from creative learning include not only exciting and original work but also a capacity to take risks and try new ideas.

Review 15.1 Providing an environment for creativity

1   What am I doing to develop my children's creativity?
2   What opportunities for being creative do I offer them? Do these go across the curriculum encouraging a creative approach to most subjects?
3   Am I creating the right sort of atmosphere in the classroom to encourage children to have ideas and explore them?
4   Do I give my children enough opportunities to suggest ideas which they would like to explore further?
5   How do I react when a child comes up with an idea I've never thought of and which doesn't seem to me to make much sense?

Creative teaching and learning

Creativity is involved in both teaching and learning. The way in which you ask children to work can give rise to many different ideas if this is what you set out to do. Creative teaching involves using approaches which allow learners to use their imagination and experiences to help them to learn. Craft (2005: 36) suggests that 'the heart of creativity is possibility thinking'. She points out that 'though creativity may be different in different subjects, it is nevertheless driven by the same underpinning curiosity combined with imagination'. She goes on to suggest that this involves:

- encouraging young people to believe in their creative identity;
- identifying young people's creative abilities;
- fostering creative ability by encouraging curiosity, becoming more knowledgeable about creative processes and providing opportunities to be creative.

The creative school and the creative classroom

A conference organised by the National College for School Leadership in 2003 brought together a number of primary school headteachers who ran schools which were were known for creative teaching and learning. The conference concluded that 'At the heart of these successful schools lies a culture of creativity that can best be described by a combination of relationships, organisation, teaching and learning.'

These headteachers said that they thought that it was important at an early stage to establish some guiding principles and an underlying philosophy together with a vision and a value system followed by action, and to create a culture of trust and mutual respect for everyone in the school.

There was evidence too that these heads responded creatively to external pressures and did their best to make space for the development of teachers' professional autonomy and confidence.

They suggest that 'creative learning is much more than an allocation of more time for humanities and the arts'. These schools had a culture of creativity which they describe as a combination of relationships, organisation, teaching and learning. They described some of the features of teaching and learning which prevailed in the creative classrooms in their schools:

- an emphasis, wherever possible, on problem-solving and an enquiry-based approach to learning;
- a willingness to take risks (presumably on the parts of both teacher and children);
- a culture of professional support that extends throughout the school;
- the celebration of innovation and imagination in teaching and learning;

- the encouragement of collaboration between pupils and between teachers;
- the integration of ICT throughout the curriculum;
- a recognition of the need to take account of preferred learning styles;
- opportunities for pupils to work independently, collaboratively and to learn collectively;
- time for pupils to persevere with extended pieces of work;
- use of the knowledge and skills of visitors and members of the wider community;
- the enrichment of learning, wherever possible, by first-hand experience.

Attitudes, behaviours and relationships

- The schools are warm and welcoming.
- There is a sense of community.
- The schools are inclusive.
- A shared vision gives the school a strong sense of purpose and direction.
- Respect and trust extend across the whole school community.
- Members of staff are willing to support one another.
- Pupils show enjoyment, excitement and enthusiasm for school.
- Challenge is evident throughout the school.
- Pupils are keen to explore.
- Pupils display high levels of interest.
- They have high levels of confidence and self-esteem.
- Pupils' opinions are valued and their needs are recognised.
- Pupils enjoy peer support or buddies.

Features of organisation

Creative approaches to learning were made possible due to creative approaches to organisation such as:

- imaginative use of budgets;
- creative solutions to problems;
- creative use and organisation of time;
- whole days or longer blocks of time for special projects;
- work based on themes that make links between subjects;
- imaginative ways of grouping pupils together;
- careful appointments made as a result of thorough selection processes;
- creative use of staffing to secure the best possible adult–child ratio;
- using the school environment to reflect the commitment to creative learning.

This was apparent in the displays of pupils' work and the careful use of colour and texture in the classrooms and shared spaces throughout the school.

Looking for opportunities for creativity

You need to be very conscious of the need to foster children's creativity, encouraging their ideas and trying to think of creative approaches to many aspects of the work. This means taking your own creativity seriously and being creative in your teaching whenever you can. Remember that opportunities to be creative usually foster enthusiasm in children and this can help in many aspects of their learning. Many learning activities offer creative opportunities if you look for them and they can make learning more interesting for children. Even quite everyday demands can provide creative opportunities.

Imagine, for example, that you are planning an exhibition of children's work of different kinds for a parents' open day. You will, of course, have ideas about this yourself, but it is an excellent opportunity to draw on children's creativity to plan parts of the day. What could they do to show their parents what they have been doing since the last parents' open day? What ideas have they about ways of showing how well they have worked? Would some drama be a good idea and if so, what should they aim to do? What should they put on exhibition and how should they choose work for this?

This kind of event provides many opportunities for creative thinking on the part of children. It may be a good idea to get them to work in groups to think up ideas and plan them. Then each group can tell the rest of the class what they have planned and they can all think together about how to put the plans into action. Many quite ordinary activities have this kind of potential.

Another approach is 're-framing' or trying to view things from a different point of view. For example, suppose you take a story like that of Cinderella and her ugly sisters. The story is always thought of from the point of view of Cinderella. However, suppose you ask the children to imagine being one of the ugly sisters and think about the story from that point of view. This kind of exercise needs quite a lot of time for discussion, but it starts a whole new line of thought: one which perhaps has some relevance to the way we view other people in our lives today.

Sometimes it may be a good idea to describe a mystery to the children. Imagine a situation in which something you value has mysteriously disappeared from your bedroom. So far as you know, only you and your parents have been there in the past week or two and it was on your windowsill last Monday. What could have happened to it? Children could make up this kind of story for each other, first talking with a partner about what they think could have happened and then writing about it.

There will often be opportunities for this kind of work and you need to take advantage of them when you can because creative thinking becomes more real when it leads to an outcome.

Planning for creativity

You need to build creativity into your overall planning and preparation. Look for creative opportunities in your schemes of work. When you work out your lesson plans for the next week or the next month, ask yourself what will give rise to creative opportunities and then think through how you will use these to strengthen children's learning and develop their creative abilities. Be clear about your objectives, for creative development as well as for the acquisition of knowledge.

Part of your planning for creativity will involve consideration of the various possible creative media, and the learning about each medium the children will need to be able to use it creatively. While it is true that very often children happen upon exciting forms of expression almost by accident, they gradually need to acquire the skills which allow them to be in control.

Work which is open-ended is more likely to offer creative opportunities than work in which everything is laid down. Encourage children to generate ideas, then question and explore them. Praise imaginative suggestions and encourage an element of risk-taking. Try to stand back sometimes and let the children take the lead.

Individual children and creativity

This chapter starts from the premise that all children have some natural creative ability and that given the opportunity they will show this. However, some children are naturally more creative than others and you need to be aware of them from an early stage and help them to use their creativity in a positive way. They are likely to be imaginative and see possibilities. They will have many ideas and want to try them out. They may want to develop a piece of work in a way different from the one you have suggested and you will have to decide whether to let them pursue their ideas or insist that they do what you have asked. You may have children gifted in particular directions, such as in writing or painting or movement or music; it will be important to provide opportunities for them to pursue work in these areas and develop it further, perhaps working together on some occasions.

There will also be others who are very hesitant about being creative. They may have been discouraged by their parents or perhaps compared unfavourably with an older sibling. A teacher they have encountered earlier in school may have been discouraging. The result of all this discouragement will be that they don't really want to try anything at all challenging. It will be very important to identify such children at an early stage and do all you can to encourage them to try new things, to pursue their own ideas and so on. You will need to give them extra attention and praise their attempts as often as you can.

Review 15.2 Creative teaching and learning

1   Am I looking for opportunities for creativity in the different aspects of my planning?
2   Am I providing for creativity in most aspects of children's learning?
3   Are my children finding ways of being creative using ICT?
4   Have I some children who have real creative gifts in some aspects of their work? What should I do to encourage and develop these abilities?
5   Are there some other children who are very hesitant about creating anything original? What should I do to help them?

Chapter 16

Personal and social education and citizenship

While these subjects are not a compulsory part of the curriculum for primary schools, no primary school teacher can escape the need to help children to develop in their personal and social relationships. It is part of everyday life when working with young children and your influence on their social development is crucial. It is therefore essential that this subject is given proper attention at all stages in primary education.

There are many skills involved in personal and social education and you need to be concerned with them throughout all your work in the classroom.

Self-knowledge

We looked at the way children develop in Chapter 3. Throughout the years of schooling each child is developing a view of him- or herself which is made up from the reactions of those around, both adults and children.

Initially a child's parents are very important in forming an early self-image, but teachers are also very powerful at the primary stage and the peer group plays an increasing part as the child grows and develops. It is very important that you, as teacher, recognise that this is happening and that your recognition of each child's progress and success counts with the child. It is also essential that you see that there are opportunities for every child to succeed in some way and for every child to take responsibility and contribute to the class community.

A child also needs gradually to know and come to terms with his or her own strengths and limitations. Children need a range of opportunities, encouragement to try new things and help and support in overcoming difficulties. It may be helpful to discuss a difficulty frankly with an individual child and together make a plan to overcome it so that you can genuinely praise each step taken.

The development of self-confidence

The development of self-confidence is closely related to the development of the self-image. Children need to be confident in themselves as people, in their ability to learn and tackle new tasks successfully and in their relationships with others.

You need to help all children to develop a confident attitude to at least some part of their activity. The secret of this is to match tasks to the level at which a child who tries can succeed. This is not easy, but it is more important for some children than for others and you can see very quickly those who lack confidence and need success. In the first days with a new group it is worth concentrating rather more attention on these children so that they achieve fairly early and gain confidence in you and become ready to try new things. Your reaction to their ideas and contributions is crucial in the early stages. This is something you need to share with your assistant so that you can work together to encourage children who lack confidence.

Children are influenced not only by the example, teaching and behaviour of teachers and assistants but also by their peer group. We tend to forget the learning that goes on between child and child. Parents often have this in mind when they choose to send a child to one school rather than another. This is not necessarily because they think the teaching is any better but because they want their child to be with children from similar families rather than learning a way of life from other children which they see as alien.

Ability to live and work with others

Learning to work with others is an important part of the curriculum. The ability to do this is a valuable skill in adult life and involves a number of subskills.

Developing social competence

We want all children to be socially competent, knowing what to do in different situations. There is also a case for seeing that all children learn the conventions of social behaviour, such as greeting people, making and responding to introductions, thanking someone, making a complaint politely, making an enquiry and so on. The teacher's example is important here, but there is also a need for specific teaching and plenty of opportunities to practise. Drama lessons may well offer this kind of opportunity.

In adult life many people may be expected to work with others to an agreed end from time to time. We want children to be able to get on with others and live and work with them to achieve group goals, sometimes leading and sometimes following.

Sensitivity to others

We also want children to be sensitive to others. Sensitivity is closely linked to the ability to see through the eyes of another person. A teacher needs to find ways of extending children's understanding of how things look from other points of view. Stories are often a help and it is worth trying to make a collection of stories which help to develop such understanding. Drama or role-play games in which each child has to study the part he or she is playing and see things from the point of view of a particular character may also contribute.

Discussion about this is important and it is often possible to use the occasion when a particular child's behaviour has hurt someone else to try to get that child and perhaps others to see how it looked from the other person's point of view. Very young children find this difficult to do, but development is likely to come from encouragement to think about other views. As children grow older they need continued help and constant encouragement to view things in this way.

Moral education

Moral education is important at all stages of education and it has a particular place in the primary school, where children are learning how to get on with other people outside their families. It is part of many aspects of primary education and begins to be important as children learn to work and play with others. Many situations will arise in schools and in the playground which create opportunities for talking about and thinking about ways of behaving and their effect on other people.

At the primary stage of education teachers can do a great deal to help this development. At the beginning of the primary stage, children need to be bound by the rules of the adults in their world, whether parents or teachers, because they are not yet ready to generate their own rules for living. Teachers need to create lots of opportunities for children to talk about how they might behave in different situations and the good and bad things about the different possible courses of action. From this kind of discussion children will eventually be able to go on to generate their own principles for behaving in situations where there is a moral choice. By the time they leave the primary stage, some are already examining the principles offered by adults and thinking deeply about how to deal with moral situations in their own lives.

In order to act morally a person needs to be able to weigh up the facts in a moral situation, look at it from different points of view as well as his or her own, generate or refer to principles and see if they fit the situation, and then make a choice and act with intention. Children can gradually learn how to do this if you provide opportunities for discussion about how to make moral choices.

Developing a framework of meaning for life and a value system

Children start to develop a framework of meaning and a value system during their years at school and this begins in the primary school. As they grow they gradually develop their own frame of reference by which they make judgements about people, events and things. Everything that happens to them contributes to this, rather as it does to their self-images.

Initially, children take on the values and ideas of their parents, and these are gradually modified and developed as teachers and other adults and children put forward different ideas. Eventually, children reach the point where they have an internal set of references which will go on developing until the child becomes an adult and they will use this to make judgements about new people and new situations.

Each person's frame of reference constitutes a view of the world and life, and, where people have widely differing views of what constitutes good, their views may be difficult to reconcile. You may find, for example, that the parents of some of your children have views about bringing up and educating children which are very different from your own, particularly if they come from a different culture. You have to work out how best to deal with these differences, so that you don't undermine the influence of the parents, but at the same time help children to see a different point of view where behaviour in school is concerned.

Those with religious faith accept with it a set of values, many of which they make their own, so that the values enshrined in their faith become part of their frame of reference. There is an important sense in which Christian values are part of the frame of reference of most British people because they are part of British history and culture and much of our thinking is rooted in the values of Christianity. This may change as the other cultures in our midst influence the way we think.

Review 16.1 Personal and social education

1 What are my children learning about themselves and what are the sources of this information?

2 Are there some children who lack self-confidence because of the way they have been treated by others? What can I do to help them be more positive about themselves?

3 How many of my children find it difficult to relate to other children or to adults? What can I do to help them?

4 Are my children learning to see from other people's points of view? What can I do to help them develop this skill?

5 Am I giving my children opportunities to learn how to work together? Have we discussed how best to do this?

6 What sort of a value system are my children developing? Do we discuss values?

7 Are my children becoming moral people? How can I help this process?

Health education

A good deal of health education is incorporated in the science curriculum and some aspects should be dealt with as part of physical education. Children should learn about the importance of regular exercise and its effect on their bodies and on their health. They also need to learn about healthy eating and the effect of their diet on their health and fitness.

At Key Stage 1 children learn about parts of the body, growth and development, personal hygiene and rules for keeping safe. At Key Stage 2 they learn about a healthy lifestyle, the onset of puberty and the physical and emotional changes this may bring about.

Teaching about drugs, including tobacco and alcohol, should be introduced at this stage, because these now present a considerable social problem with adolescent boys and girls in secondary schools and your children need to be prepared for this.

Primary schools have a choice about whether to include sex education in the curriculum in addition to the teaching about reproduction, which is part of the science curriculum. There is much to be said for talking to the older children about sex, and warning them about teenage pregnancy. It is important to get this in context, stressing the need to provide a loving and caring environment for children, which is especially difficult if you become a mother unintentionally and have to bring up a child without the support of a husband or partner and perhaps without a permanent home.

Citizenship

Children need to know something about how democracy works nationally and locally and this is reinforced if you use opportunities which arise to make democratic decisions in the classroom, and the school has a democratic school council. You can then relate this to local and national decision-making.

Some aspects of citizenship are likely to be covered in the history programme, which should introduce children to some of our historical and cultural background and that of other groups and nations. It is also important that as children grow older, they learn something of how people behave in groups and something about the way our society functions, including its institutions and practices, the way we are governed, the need to generate wealth and the way present-day life differs from that of the past. Children, as they grow older, also need to learn about the part played by industry and the rule of law. Some of this may come from relevant visits or visitors, such as the police or members of the fire service.

Social values

Children should be introduced to those values in our society which are commonly held. There will be many opportunities to introduce the values of the school which are also part of wider values. This will go on developing until the child becomes an adult. They may use this knowledge to make judgements about the school values, which will be evident in the way teachers and assistants deal with children and encourage them to deal with each other and with other people and in the way the school tackles children's misdemeanours. Assembly is traditionally a way of reinforcing values.

In today's multicultural schools there are considerable problems about putting over values because different groups within our society have different values. However, there is a good deal in common on which early work may be based. As children grow older it may be possible and useful to discuss some of similarities and the differences.

Environmental education

One of the most important issues for children to learn about at the present time is that of the environment. They need to know what is happening to the world in terms of the greenhouse effect and the human behaviour which is creating it. They also need to be concerned about maintaining an environment in which we can live in comfort with areas for leisure and recreation as well as places for work. We need to give thought to the way we want our towns and cities to develop. Much of this work will come in geography and in science and some in technology.

In thinking about the environment it may also be sensible to think about human behaviour and ways in which we might change it. Discussion about issues such as graffiti and vandalism, football hooliganism and drugs at the primary stage might have an effect then which would be more difficult to achieve when the children are older.

Multicultural education

Schools in areas where the population is ethnically mixed have usually done a great deal to help the various groups appreciate each other. There is much work in celebrating each other's festivals, helping children to understand other points of view and encouraging them to respect and tolerate differences. This may not always be successful but there is no lack of appreciation of the need for such work to be done. There continues to be a need to combat racism in all its forms, and every school needs to consider how incidents of racism should be dealt with and how children can be helped to realise its dangers.

There is a different and more difficult task to be done in schools where there are few children from minority ethnic communities, and there is often a lack of realisation that in these circumstances there is also much to be done. The Swann Report (Department of Education and Science, 1985: 236) makes the following comment about attitudes in schools:

> A major conclusion which we feel must regrettably be drawn from the findings of this project, is in relation to the widespread existence of racism, whether unintentional and 'latent' or overt and aggressive in the schools visited ... The project revealed widespread evidence of racism in all the areas covered, ranging from unintentional racism and patronising and stereotyped ideas about ethnic minority groups combined with appalling ignorance of their cultural backgrounds and the facts of race and immigration, to the extreme of overt hatred and 'National Front' style attitudes.

Although this report was written a long time ago now, the points it makes are still relevant in schools today and we need to act on it to see that prejudice is gradually overcome and children come to appreciate each other's backgrounds. Children in 'white' areas, and their parents also, often have a very limited idea of people of other nationalities, especially those of Afro-Caribbean background, and the school has an important job to do in broadening this view. Contacts with schools where there are substantial ethnic minority populations would be valuable, but there should at least be discussion about people who are different in various ways, including stories and films about other nationalities and some work on festivals. There is also value in stressing the idea put forward in Chapter 14 of thinking about what all human beings, past and present, have in common.

Education for equal opportunities

Concern for equal opportunities for everyone whatever their race, gender, social class or background is important in all schools. Most young children come to school with fairly firm ideas about male and female roles. In most households it is still the mother who stays at home while the children are very young, although this is changing, and she is therefore the person with the time to undertake the household chores and feed the family. Small children naturally take this as the norm, as is evident from the way they play in the home corner and elsewhere.

A view of women as subservient to men is also reinforced in schools where the headteacher is male. The school has a substantial task to do in helping children to appreciate that women need not take the background role but can offer many of the contributions made by men except those which require physical strength and also many valuable and rather different contributions of their own. Boys also need to appreciate and learn that men are no less masculine if they are sensitive to others and take their share of domestic chores.

This task is made more difficult by the fact that children are themselves trying to sort out their own roles as future men and women. Boys are under pressure to seek macho behaviour and avoid anything which has overtones of the feminine. Girls experience less pressure in some senses but are growing up in a society which is still somewhat uncertain about the role of women and this can sometimes make life difficult for them.

There is also a need to consider issues of equality where children with disabilities are concerned. Are they being treated in the same way as other children as far as this is possible? Are they getting all the opportunities that other children have where and when they are able to gain from them?

A further area in which there is the need for equal opportunities is in social class. It is easy to favour middle-class children without really appreciating that you are doing so, by giving them more opportunities for taking responsibility, more praise, more opportunities in the classroom, and so on. Working-class children quickly pick this up and you need to work at raising the self-image of children from working-class families.

You need to be constantly watching the way you work with children. Are you unintentionally treating some children differently from others without realising it? Do you ask more questions of boys than girls or vice versa? Do you make more critical comments about behaviour to Afro-Caribbean children than to others? Do you tend to have higher expectations of middle-class than working-class children and is this always justified? Are responsibilities around the classroom equally distributed among girls and boys, children of different ethnicity, able-bodied and those with disabilities, middle-class and working-class children?

Preparation for adult life

It might be argued that all education is about preparing children for adult life. It might also be said that certain aspects of this preparation, such as preparation for employment, marriage or partnership and parenthood, are really the province of the secondary school as it is then that children begin to look forward to adult life and experience work related to possible careers.

Yet preparation for adult life is really a continuum which starts before school and continues into the nursery school and reception class, with children playing out the adult activities they see taking place, such as shopping, cooking, caring for the home and children, visiting the doctor or hospital and so on. Some of these activities become more directed as children grow older and they experience cookery or perhaps gardening or caring for animals and learning about how babies are born and grow as part of the curriculum. None of this is a very conscious preparation for marriage or partnership and parenthood, but it is a starting point and a valuable contribution that is likely to affect later attitudes.

Schooling at any stage may be regarded as induction into the adult world. Part of the induction process is introducing children to their cultural legacy, teaching them about their past and that of other groups, reading and telling stories, hearing about great men and women and events. This is one of the reasons why the study of history is important.

Children learn a great deal about living with and working with others at all stages in their schooling and the ability to share, to work together, to take responsibility, to lead and to follow are all useful parts of learning to be a member of a community.

A further aspect of adult life which has its roots in the primary school is the development of leisure interests, skills and hobbies. This involves opportunities for learning to enjoy music, dance, drama, art, practical opportunities for developing craft skills and playing games, the development of interests such as reading, electronics, photography, astronomy and many other likely and unlikely studies, depending on the enthusiasm and skills of teachers and anyone outside the school willing to be drawn in.

Teaching and learning are not tidy pursuits. A good deal of important learning goes on outside the curriculum and much that is important is apparently learned incidentally. No teacher can do everything and none of us can do everything at once. The value of considering a set of aims is that it gives you a frame of reference for your teaching and enables you to look at what you are doing from a wider perspective from time to time.

Review 16.2 Other aspects of personal and social learning

1　Are my children learning how to live a healthy life?

2　Are they learning something about democracy and how we are governed?

3　Do I provide any opportunities for them to experience democracy by giving them opportunities to discuss and make decisions about some aspects of the organisation of their work as a class?

4　Do we discuss issues such as climate change and global warming and think about what we can do to help this problem?

5　What sorts of attitudes are my children developing towards people of other cultures? What am I doing to influence their thinking about this?

6　What sorts of attitudes are my children developing about the roles of men and women in our society?

7　What am I doing which will prepare children for adult life?

Chapter 17

Classroom management

The range of children in a school is decided by the LEA, which determines the age groups for which a school has to cater. The way children are organised within the school is the decision of the headteacher and staff, with support from the governors. Classes and groups can be formed on the basis of age, ability or stage of development or achievement in a particular activity. Children can also be grouped randomly or by friendship and family. A school may choose to have some re-grouping or setting for the older children in some areas of curriculum. The problem about this is the fact that the least able children are made aware of the fact that they are not doing as well as some of their contemporaries.

It may be that in the future, you will more easily be able to cater for a wide range of abilities because computers are gradually making it more possible for children to do work matched to their abilities but it will probably take a lot of careful organising and we haven't yet really reached that stage. As teacher, you may work solely within one class or you may take some subjects with another group or you may sometimes work with other teachers taking joint responsibility for more than one group of children.

Working with an assistant

The advent of teaching assistants has given a new dimension to classroom organisation. There is now another adult available to work with you and to help children. You need to come to an agreement on your assistant's role, taking into account the particular skills she brings to the job and how she can best complement your own work. Her presence should make a considerable difference to your organisation.

The overall effect of the way you organise

The way you organise work within the classroom has a hidden or partly hidden agenda which should be considered from time to time so that it ceases to be hidden.

The extent to which you work with the whole class or with individuals or groups affects the kind of contact you have with each child. Your organisation also has implications for the development of study skills and independence in learning. The extent to which you encourage competition or co-operation will affect attitudes to learning and to other people. Encouraging children to work together or compete with one another will have implications for social behaviour and the extent to which children eventually come to regard others as fellow workers or rivals.

Grouping by ability

Sometimes you will group children for learning, so that each group contains a balance of able and less able children and boys and girls, with the idea that the less able will be helped by the more able and the views of both sexes will be represented. This has the advantage that the less able children may not feel labelled as being less able, as they would in setted groups. On the other hand, a grouping by ability, carefully done within a class, may provide opportunities to ensure that very able children have the chance to be stimulated by equally able peers, and less able children may benefit from having only the competition of other children with difficulties, rather than a group where others get all the answers before a less able child has had time to think. There is a place for both which could give you the advantages of both these ways of organising.

Few primary schools use setting as such, with different ability groups taught by different teachers in different places. Research on attainment in setted groups tends to be somewhat inconclusive. It would seem that setted groups benefit the able but tend to have a more negative effect on the less able. The able are challenged by being with others of similar ability, while the less able not only are made to recognise their lower ability but also lack the stimulus offered by being with more able children in a group.

It is nevertheless important to be aware if you have in your class children at the extremes of the ability range. It is very important that both of these groups and individuals have the opportunity to fulfil their potential and you need to be continually watchful to see that this happens.

We saw in earlier chapters that the way a teacher organises work is a very personal matter and that here are many good ways of working, each with its own collection of strengths and disadvantages or pitfalls. No one way of working suits everyone. At the same time there is a certain amount of research evidence which suggests that some ways of working yield better results than others, and Chapter 7 listed some of the findings of research about effective teaching.

Keeping a balance in teaching approaches

HMI (1997), studying the teaching of number, found that the more effective teachers had a good balance of teaching the whole class, work in groups and individual work. Less effective teachers tended to have too much emphasis on individual and group work. They also found that effective teachers ended the lesson with a plenary session summing up what had been learned and checking how much the children had understood. These approaches have also been incorporated into the literacy and numeracy strategies.

Developing independence in children

It is important to find ways of enabling children to be as independent as their stage of development allows. The more that children can be independent in different aspects of their work, the more you will be able to use your own time effectively and to help individual children – both the less able who may need individual help and also the more able whom you can encourage to explore new areas of learning and develop particular interests. The way you organise the classroom can help the development of independence. Are children able to go and find what they need for particular work when they need it or do they need your permission first? The routines you establish can help independence or make children more dependent. Children's ability to work independently takes a long time to develop, but it is a goal to keep in mind.

Learning how to learn

An important part of becoming an independent learner is learning is how to learn. This is a basic skill which children will need throughout their education and probably throughout their lives. It is also one which can make a difference to a child's overall progress. Children can sometimes be helped by being encouraged to classify what they are learning into different categories. In learning spellings, for example, children often feel that they should learn by simply repeating the letters of the words. It is better if they are encouraged to look for patterns in spelling. Which words are like other words? Can words which are alike be grouped?

Are there any rules which can be learned? For example, do they know that words ending with 'y' change the 'y' into 'ies' when the word becomes plural? Can you put them in a position to work this out for themselves? What about words ending in 'ey' such as donkey or monkey?

They need gradually to learn how to classify and group ideas, to generalise from one idea to another. Some of these abilities were discussed in more detail in Chapter 6. Different children may learn in different ways and you need to discuss with them how they learn and to sometimes give them the opportunity to discuss this in groups and report to the class on their conclusions.

Learning how to plan work

As they grow older children can also be encouraged to think about how they plan their work. This too is something which it is useful for them to discuss in pairs or groups and then report on their conclusions. For example, you might discuss with them how to set out the outline for a story and then get them to do something similar in preparation for writing a story. Groups and pairs can be encouraged to work together to plan work on a topic. You might introduce a topic which you want them to be involved in, giving them a rough idea of what will be involved and then asking them, again in pairs or small groups, to make a plan for the work.

Making good use of resources

Part of independent learning involves being able to make good use of books and the internet. Children need to be taught how to use catalogues and indexes and content lists, and how to scan a page searching for the information they need. They also need to learn how to use the internet and email. The more you can help children to become independent learners, the more you will be able to direct your time where it is most needed.

Children also should be involved in helping to manage the classroom, perhaps looking after different resources, caring for classroom pets, seeing that materials are properly tidied away after use, and so on.

Review 17.1 Learning how to become an independent learner

1   How can I help my children become more independent as learners?
2   Does my classroom organisation contribute to this goal?
3   In what areas do I want the children to become more independent?
4   What can I do to achieve this?
5   Have we talked about how we learn as a class or in groups?
6   What evidence do I need to know whether this work is succeeding?

Monitoring what is happening

Another important point is that of monitoring. You need to be aware of what is happening in the classroom at all times. Children should be able to read your body language and be aware by your actual behaviour that you know what they are doing. Effective teachers are able to deal with more than one thing at once and move smoothly from one activity to another. You need to cultivate the habit of scanning the room and catching the eye of children who are not on-task or who need help. Monitoring also involves being aware of the work that children are doing and how it is going.

Classroom routines

If effective teaching and learning is to take place, it is essential that the classroom is well organised. Bennett and Kell (1989) described poor classroom organisation which showed itself in a lack of pupil involvement, children wandering about, lack of interest or motivation and poor use of resources. Children played about without the teacher apparently being aware of it. The same study was critical of some of the use of play activities in the youngest classes where children were fighting, throwing things about and generally working with a lack of purpose.

Many writers in the past have commented on the problems of the primary school teacher in dealing with individual children. They report long queues to see the teacher in some classrooms, particularly where the teacher liked to mark work with the child present. This problem, while it still exists to some extent, should be helped considerably by the presence of a teaching assistant, who can deal with many of the minor queries which children raise and undertake many of the tasks which took up teachers' time in the past. However, it is still important for the teacher to develop a structure in which children know what to do when they have finished a piece of work.

Children should also be encouraged to look at information around the classroom and perhaps ask advice from other children before going to the teacher or assistant for spellings or similar information.

A well-organised classroom has routines, so that children feel secure in knowing what to do. You need to have rules about all of the following issues.

Movement about the room

Children should know when they are allowed to move freely about the room and when you expect them to sit at their tables. They also need to know how many people are allowed to undertake any one activity at the same time.

The things for which they need your permission

This needs to be made very clear to children from the beginning. Most teachers would expect to have to give permission for children to leave the classroom, although where there is working space outside further definition may be needed.

What to do when they come into the classroom

First thing in the morning and after breaks in the day, you may want them to continue with the work in hand or have some other task for them to do. Whatever your routine is, they need to be clear about what is required.

When they are expected to be quiet

There will be times in the day when you want quiet. There will also be situations when you want attention from everyone. You need to have an understood signal for quiet, such as clapping your hands or raising one hand, and you should insist that everyone stops and listens when you give this signal.

What to do when they have finished their work

Try to avoid the situation where children come to you every time they finish a piece of work. If you give them more than one piece of work at once, the occasions when they need to come back to you will be fewer. You may also be able to provide some materials that have a structure which makes it clear what comes next, and there may be materials about the classroom from which children may choose when they have finished other work. At the same time you need to keep track of some individuals who may avoid coming to you at all. If everyone is kept busy it becomes possible to call on those you want to see. Again, your assistant will be able to help in these situations.

Forms of organisation

There are a number of different ways in which a class can be organised for learning and you need to select your approaches to suit the material to be learned and the mood of the class.

Whole-class teaching

The literacy and numeracy strategies have made the case for an important place for whole-class teaching which is interactive and involves individual children while maintaining the attention of the whole class. It is useful in number work to involve individuals in answering different parts of the problems the class is discussing. This is all made so much easier by the interactive whiteboard where the children can be involved in adding things to it as you go along. The introduction of 'big books' has made whole-class teaching of reading more of a possibility. A good teacher can also do much to stimulate and inspire children in a class group. It is particularly useful for starting a new topic and for drawing together the work as a topic nears completion.

Children work at the same subject at different levels

The numeracy and literacy hours and some other studies are likely to involve work in groups after the initial introduction, sometimes with different work set for each group and the teacher working with the groups in turn, and sometimes with everyone doing the same work but at a level determined by his or her ability. This requires good organisation to keep everyone going so that you are free to work with a group at a time. It can work best if your materials are set out in an order which children recognise. Children need to know what to do if they need your help but you are teaching a group. There should be alternative work for them to do so that they can get on with something useful until you are free to help them, or they can call on your assistant.

Children work on individual programmes

There is a place for this, particularly in topic work where children may have a choice of activity, but evidence suggests that children make less progress in this form of organisation if it is too widely used.

There is, nevertheless, an important place for individual work which may involve any of the following situations.

- Children work at individual tasks which may be chosen by the child or given by the teacher. These tasks could arise from topic work or a class activity or be a development of the child's own ideas. Individual work is part of the literacy and numeracy strategies.
- Children work at their own pace through a structured scheme of work. This may mean that everyone is doing English or mathematics but the actual work each child is doing may be different. This should not replace direct teaching as a class or in a group.
- Children work at individual tasks which are part of a group activity. Each child's work contributes to the group's findings or presentation.

Individual work in one or other of these categories would seem to be most appropriate in the following cases.

- A situation in which there is a wide range of ability within the class, but a common theme. For example, an environmental study might involve a variety of different questions and working plans so that the work could be matched to the ability of the children.
- Learning which needs to be step by step, such as those aspects of mathematics which are concerned with individual understanding and practice.
- Learning which is matched to individual need and differentiates children according to their ability, stage of development and the stage they have reached in the work in hand and in the National Curriculum.
- Providing individual opportunities for creative and practical work, although this may also contribute to a common goal.

Children work together in pairs or groups

The smallest group is a pair and this is usually very easy to arrange without rearranging seating. Children can be encouraged to help each other, check each other's work, discuss how to tackle a problem, plan together for written work, teach each other and so on. You need to be alert to possible time-wasting but much valuable work can be done in this way.

Group work might be divided into two broad categories. The first is grouping by ability, in which the teacher may work with a group at a time giving them work matched to the ability and stage of development of the children within the group. Both the literacy and numeracy strategies involve this kind of grouping and the number of such groups should be kept comparatively small, probably no more than three or four groups in the class. If there are too many groups you will not be able to deal with them adequately.

The second kind of grouping is grouping for co-operative work. Here the groups should be small: three or four children in a group would be a good size.

Collaborative group work has much to offer as a way of learning. Children working together in a group can generate more ideas than individuals working alone. There is some evidence that self-confidence and self-esteem are improved. Working together can be enjoyable and children can sometimes help each other very effectively. Group work can also free the teacher from some demands because children can use the members of their group as a point of reference rather than always turning to the teacher for information. The ability to work in groups is also an important skill for adult life where much work involves working with others. School should train children to do this as part of preparation for adult life.

Review 17.2 Organising for learning

1   What different forms of organisation do I like to use in my classroom?
2   For which aspects of work do I like to use class teaching and discussion?
3   For which work do I find grouping necessary or preferable?
4   On what basis do I form groups for learning? Is there some work for which I find ability grouping the best arrangement? Are there any snags about this?
5   Do I sometimes use friendship grouping? For what do I use it and has it any disadvantages?
6   Do I discuss with the children the skills involved in working together?
7   Do I sometimes provide children with work on an individual basis? What are the advantages and disadvantages of this?
8   When children work in groups, how do I see my role and that of my assistant?

Aspects of group work

Group work can vary in the degree of collaboration involved. In some classes children are seated in groups but work individually. Children can also work individually on elements of a task for a joint outcome such as the production of a group story or newspaper or the forming of a set of objects as in a mathematical activity on sets. This requires a certain amount of co-operation. In a fully co-operative situation children work jointly on a task for a joint outcome or discuss a topic together.

The role of the teacher and the assistant during co-operative group work is to monitor unobtrusively and encourage children to put forward their ideas. It is important not to join in in ways that discourage children. Delamont (1987: 40) found that children resented any takeover. She quotes a child who comments 'You have put all that work into it and then the teacher suddenly changes it'. It is not an easy role for you and for your assistant and requires great sensitivity on the part of you both.

Group discussion

Bennett and Dunne (1994) analysed the conversation which took place in groups studying different aspects of the curriculum. They found that when children were genuinely working together, task-related talk was very high, averaging 88 per cent of the time, being highest in technology and computer tasks and lowest in language work. Children working in groups where they were expected to achieve the task demonstrated much greater involvement in their work, and the amount of task-related talk was 22 per cent higher than in groups where children were working individually. Language tasks, in particular, appeared to generate a good deal of abstract talk, although this might be the effect of the nature of the tasks set. Talk about action predominated in all the groups. The majority of teachers in Bennett and Dunne's study were delighted with the perseverance of even the youngest children and of children with the lowest ability. They felt that the children produced better results than usual in the action tasks. In addition, more able children tended to take on the role of the teacher, leaving the teacher free to stimulate by asking questions and encouraging higher order thinking.

Group formation

Children can be organised for learning in groups of many kinds, varying in size, composition and permanency. Each type of grouping has its advantages and disadvantages for particular activities and particular children and there is a place for work on an individual basis, for work in a variety of different groups and for work as a whole class.

Most classes now have help from teaching assistants and/or volunteer parents and this may have a bearing on the way that children are grouped. Teachers need to ask whether a particular size of group and composition is the most efficient and effective way of teaching a particular thing or of providing opportunities for practice and discussion of a particular topic or achievement of a particular task. Groups can be formed in different ways.

Pairs and trios

This form of grouping is easy to organise, has a good deal to offer and is probably insufficiently used. A pair of children tackling a mathematical or scientific problem may benefit considerably from talking it through. This not only helps the mathematical or scientific learning but it also makes demands on the child's spoken language ability. This also applies to the situation where one child teaches another.

Small groups (five or fewer)

Groups of this size are valuable for a variety of activities. It is a good size of group for the kind of collaborative work which might be the outcome of a topic or environmental study. Groups of four may be a good size for reading, with each group reading from a book chosen to match the group's ability.

Large groups

A large group can be anything from a class group to the whole school. A large group does not lend itself to discussion as well as a smaller group and it is much easier for a child to opt out in a large group. On the other hand, there are activities such as aspects of music and dance where the large group provides an experience of involvement and participation which is very valuable. Large groups require much more detailed preparation than small groups.

Grouping for different activities

In considering what may be appropriate grouping for different activities it is useful to consider grouping from the child's point of view. We actually know very little about how children view the groups they are in. Does a five-year-old, for example, know all the children in the class? At what stage does an assembly of the whole school have meaning for a child and to what extent are some children frightened by being part of such a large group?

In a small group it is difficult for an individual to opt out or day-dream. While day-dreaming too much or at the wrong time may be a nuisance or worrying, there may be a case for providing some opportunities for children to be inactive and to think. This is probably more difficult in today's active classrooms than it was in traditional settings, where class teaching sometimes became a background for a child's own thoughts. Times are needed when everyone is quiet not only for the teacher's peace of mind but also in order to allow the children to reflect.

The formation of groups

Another important question about grouping for teaching concerns the criteria by which the groups are formed.

Different kinds of groups are needed for different purposes and different activities, and it is better not to have groups which are too fixed. Ability groups for working with the teacher may be fairly stable over a period but even these should be reviewed fairly frequently so that children can be moved to a higher or lower group if their progress warrants it. However, it will be important not to make too much of the idea of higher and lower groups because the sense of being in a lower group can be discouraging for children. For other purposes groups should be variable so that children have experience of working with a range of different people.

There is much to be said for structuring the groups for collaborative work so that there is a good mix of abilities and there is some evidence that mixed-sex groups do better than single-sex groups, although as the children grow older they tend to be negative about this. Dunne and Bennett (1990) found that both high and low attainers worked well in mixed-ability groups. Groups of high attainers worked well but groups of low attainers did not. This seemed to be because of a lack of understanding of the task: low-attaining pupils in low-attaining groups were not drawn into the task as they were when they worked in mixed-ability groups.

Grouping for class management

There are many situations where the teacher needs to divide the class in order to undertake particular activities. This kind of grouping is very common in physical education and in art and craft and technology activities because there may be a limited amount of space, or equipment which has to be shared. It is also necessary to group children from time to time in order to make the teacher's work easier. For example, you may wish to demonstrate or show something which cannot be seen properly if the group is too large.

Grouping by age

Primary schools tend to group children in classes by age when the school is large enough to do this, but there are many schools in which children are in mixed-age classes, sometimes by choice and sometimes because the school is very small. Teachers need to be aware of age differences whether the class is of a single age group or a mixed-age group.

A child's date of birth may have all sorts of consequences for his or her education. A child who is among the oldest in the class may appear to do well and this can be motivating. A child who looks mature may be treated as older and is thus encouraged to behave in more mature ways. A child who is one of the youngest may be stimulated to emulate the older children and thus make good progress. On the other hand, such a child may become depressed about doing less well and develop a self-image which suggests that s/he is a person who is not very competent and consequently may cease to try very hard.

Mortimore *et al.* (1988: 163) found that teachers 'were found consistently to have judged pupils born in the summer months as being of lower ability and having more behaviour difficulties'. Younger pupils themselves were found to have a less positive view of school than their older peers'. When a child is small and immature as well as being young, teachers and others will speak to him or her as to a younger child and their expectations may be lower than the child's ability justifies. There may therefore be a case for grouping by age in classes containing only one age group.

Grouping by ability

Studies of ability grouping suggest that teachers need to be aware of under-estimating the less able, who tend to do better in mixed-ability classes. Teachers have also been shown to believe that they review ability groups and move children from group to group more often than they actually do.

The attitudes and expectations of the teacher and the school make all the difference to the way children view ability grouping, whether this is by sets across a year group or within the class. A good teacher can make each group feel that they are special and deserving of the best attention. It is also important that the school encourages more able children to be sympathetic to less able peers.

Ability grouping may be the most efficient and effective way of teaching some things, offering the right level of group stimulus to the children and using your time most effectively. For example, some aspects of work in mathematics may best be carried out in ability groups, although there is also mathematical work which can be carried out effectively in a mixed group. There is a particular case for sometimes working with the most able and the least able in separate groups.

Other work may gain from a mixed-ability group. This is particularly true of the creative types of work such as art and drama and the content, although not necessarily the presentation, of personal writing.

Friendship groups

Most of us like to work with our friends and there will be occasions when friendship groups work well. There are some caveats, however. At the junior stage friendship groups will nearly always be single-sex and there may be occasions when a mixed-sex group would be preferable. Research suggests that mixed groups tend to work better than single-sex groups. There is also the problem of the child whom no one wants and the group where one dominant child does all the work. You may need to do some engineering in these cases.

A teacher needs to use a mixture of groupings, sometimes forming ability groups or groups at the same stage of learning, sometimes deliberately structuring groups – so that children learn from one another – and sometimes using friendship groups. This enables children to gain from the differing contributions of other children.

Questions to ask about grouping

The questions you need to ask in planning grouping might be as follows.

Which activities need homogeneous groups?

Mathematics is one area which is commonly expected to need homogeneous groups. Some activities can be undertaken with the whole class and children can follow them up according to their ability, perhaps with differentiation into groups with different tasks. Nearly all work benefits from discussion and you need to consider what can be discussed as a class and in groups.

Reading is another area where you will need ability groups, with each group reading a particular shared text matched to their ability.

It could be argued that physical education and music are subjects where work might be more effective if children worked in groups of similar ability, but it is unusual to find this.

Which areas of curriculum gain from being undertaken in a mixed-ability group?

Most creative work provides a situation in which a mixture of abilities is possible and often useful. Inventiveness and creativity are not solely the province of the more able and this is likely to become particularly evident as the technology curriculum develops.

Any area of curriculum where pupils are asked to work collaboratively can be undertaken effectively in a mixed-ability group. Topic work and work in history and geography, environmental studies and science all lend themselves to mixed groups.

Does the organisation I provide offer children a chance to work in different kinds of group in the course of time?

If different types of group offer different learning opportunities, this suggests that it would be beneficial for children to have experience of different types of groups over a period. There should also be an opportunity for every child to work with different children over a period.

Am I training children to work together rather than alongside each other?

Children will work together without a great deal of encouragement as they grow older, but their ability to do this is likely to develop more quickly if they are given encouragement and training in the skills of corporate working.

Training children to work in groups

Working with a group towards a common end involves a different set of activities from working alongside others with similar tasks. It requires certain skills and is important for adulthood.

Children need training in working together if the intention is to do co-operative group work. Teachers of infant classes are usually concerned about the way children are reacting to each other and training in group work skills starts here with such elementary tasks as learning to share, to take turns and to listen to other people and try to see their point of view. Children advance from this stage to develop readiness to contribute to common goals and to sink personal differences in order to achieve something. These continue to be necessary skills as children grow older.

Training may involve discussing with the class how to listen to each other in a group and how to encourage each other to contribute. After a session of group work, groups can be asked to consider how well the group did these things. Was there anyone who did not contribute anything? Why was this? Were everyone's ideas considered? How did the group come to conclusions?

The role of the group leader

Some thought needs to be given to the skills of leading a group, especially with older children who can take turns to be leader. Good group leaders make sure that everyone has a chance to contribute and is listened to. They sum up what has been said from time to time and move the group on when people seem to be getting nowhere. They are sensitive to people wanting to say something and encourage everyone to contribute. Groups might consider at the end of a session how successful their leader has been. The following are useful tasks for group leaders to practise in the context of a piece of group work.

Getting ideas from the group

A group leader gives shape and direction to discussion about a task and the action required; for example, a group leader asked to prepare the group for a visit to a local farm might start by getting the group to list what might be available for study at the farm.

Sharing out the tasks

When the lists of possibilities have been made, the leader has to see that the tasks are reasonably distributed. This is more a matter of saying 'Who would like to do this?' than of telling others what to do. It will include seeing that all the tasks are covered and that they are fairly distributed, taking into account the particular people in the group.

Pacing the work

The group leader needs to keep track of what is happening and to see that anyone left behind is helped to catch up. He or she may also need to discover whether anyone finishing early has a further contribution to make.

Encouraging and supporting

Encouraging others is an essential part of leading a group and often makes all the difference between a person who leads well and is accepted as a leader and a person who cannot get others to follow him or her. Very few people do this without being made aware of its importance and you need to encourage children who are leading groups to tell others that they are doing well or to thank them for contributions. The teacher's example will be important here.

Considering the way the pieces fit together

If the group is to present its findings to others, the form of the presentation has to be agreed and the leader will need to keep a running check on how the various contributions fit together and how each contributes to the whole, bringing the group together to discuss this.

The existence of a leader in a group implies the existence of followers. If a group is to work well with a leader, its members must accept the leader's role and work with him or her. This can be difficult for children who are natural leaders if they are not chosen to be the leader, but it is an important piece of learning for them. As many children as possible should have experience of leading a group so that they can learn the skills involved. You need to make a point of praising children for being good group members.

It is also worth considering the various other tasks which children may undertake within a group and discussing how best to fulfil them. This will vary according to the age of the children but roles considered at an appropriate point in time might include chairing a group, summing up the discussion, questioning individual group members, teaching other group members, recording important points in the discussion and making some decisions about the next steps to be taken.

The contribution of classroom support

Most teachers now have a certain amount of support in the classroom, sometimes from paid classroom assistants and sometimes from volunteer parents. There may also be learning support assistants working with the SENCO and employed to help particular children with special educational needs. It is very important that these valuable resources are fully used. Suggestions for the role of teaching assistants were given in Chapter 4.

All assistants, whether employed or volunteers, need to be briefed fully on the tasks they undertake. Ideally they should be trained in tasks such as hearing reading, overseeing children involved in practical activities, extending the learning involved in play activities with very young children and so on. There is an increasing amount of training now offered for assistants, sometimes within the school and sometimes by the LEA, and you should certainly encourage your assistant to take advantage of this. With a newly appointed assistant you will need to do some training yourself from day to day, explaining how you like to work and how you would like to involve her in the tasks that you will be delegating.

Each day you need to plan exactly how you are going to use the services of your assistant at each stage of the work. You also need to brief her for supporting your work as teacher explaining what you are aiming to do, how you are going to set about it and what her role will be. It is also a good idea to try to find some time at the end of a session to talk over how things went, using this as an opportunity to get some feedback from someone who has been observing and also to discuss any difficulties the assistant has encountered. During the lessons you need to be alert to such difficulties and ready to intervene or offer advice later.

Review 17.3 Further consideration of classroom organisation

1   Do I have effective and established classroom routines which children follow?
2   Is the balance I have of class teaching, group and individual work effective for children's learning?
3   Are my children really learning to work in groups? Should I provide more training for this organisation?
4   Is the grouping that I am using satisfactory for its purposes?
5   Do the children have the chance to work in a variety of groups?
6   How well am I able to match work to individual children?
7   What opportunities do I offer children to contribute to the planning of their work? How effectively are they able to do this?
8   Are they becoming independent learners?
9   Have I the right balance between teacher-directed work and choice by children?
10 Am I providing enough opportunities for discussion in pairs, small groups and as a class? How effective are the discussion opportunities I have provided?
11 Am I making the best use of any support I have from assistants or volunteer parents?

Chapter 18

The use of time and space

Organising work in the classroom involves not only managing the children and planning the curriculum but also managing time, space and resources. The time and space you have are relatively fixed and cannot be expanded. You can only plan to make better use of them. Resources can be increased if there is the money for them and if you are prepared to make some of them.

The use of time

Government demands and continual new developments have created a pressure on time for teachers. There is now a great deal to do in the time available, and since a primary school teacher usually has considerable freedom to plan the programme of work in a way that seems best for the children within the constraints which have been created, the use of time requires a good deal of planning. There may be some fixed points because of shared use of some facilities or because the school does some specialist teaching and teachers now have to incorporate so much into the day. There will also be some fixed breaks in the day but generally speaking you should still have a good deal of time to use for your planned programme as seems best for you and your children.

Since time is limited, you need to be very conscious of how you and the children are using it. While it is almost certainly impossible to organise so that you and your children are always using time to the best advantage, this is, nevertheless, the goal you should be trying to achieve.

The problem about organising time in the classroom is that the time individuals need for learning and the practice they need are so varied. The mixture of class, group and individual work that you plan needs to allow for this. Your aim should be for every child to be working profitably with no one simply occupied because you haven't time to deal with him or her. This means that for much work you will need to provide for a variety of levels or provide work which can be carried out at different levels according to ability.

Studies of the use of time

Research suggests that particularly where the younger children are concerned a great deal of time is needed for routine activities such as registration, toilet visits, lining up, tidying, meals and playtimes: and this means less time for work activity. If you also take into account the fact that some children will only be working for part of that time and perhaps spending the rest day-dreaming or thinking about something else, this suggests that actual learning time is quite limited.

Hargreaves (1990: 78) found that on-task behaviour was better in small primary schools. In his study, he found that:

> The striking feature of both the infant and junior levels is the high level of task work. Seventy-one per cent of observations were task-focused, and this increased to 80 per cent if routine task-supporting jobs, such as sharpening pencils or ruling lines, were included. Only 13 per cent of the observations were counted as off-task or distracted behaviour such as chatting or day-dreaming.

Alexander (1992: 69), in the course of evaluating a project in Leeds that set out to improve performance in primary schools, found that on average children in the classrooms in his study spent:

- 59 per cent of their time working;
- 11 per cent on associated routine activities (getting out and putting away books and apparatus, sharpening pencils and so on);
- 8 per cent waiting for the teacher or other adult;
- 21 per cent distracted from the work that had been set;
- 1 per cent 'other' (unspecified).

Mortimore *et al.* (1988) found that there was a significant positive relationship between the time spent with the teacher interacting with the class and progress in a wide range of areas.

Overall the studies of the use of time appear to suggest that the amount of time spent on-task is more limited than most teachers would like. There would seem to be scope for improving the use of time by both teachers and children.

The teacher's use of time

As a teacher, you are responsible for the way you use your time and the children's time. It is not easy to fit in all the aspects of the National Curriculum and it is therefore important to consider the areas in which one subject overlaps with another. For example, the National Curriculum in English can be met through work in geography and history and other subjects as well as in English lessons. Mathematics is often needed in work in science and technology and so on. It is also important to consider how the time available in the week and the term can best be broken down to ensure that every subject is getting a fair share of attention.

How you use your time depends also on your teaching style, but it is very easy under the pressures of day-to-day classroom life to believe that you should be using time in a particular way and end up using it completely differently, sometimes without realising it. Having a teaching assistant working with you would seem to help in that you can delegate some things to her, but in practice this may make you even more aware of how much there is to do.

A good starting point, therefore, may be to work out how you think you ought to be using your time, your assistant's and your children's time, and then to check how you are actually using it. Your assistant could help with this. She could note your use of time against a check-list which you had prepared for her. You could use Review 18.1 for this purpose. Most studies show some differences between what teachers think they are doing and what they actually do, so don't be surprised if this is true for you.

Another possible starting point is to have a recorder running for a time, recording what is going on. You can then listen to it and decide on the categories of activity which could be checked with a list as you work. If you record day by day for a short period you can see whether you have a different pattern of using time on different days. You may also like to note the time spent on routine activities which do not contribute to the children's learning.

Review 18.1 Teacher's time log

Please tick each activity listed as you undertake it and if possible write the approximate time it took.

1   Talking to the class as a whole
2   Questioning with the whole class
3   Using the whiteboard and involving children
4   Working with a particular group or a number of different groups of children
5   Working with children individually
6   Organising activity or practical work
7   Hearing reading, checking work
8   Watching television or video

Children's use of time

Studying your own use of time will inevitably involve studying aspects of the way the children are using time. How you set about studying this must depend partly on the age group you teach and whether the children are able to make some observations of their use of time for themselves, perhaps as part of mathematical work on time.

Alternatively, perhaps with a younger class, your assistant could make detailed observations of what a sample group of children are doing at agreed intervals. The involvement of older children in studying their own use of time might become part of graphical representation. Doing this kind of study may help children to be more aware of how they are using their time and help them to concentrate more. The log sheet for children, which follows as Review 18.2, can be adapted for your particular class.

Give every child a copy of the log sheet and discuss what each item means. Bring in a pinger egg timer and set it to ping at regular intervals: every ten minutes might be a good starting point. Give a child the task of resetting it each time it pings. When the pinger goes everyone puts a tick beside the item on the list which shows what he or she is doing.

Although this may seem to be a bit disrupting, what you may find is that the number of children doing what they should be doing when the pinger goes actually increases because they want to be able to write down that they

Review 18.2 Children's use of time

When the pinger goes put a tick beside what you are doing then. Please be honest about this. You won't be asked to put your name on your paper. Please write in the actual time which the teacher will tell you, and put B or G at the top of your paper to say whether you are a boy or a girl.

- Listening to the teacher
- Answering questions/class discussion
- Working with a partner or in a group
- Writing
- Reading
- Number work
- Practical work
- Using a computer
- Talking about work
- Talking about other things
- Getting ready to work
- Getting help from the teacher
- Doing nothing in particular

are doing the right thing. Ideally you want to do this on several occasions over a number of weeks, so that you get a fairly typical pattern.

When you have put together the overall findings they can be discussed with the children, who can then consider how they can increase the amount of time they are on-task. It may be an opportunity to discuss with older children different possible ways of studying and to then provide an opportunity for each child to choose the order in which s/he does some of the work and discover his or her best way of working. We all have our own best ways of using time and we need to know whether we work best in short or long spells. Children may like to set personal goals to improve their patterns of working, and it may help them to identify and state something they plan to improve and to keep a log of whether they are achieving this. It is all part of the process of becoming an independent learner.

Further investigations and action

These exercises will almost certainly throw up things you will want to do something about. Your areas of concern will be to some extent personal to you, but the following suggestions for considering your findings may be useful. If you made a statement earlier about the way you thought you should be using time, this will give you a useful yardstick against which you can assess how well you and the children are doing.

Consider the balance of class, group and individual work

A recent study of children in Year 7 asked children in a questionnaire which teaching approaches they felt did most to enable them to learn. The results showed a strong preference for class discussion, work in pairs or small groups and practical activities. Individual work scored lowest, and exposition and explanation by the teacher came midway. Although this was a secondary school study its findings would seem applicable at least to the older children in a primary school.

The grouping of children for learning was discussed in a previous chapter. Here we are looking at whether the balance of class work and grouping you are using is the best for your class in terms of the time spent in each kind of organisation. This means studying the differences in children. These include not only differences in ability, skill and knowledge, but also differences in learning style. There are normally considerable differences in the way boys and girls respond.

The following may help you to take your analysis a step further. Select a time when you are working with the whole class using exposition and questioning and discussion. As soon as possible afterwards go through the class list classifying children as follows:

- those for whom what you did was probably exactly right;
- those who had either learned what you were doing already or could have learned it much more quickly;
- those who needed more work and explanation before they grasped what you were talking about.

Most of your children should come into the first category and you will probably have made use of those who knew it all to stimulate the others and make them think, perhaps also asking some open-ended questions which challenged the thinking of the most able and took their thinking further. Those in the third category will have made a start which you will be planning to follow up.

If you can honestly say that this is what happened in your class then you have probably spent time profitably. But if you find that you have quite a number of children in the second and third categories, then you should consider whether you might have done better to teach them group by group.

You might also look out for differences in reaction from boys and girls when you are teaching the class. Do you get equal contributions from both? What seems to stimulate each group? What particular interests do they each demonstrate?

You also need to consider whether the time spent in group and individual work is being well used. There are a number of ways you could look at this.

- Take a point in the day when everyone should be working individually and look around the class noting how many children are really engaged and involved in what they are doing, as far as you can tell. Then look for those who seem to be dreaming or looking round to see what everybody else is doing or otherwise not working. Do this several times over a period. Note the children whose names occur most frequently among those not involved and consider whether a different form of organisation might do more to engage them.
- Note over a period of time which children respond best to teacher-stimulated and teacher-directed activities and which do better given more freedom to work on their own.
- Listen to what happens when you ask a group of children to work together at something, thinking about the skills involved in group work and considering whether you need to do more to foster them.
- Set up an experiment by selecting two very similar topics and then deal with one as a piece of class teaching and the other on an individual or group work basis. Check at each stage how many children are fully involved in learning in each case.
- Ask each child to do a week's work in one notebook, differentiating in your own mind which pieces of work arose from class work and which from individual or group work. While written work is by no means the

only way or even the best way of assessing what children are learning, this will nevertheless give you valuable information. It will show how much each child actually does in a week and the notebooks can be kept and used in this way perhaps once a month or once a term. This provides a very useful long-term record.

The outcomes of these investigations into the use of time may not change your practice all that much and, of course, you can never cater equally well for all the children. Nevertheless, they should provide some food for thought and perhaps a greater awareness of the children who would benefit most from different approaches. This may give you some criteria for deciding how to set about a piece of work.

Study the occasions when you are speaking or reading to the whole class

The value of these activities lies mainly in the extent to which you can stimulate interest and thought. The review suggested above, when you check through the register thinking about what children have gained, is probably among your best checks on the value of whole-class activity, although you need to remember that some of your inputs may not have immediate outcomes but yet have important long-term benefits. Much reading and storytelling might come into this category.

If you are near the beginning of your career, you may have doubts about your ability to stimulate children in a large group. The skills involved come with practice. It is easiest to stimulate others if you are enthusiastic yourself.

Examine your work in questioning and leading discussion

This is a most valuable way of supporting children's learning. You need to consider whether you do enough of this kind of activity or too much and whether you are happy with the quality of what you do. Stimulating questioning at the right moment which demands thought and goes beyond questions which are a matter of recall may do a great deal to help children assimilate their learning and explore ideas. The ability to draw thinking together through discussion is also valuable.

It would be valuable to record some question and answer sessions to get a clearer idea of what actually happens.

Further investigation here must be concerned with quality as well as quantity and you may find it helpful to record two or three sessions for analysis. You may like to turn back to Chapter 7, where there is an analysis of the different kinds of questions which you can use to help you analyse the questions you actually asked. You can also speculate about what was achieved perhaps by working through the following questions.

- Which questions got the most response and which the least? Why do you think this was? If you changed some questions a little would you get a better response?
- How many children actually gave or wanted to give answers? It may be useful to make a seating plan and you or your assistant can tick each child who answers a question. This will give you several pieces of information. It will tell you which children actually answered questions and which children were silent or not called upon. You will also be able to check whether there was any pattern about who answered and speculate about whether this was the result of your selection of children or lack of contributions from some children. Do the children who contributed most, for example, come from any particular part of the classroom? Are you unwittingly missing some children because of where they are sitting? Are girls answering fewer questions than boys or the reverse and is this because of your selection of children to answer or the natural behaviour of the two sexes?
- What was the quality of the answers given by different children? What does this tell you about them?
- How did you respond to children's answers? Were there any children who might hesitate to respond again because you were not encouraging enough? How did you deal with incorrect answers or answers which did not contribute to the work in hand?
- If you go through the register, for which children can you say that this session was a valuable use of time? For whom was it of some value and for whom was it of very little value? How many would have learned more from personal reading? How many didn't need the session anyway? Could you, by better planning, better questioning and better follow-up, have increased the number for whom the session was valuable?

Study the time you spend on organising children, space and materials

Many of the studies of the use of time in school show that teachers spend quite a lot of time on this kind of activity. One researcher found that on average the teachers in an Inner London junior school project spent about a tenth of their time on classroom management. We saw earlier that Tizard *et al.* (1988) found that in top infant classes much time was spent on routine activities. This is time which it is in everyone's interest to reduce to the minimum.

It isn't easy to check the detail of this type of use of time, but you can note how long clearing up takes and consider whether there is any way in which you could do it more quickly and efficiently. You can also study the extent to which your organisation is making you use time inefficiently. If you keep a copy of the list in Review 18.1 beside you during a morning or afternoon and tick it when you deal with any of the matters listed, you will begin to see where some of your time goes and you can then consider whether you can reduce the time you are using for these kinds of activities.

Using Review 18.1 should help you to see which activities are using too much time. Each of the activities can be considered in turn.

Tell children what to do

The following points might be considered.

- Could you more often give children their work in writing, particularly where you are providing different work for different groups? Even with quite young children you can build a vocabulary which allows this to some extent and the instructions can give reading practice. With older children more can be done, and this too will provide practice in reading comprehension.
- Could you organise materials so that their sequence is more evident to children? In a number of areas of work there is a sequence and if children know, for example, that the blue mathematics group is working through the next four cards or exercises in the book they can get on without coming back to you at frequent intervals to check on what they should do next. This gives you time to intervene and direct your attention where you think it necessary rather than using your time at the children's behest.
- Children who have genuinely developed skill in working in groups will often turn to each other to ask questions which in other circumstances they would ask the teacher. This is to be encouraged.

Explain work to an individual who hasn't understood

The best way to cut this down is to look at the kind of questions that children are asking you and then to use the information about problems that this gives you to modify the way you give out work. It may be, for example, that the language you are using is too difficult, perhaps not so much in vocabulary but in language structure. You may also be unwittingly referring to things outside the children's experience. You may be giving too much information at once and it will help to have some of it in writing on the whiteboard, so that a child can check it over when you have finished speaking. Preparing work on the whiteboard and leaving it up for reference after you have talked about it may be helpful.

Another approach is to get a child who has understood to explain it to one who hasn't but in such a way that it is clearly seen as the responsibility of the explainer to see that the child to whom he or she is explaining really has understood.

Answer a child asking what to do next

This links with your arrangements for giving work to children. However, there will be children who are working individually, who may need your guidance. There will also be the attention seekers, who ask questions in order to make contact with you. However, if you start getting a lot of questions on a particular aspect of the work then you should take a look at the following issues.

- Your organisation and the way you gave children their work.
- The need to do more to train children to work independently. We noted earlier that there is a need to train children in study skills. You need to identify the way you want children to work and make sure that they gradually become more independent.

Answer a child raising a query about work

Some such queries are inevitable, but you need to minimise them. Your assistant should be able to deal with a number of them and the number she can manage should increase as she grows more experienced. The following are very common queries.

- How do you spell ...? There are various ways of dealing with this. You can encourage the use of dictionaries and word lists. For some children it may be useful to ask another child before asking the teacher, although one has to watch for the problem of some children being constantly interrupted in their work. Your assistant should be able to deal with these questions.

    You can also ask children to have a go before they come to you or suggest that they write the word in rough, without worrying about spelling and then discuss it with you when the rough draft is finished before going on to make a finished copy. There will also be spell-checkers on your computers for children to use and there are free-standing spell-checkers now on the market which allow the writer to check the spelling of a word.

If you press children too much about always spelling correctly, they will tend to use only words that they know they can spell. This makes it more difficult for you to help them enlarge their spelling vocabulary because you can't tell easily what is in their spoken vocabulary. An approach which encourages children to have a go allows you to pick out words on which the child should concentrate attention.

- How do you do this sum? This is more difficult than spelling because you really need to explore a child's thinking and level of understanding in order to help. This again is something your assistant can learn how to do. If you are getting many enquiries about a particular piece of work, however, you are obviously pitching it at the wrong level for a number of children. It is also helpful to try to note the types of query you get over how to do something. It could be a matter of not understanding the language involved, inadequate number concepts or understanding of number operations or one of several problems. By generalising from the range of queries, you can often improve the ability of children to cope without recourse to you.

- What does this mean? Try to get children to rephrase this as 'Does this mean ...?' This encourages them to try to understand before coming to you.

- Answer a child checking that he or she is doing the right work. The children who constantly turn to you or your assistant to ask this kind of question tend to be the children who are a bit insecure. You need gradually to build up their confidence in themselves and in you, so that they know that you won't be cross with them for doing the wrong thing. It may be a good idea to check at the beginning that children who tend to ask this kind of question have understood and at an early stage, if possible, make encouraging sounds about what they are doing so that they know they are doing the right thing.

- Answer a child asking permission to do something. A teacher normally expects children to ask permission to go out of the classroom unless there are work areas adjacent, but as you work with a group of children you should be able to reduce the number of other occasions for asking permission to a minimum. Note the occasions when children ask permission and see if you can organise so that some of these requests are not needed.

- Make disciplinary comments. These include both telling a child not to do something and praising a child for doing the right thing. There is a lot of evidence to show that the latter is more effective than the former and that it is used more rarely. As your class gets to know you there should be a declining need for negative comment, although there will always be children who need to be restrained from time to time. It is also useful to look at the children to whom you offer each kind of comment. It is not unusual to find that some children get negative comments all the time and research suggests that these tend more often to be boys than girls and more often boys of Afro-Caribbean origin than others. If you find that this is so, you need to look for situations in which positive comments might be made, because quite often some children will misbehave in order to get attention and attention for doing the right thing may satisfy this need and reduce the number of occasions when negative comments are needed. Remember that behaviour which attracts positive comment is likely to be repeated while behaviour which attracts negative comment tends to disappear only temporarily. Just looking for something positive to say to a child who always seems to be doing the wrong thing can sometimes be productive. Here again it is useful to check on the comments you make from time to time.

A major problem for teachers is finding enough time to make assessments. A number of the suggestions above may be relevant in helping to create more time for this, which is a part of both the literacy and numeracy strategies. You also need to have some types of work which you know children can be left to do without interrupting you when you want to check on an individual child's learning. Reading is an obvious task with older children and various forms of play may occupy younger children, although play is less useful if no adult is involved. It may be possible to give children more than one task to do at a time so that they can go on to another task if they find difficulties with the first one. Your assistant should usually be able to deal with many of the problems while you are dealing with an individual child.

Review 18.3 My use of time

1 What are my first priorities for the use of my time in the classroom?
2 Are there aspects of my work which seem to get neglected because I can't find time for them? What can I do to change this?
3 Which aspects of my work take up more time than I feel they should? Why is this? Is there anything I can do to change this?
4 Could my assistant do more to enable me to spend more time on the things I see as a priority?
5 Could I do anything to help my children to become more independent of me so that I can direct my attention to those whom I feel need it most?
6 How much time are the children on-task? Could I improve the way they are using time?

The classroom environment

Children learn from everything that happens to them and the classroom environment is no exception. You can use it as a tool to influence the children in the following ways.

It can set aesthetic standards for children

Children should be able to get pleasure from what is around them. This has several benefits. What we know about learning suggests that attitudes towards school and towards learning are formed early. A pleasant environment is likely to contribute to the formation of good attitudes.

We set standards by the environment we offer to children. We need to provide things of quality and give children a chance to enjoy them. Plants and reproductions of paintings are comparatively inexpensive and objects which can be handled may be included along with examples of good work from children. This is how standards are formed and maintained, and the less likely children are to get such experience at home the more important it is for the school to offer it.

The classroom displays can set standards of presentation

The teacher and assistant should set a standard of displaying work and teaching materials which will be reflected in the children's own work. This should lead gradually to children putting up displays themselves and learning about how to display material effectively.

Primary teachers often feel that they could do with more display space than they actually have. Pinboard is a very desirable wall covering but if you have only a small amount you can add to it in various ways.

Hessian wallpaper which takes pins is a very attractive surface which can be stuck directly onto plaster or over pinboard which has become unsightly. Corrugated card can be used in many ways and lengths of it can be pinned to a small amount of pinboard and so provide extra display space. Carpet tiles of the cheapest kind make a good pin-up surface and have the advantage that they absorb noise. They are more expensive than pinboard but provide a more attractive background for display and can be bought a few at a time.

The classroom environment should be easy to maintain

You need good arrangements for getting things out and putting them away and with a new class you need to spend time training children to do this. One simple approach is to make every child responsible for the tidiness of a small area of the classroom. The child's name is stuck to the section together with a list of what should be there. There should be a definite place for everything and each place should be labelled appropriately so that it is easy to see where things go. At the end of each session each child checks the list and tidies his or her area. It is easy for the teacher to see whether the work has been done and who should be doing it. This enables you to clear up very quickly and ensures that everyone takes a fair share of the work.

The classroom should stimulate children

This means that you display some material designed to start children thinking and asking questions and sometimes to start them working. It also means that you need to change the display fairly frequently and check that what is on show is really looked at and used. It is not unusual to find a classroom with a considerable amount of attractive material displayed but having no impact because the teacher has not stimulated the children to look at what is there. You need to train children to look at displays and to see what is there and provide opportunities for discussion about what they see. It is sometimes better to display less, use it more and change it more frequently. It was suggested in Chapter 4 that teaching assistants could do useful work in looking after displays.

You can also stimulate children in the way you set out materials for their use. A good collection of scrap papers and fabrics for collage may spark off interesting pictures. Other scrap materials may stimulate development in technology.

Organising the use of space and resources

The classroom should provide for the work you want to do. This means careful thought about storage and the way in which the grouping of children and the pattern of work relate to the environment and the resources available. Are you getting the best use of the resources you have at your disposal? Are the computers in your classroom used for as much of the time as possible? Could you make more use of this resource if you organised differently? Are you sure you are using everything that is available? It is surprising how often a teacher who is clear about what is needed finds ways round limited funding. There is very often equipment and material lying unused in someone else's cupboard and schools need to make sure they are sharing what is there, perhaps keeping a list of what is available which states where things are so that teachers can borrow them when needed.

Managing the space

In most primary classrooms the vast majority of the week's work has to take place in the same space, with only a small amount of specialist space available, if any. The classroom has to be used for many different activities, some of which don't go too well together. It is never very satisfactory to have to use such materials as paint and clay in the same space as clean work, however carefully you clean up.

In thinking how best to use your room, you may find it helpful to work through the following questions.

What space is actually available?

Is there space outside the classroom but nearby, which could be used for some of the time? This might be corridor or cloakroom or shared space. Draw a plan of all the space you have available for use in planning.

*What activities will need to take place in the space you have
available in the course of the day or week?*

Most teachers will have a list which includes reading, writing, mathematics,
science, technology, discussion, drawing and painting and working with
materials (both clean materials such as fabric and messy materials such as
clay and foodstuffs). Working with computers is also an important aspect of
classroom life which requires them to be easily available. The list may also
include music-making and drama. You need to think too about the balance
of whole-class teaching, group and individual work and plan the use of
space with the demands of these organisations in mind. With very young
children you will need to think about the play opportunities you want to
offer. You also need to think about the storage you need. Each child will
need somewhere to keep his or her things and you will need places for the
equipment for each area of curriculum.

*What does each of these activities require in terms of space,
equipment and storage?*

How can the space available best be used to provide for all these activities?
Inevitably you must compromise to some extent. If you have drawn a plan
of the space available roughly to scale, you can go on to make cut-outs of the
base of each piece of furniture. This allows you to find different ways of
arranging them. You may want to designate particular areas of the classroom for particular activities, even if this is just a matter of arranging the
storage for particular materials and equipment.

When you have arrived at an arrangement of furniture which seems to
meet your needs, try to find time to check how it is working out and whether
there are modifications needed.

The seating of children

As teacher you decide the way children are seated. Children in primary school
classes are often seated in groups, but research suggests that comparatively
little use is made of this form of seating for co-operative work.

Wheldall and Glynn (1989) studied two Year 3 classes, one of twenty-eight
and one of twenty-five children. The classes were observed for two weeks
seated round tables looking at the amount of on-task behaviour which took
place which was defined as doing what the teacher had instructed. Tables were
then moved into rows and the children were observed for another two weeks.
Finally, tables were moved back to their original position for a further two
weeks. These are the researchers' findings.

The on-task behaviour of the first class rose from an average of 72 per cent to 85 per cent in rows and fell back to 73 per cent when tables seating was resumed. Similarly the performance of the second class rose from averaging 68 per cent on-task behaviour during baseline (tables) to 92 per cent during rows, and fell to 73 per cent for the final tables phase. They found that the seating arrangements had the most noticeable effect on children whose on-task behaviour was low. In some cases there was an improvement of 30 per cent. The children themselves said they preferred to be seated in rows. Another study of seating patterns had similar findings. The children's involvement in their work and the quantity of work completed rose significantly when the children were seated in rows rather than in groups. These findings suggest that children might get more work done if they were seated in rows rather than in groups. However, this is less convenient for co-operative work, although it is fairly easy to form groups of four by turning chairs round. Seating in rows is also less convenient for class discussion, because children cannot see each other. One alternative which may be better is to sit children in a horseshoe if there is enough space in the classroom to do this. This is good for discussion and is not difficult to rearrange into groups for co-operative work.

Wheldall and Glynn also studied the effect of mixed-sex seating. In a Year 4 class the level of on-task behaviour was 90 per cent during mixed-sex seating and fell to 76 per cent when children sat with same-sex partners. It rose again to 89 per cent when mixed seating was resumed. There was also less disruptive behaviour. They point out, however, that more on-task behaviour does not necessarily mean that the work is of higher quality. They also found that children thought they concentrated less when they were in same-sex pairs and worked harder in the mixed groups.

These findings are thought-provoking. Mixed-sex seating would undoubtedly be unpopular with children but you might try experimenting to see whether you have similar findings to the researchers.

Whatever your seating arrangement, you need to think about sight lines. It is easy to miss children who are at the extreme right and left of you towards the front of the classroom. A check on who answers questions will help to ensure that this doesn't happen.

Storage

It is rare for a teacher to get exactly the furniture he or she would like and rarer still to get a sufficient amount of storage. Most teachers have to make the best of what they have and do a good deal of improvising and arranging things to meet the needs of their children's work.

Storage is a problem in most classrooms. You need to store things in such a way that they are easy to find, placed so that children do not have to wander about the room to collect things to do one job, are easy to return and keep tidy as well as using space as economically as possible. Start thinking about storage by considering what you need to store for each aspect of your work and then see how this matches up with the space available. Look for spaces which could take additional shelves, including some high shelving for things not often needed. Look also for existing shelving which uses space uneconomically which might be adapted for better use.

Cupboards are often more useful and easier to keep tidy without their doors, or you can plan that when the doors are open your storage is carefully set out and the doors used for pinning up information or suspending material in pockets. It is a good idea to mark shelves with outlines or labels of what should be stored there so that everyone can see the space to which it should be returned.

Flat materials can be suspended in bags hung from wire coat hangers which in turn can be hung on a rail.

Trolleys are always useful, particularly for materials such as paint, where you need to clean the surfaces where they are stored fairly frequently. A deep box trolley is very useful for various kinds of scrap material and for clay, providing it has a lid.

Pegboard is useful for storing tools and each tool can be outlined on the pegboard so that it is easy to see where it should go and whether it has been returned.

You may analyse your use of time, space and resources in the classroom using the questions set out in Review 18.4.

Review 18.4 The use of time, space and resources

1 Am I using space to the best advantage?

2 Is the seating arrangement I have for children the most conducive to on-task work?

3 Does what I have displayed at the moment include both children's work and material to stimulate? How long has it been in place?

4 Does everything in the classroom have its proper place? Are all the places labelled?

5 Are resources easily accessible and close to the places where they are to be used?

6 Have I a good scheme for getting everything returned to its proper place after use?

Chapter 19

Providing for individual needs

Catering for individuals within a class is never easy. In every class there will be some children who not only need individual help with some of the work but also, for some of the time at least, an Individual Education Programme (IEP). The development of ICT is beginning to make personalised learning more of a reality and you need to seek opportunities to use this facility to help in catering for different needs.

Children with special educational needs

You may have children in your class who would formerly have been in a special school and who make considerable demands on your time and attention. There will also be others who have special educational needs of one kind or another. Your school, if it is large enough, should have a teacher who co-ordinates work with children with special educational needs (the SENCO) who should be in a position to help you to provide for such children in your class. There may also be a special needs assistant who will be able to work with some of the children who have special educational needs. This group is likely to include children with:

- low ability;
- specific learning problems, e.g. dyslexia;
- emotional and/or behavioural difficulties;
- problems of sight or hearing;
- other physical disabilities;
- gaps in schooling;
- language or speech problems, including non-English-speaking home background.

Diagnosis of needs

Your first task is one of diagnosis. You will have discovered from the records which children have major problems. Some of these, such as the child with a physical disability or a lack of English, are easy to identify and it is easy to see the reasons for the difficulties. Other problems too, such as the child who is nine but whose reading age is six, are comparatively easy to identify but it may be difficult to discover the reasons for the problem and still more difficult to know what to do about it.

If you teach a reception class you may have access to some records of pre-school experience and these may give you some information about children with learning problems and any professional diagnoses made by doctors or psychologists. There may also be some children who appear to have problems which the parent will tell you about and provide any information gathered from doctors or psychologists. You will then need to observe the child for a while, looking at what s/he does and what s/he says and whether s/he can speak articulately. You will also watch the child with other children and notice whether there is any interaction between them. How does this child move? How does s/he react when you ask the children to do something? If you have a special needs co-ordinator in your school, s/he may be able to help you.

If you teach at other levels in the school there will usually be records giving information about such children. These will probably tell you about any medical or psychological diagnosis that has been made, which should give you some clues about the child. You will also be able to talk with the child's previous teacher and find out what s/he feels has been a successful way of working. Of course, if the child in question has only just transferred to your school, you will have to rely on any records they have sent and what the parents can tell you about the child.

As you work with the child you will gradually discover more about him or her. You will find out what s/he can do and cannot do, what s/he knows or does not know, what seems to work and what doesn't work and whether there are any problems in relating to other children. You will also quickly discover if this child has behaviour problems and their nature: you will probably have heard about these from the previous teacher, and you now have to think about how to tackle them. You would be wise to keep notes about the things you discover as you go along and consider if they add up to suggest any particular way of working which might help. You also need to consider whether you should be recommending to the head that s/he should suggest to the parents that this child should be seen by a psychologist.

There may also be other problems which may pass unnoticed for a time, such as the child with an undiagnosed hearing problem. This is especially likely where the child is quiet and well behaved, and does nothing to alert you to the fact that s/he isn't hearing very well.

As your classroom assistant comes to know the children well as individuals, she should be able to help you with the process of diagnosing difficulties if you brief her carefully about what she should look for. You can also instruct her in ways of helping particular individuals.

It may be helpful at this stage to look briefly at each of the groups listed and decide which of the categories above fit each of the children you have identified, remembering that a child may come into more than one category.

Children with low ability

Children with low ability are likely to need a certain amount of special attention at every stage of schooling and this needs to be accepted and planned for. They are likely to be at an earlier stage in many ways than other children in the class and you will need to do a great deal to encourage them, praising and rewarding their progress whenever you can so that they are not too depressed by their slow progress. You also need to make your assistant aware of the importance of encouraging such children.

The extent of the special attention they will need will depend upon the class they are with. If they are in a class where the average IQ is well below 100, the work is more likely to meet their needs than would be the case if they were in a class with an average or above average ability range. A child with a much higher IQ may need special help if he or she is with a group of high flyers. This makes it difficult to talk about children with high or low ability in the abstract. Although the terms are defined by national norms of ability, the extent to which the level of ability of a particular individual affects the work of the school or class is a matter of the norms within it as well as the ways in which the child's ability differs from the norm.

It is particularly important to look at what motivates the children whose needs differ from those of the majority and to use this to help them to learn in appropriate areas. You also need to look at what they know and do not know within the core subjects and plan work to fill the gaps you discover. Teachers occasionally take the view that, since children who are slow learners are poor at reasoning, they should learn by heart. This is unlikely to be a successful ploy as they probably have a poorer memory than the majority anyway and you need to think of ways to help them fix learning in their minds. What is needed is work designed to help them to learn to reason and develop appropriate strategies for learning, so that they become more capable learners. All children need this teaching, but in some ways the need to provide this for slow learners is greater than it is for others because of the limited amount of time you have available to work with them. It also helps to get them to use sight, hearing and movement to remember. In learning to spell, for example, it can help to say the word and then write it. It may also help to draw it in the air. In number, they will need more use of apparatus than the majority.

The need to provide short-term goals and objectives

Children with low ability tend to need short-term goals which they can enjoy achieving. You are more likely to be successful in teaching such a child if you identify clear objectives with the child, encouraging him or her to identify them with your help, rather than doing this yourself. Aim to help the child to identify goals which can be achieved fairly quickly, perhaps in one lesson, or even within a shorter period. You then give praise when the objectives are achieved and perhaps record the achievement somewhere for the child to see. It is also important to praise effort, even when it does not lead to success, because much effort will be needed from the child if he or she is to succeed.

You need to discuss ways of working with such children with your assistant, who should be encouraged to learn about how best to help them.

Providing materials for slow learners

It is likely that there will always be children of low ability in your class. It is therefore worthwhile making or buying specific materials for them, firstly for developing work in the core subjects and secondly to provide for them to develop their work in other aspects of the curriculum. Material of this kind can then be used many times. If you add to this collection a little at a time and start with material you know you will need time after time, you can gradually build a collection and this makes it easy to provide for children at the right level. A similar approach is needed for very able children.

Specific learning difficulties

Children with special needs form a very varied group. There will be some who are apparently of average or above average intelligence but who are not achieving at their proper level. They may be dyslexic. This means that they may have difficulties of various kinds. They are not unintelligent but they may find it hard to take in what you are saying. They tend to find handwriting and spelling very difficult. They read very slowly and often misread words and don't understand what they are reading. All these problems can make them anxious, because they don't want to appear stupid in front of the other children or appear stupid to you. They need a lot of encouragement.

There will be others who appear to have difficulty in one particular aspect of their work while managing the rest quite well. There may be children with minimal brain damage which creates problems for them and there may also be children whose school work seems to be well below average who have problems which have not yet been diagnosed. Children in this group may need special attention for a period and may then be able to cope normally. It is particularly important to spend time analysing what they know and do not know and what they can do and not do, so that work can be directed appropriately and time is not wasted. Some of these children may have the services of a support assistant if their problems are serious and you will need to give careful thought to the way this help is used in the classroom.

Children with emotional and/or behavioural problems

Most teachers find this group the most difficult to deal with and most demanding professionally. Research suggests that the type of school situation most likely to cope well with these children is likely to have:

- warm, caring attitudes in adult–child relationships;
- improvement of the child's self-image through success;
- individual counselling and discussion;
- a varied and stimulating educational programme;
- continuity in adult–child relationships;
- firm, consistent discipline.

Successful specialist teachers of these children tend to use one or both of two main ways of working with them. They make considerable effort to know the children well and this leads into counselling about work and behaviour. It sometimes involves teaching a child how to behave in a given social situation because sometimes children behave badly through ignorance of the acceptable thing to do.

The second approach is that of behaviour modification. This involves setting very specific goals for behaviour which appear to be within the child's capacity to attain. For example, you might agree with a child that he or she will work quietly for ten minutes by the clock without getting up or speaking to anyone else. If the child achieves this goal, you reward him or her with praise and perhaps a mark on a personal chart. You then go on to set further goals. If the child is unable to achieve the goal set then you make it easier: working for five minutes, for example.

In some cases you may find that a child who is easily distracted is helped if you arrange for him to work in a carrel or booth. You can create areas for individual learning of this kind by placing hardboard between two tables or placing a cupboard at right angles to the wall. The child then sits facing the wall, where he or she is less likely to be distracted by other children. Working there should be treated as a privilege rather than a punishment, since a distractible child may wish as fervently as you do that he or she could behave like other children. You may find that other children too like working in this situation.

From time to time you may experience a child who creates a situation which challenges your authority as a teacher and perhaps tries to demonstrate to the class that he or she is managing you. The child swears at you, defies you, deliberately does something you have forbidden and creates a dramatic situation where all the children are waiting, breathless, to see what will happen. When this kind of situation occurs you usually have little time to think. The first thing to do is to retain a professional calm, acting the part of someone calm even if you are boiling inside. You can then take one of several possible courses of action.

You can separate the child from the others

You may do this in various ways. You may perhaps take him or her out of the room or at least out of earshot, if not out of sight of other children so that you can talk without an audience. This is probably the best solution and has the advantage of ending the drama. How you deal with the child then will depend upon your knowledge of the particular child and the situation, but you have a better chance of making an impression when the child is not playing to the gallery.

You can assert your authority

You may do this in any way you think may be effective. Some teachers demonstrate blank astonishment that anyone could do such a thing; others produce a show of anger, looking directly at the child and maintaining eye contact while moving towards him or her. Both of these tactics can work, but you have to feel reasonably confident that this kind of action won't lead to further defiance. It is also easier to stay in control of the situation if you are acting as if you are astonished or angry and not really feeling it. This is often difficult to do.

You can pass it off lightly

You can imply that it is not important or treat it as a joke or by saying something like 'I'm sure you didn't really mean that. How about starting again?' Then you take a later opportunity to talk to the child in question and try to find out the reason for the outburst.

You can behave as if nothing has happened

You can more or less ignore the behaviour at the time and discuss it later. If you are dealing with a child whose behaviour is known to be abnormal and recognised by the other children to be so, this is not an unreasonable thing to do, especially if you can couple it with an opportunity to retract or rephrase what was said. A comment like 'I didn't quite hear that. Would you mind repeating it?' very frequently produces something more moderate.

It is useful to keep a note of situations where a child or a group of children have been particularly difficult, recording what led up to the situation. If you do this over a period, you may be able to see a pattern in what triggers unacceptable behaviour and this may enable you to avoid situations which create problems. You can also discuss with an individual child what makes him or her angry and badly behaved and use the techniques of behaviour modification to help the child overcome the problem.

Problems of sight or hearing

You may have within your class children with problems of sight or hearing. They may be with you for only part of the time and in a school-based unit for the rest of the time, but you need to be aware of the problems they have and the implications of those problems for you as teacher. If you teach one of the younger groups, this problem may not yet have been recognised and your observation of the child may give you clues to his or her problem.

Children with poor vision need very good light for their work. They certainly need to sit near a window and if their problems are serious they may need a reading lamp. They also need to sit near the board and some will need someone to read what is on it for them. Whiteboards are easier to read than blackboards. Worksheets also need to be in black and white and may need large print.

If you have a child with serious sight problems you may need to familiarise him or her with the classroom layout when the child first joins you. It is useful to use clock face directions in describing where something is if the child is old enough to understand them.

If a child has had poor sight from birth, he or she will have developed a rather different picture of the world from a normally sighted child and this will affect the way concepts have been formed. You need to be prepared for this. The child may ask strange questions which can sometimes reveal something of his or her inner view of the world.

Colour blindness

One common sight defect which is not sufficiently noticed in schools is colour blindness. You may have a child in your class at some time who has a degree of colour blindness. This creates problems for the child when things are colour-coded as well as problems in art and craft and in daily life. This is a defect which cannot be remedied, but if you know about it you can help the child in question by giving other references as well as colour.

It is easy to check whether you have any colour-blind children in your class by asking everyone to draw a flag with diagonals on it. You then ask them to colour in each section as you do and you show them a flag coloured with some sections red and some green. Colour-blind children will have difficulty doing this because red/green colour blindness is the most common. They may, however, have learned to make up for their deficiency and will identify red and green crayons, perhaps by reading their labels or by some marking on them. They will also look to see what other children are doing. It may therefore be best to divide the class in half. One lot of children might be asked to colour their flags blue and orange, which are other colours often confused, and the others red and green and then they could change over. Look out for children looking around to see what others are doing. They are quite likely to be colour blind.

Hearing problems

Children with hearing problems also need to sit near the front and they will need to see your face as you speak if they are to understand what you are saying. Try to avoid talking while you are writing on the board or asking children to look at something on their tables while you talk about it. A child with hearing problems will find this very difficult. You can sometimes recognise such children by the puzzled look on their faces when you say something or by their comments and questions which reveal that they didn't take in what you said earlier. It is very easy to mistake this for inattention and make some critical comment about it. If this happens on more than one occasion you would be wise to find out more about the child's hearing.

A child who has had serious hearing problems from birth will almost certainly have more limited speech than his or her contemporaries and will therefore have more difficulty in understanding as well as in hearing. Speech problems may include not only pronunciation but also limitations in vocabulary and language structure and this may need explaining to other children who may find such a child odd because of the peculiar speech. It is obviously best to do this at some time when the child in question is not there.

In both the cases of visually and hearing impaired children it is important to see that they have with them and are using the aids they need. Glasses and hearing aids are essential to them but they do not always want to use them. The teacher can do much to help the child to find these aids more acceptable and help other children to be sympathetic about the child's problems.

The child with physical disabilities

You may have in your class a child with physical problems of one kind or another. It is very easy to assume that such children will make slower progress than children without such problems, but this is not necessarily the case. Children with physical disabilities probably represent the same range of ability as that in the normal population and their needs need to be assessed in much the same way.

The major problem you have to tackle with such children is what they can do physically. There will normally be advice available to you about what the problems are and how best to tackle them. Such children may have considerable difficulty with subjects such as art, science and technology as well as physical education. If their hands are affected by their disability you may need to seek out ways in which they can be enabled to do the work that others do, perhaps by working with a partner to help them or by finding a way to support them. They may be able to do some things in physical education and generally should be encouraged to join in as much as possible, providing the medical advice allows this.

You may also have children with a variety of medical conditions, including such problems as asthma, diabetes or epilepsy and some may have acquired immunodeficiency syndrome (AIDS). Each needs to be dealt with according to the advice offered by doctors and parents, but you would be wise to find out all you can about any disability or medical condition in a child in your class. Your task is to help him or her to learn and if your knowledge of the problem is good you can make this provision with more confidence.

Children with gaps in schooling

A child may have missed a period at school through illness or for other reasons. He or she may have been taught badly or missed something by changing schools. Careful analysis will be needed especially for initial reading and number. If you have new children fairly frequently in your school it is a good idea to have some appropriate test material on disc or on paper so that you can find out, for example, whether a child has all the phonic knowledge needed at the stage that most of the rest of the class have reached, or whether a child has sufficient knowledge of spelling rules, what his or her knowledge of the four rules of number actually is and so on.

It is not sufficient to find out what is missing, however. You also need teaching material you can use with such a child on an individual basis. Once again the best way to build an appropriate stock of such material is to make or buy a little at a time to meet the needs of a particular child and then to file this for future use.

Children with language problems

Language problems can range from the child who comes into school with virtually no English because this is not the language used in the home, to the child whose language is so far from standard English that he or she sometimes has difficulty in understanding and being understood. Problems also include children who stammer or have some impediment in their speech or difficulty in using and understanding normal language. Where there is a group of such children with similar problems who can be helped together, perhaps by a specialist teacher, this is less of a problem than where the situation is one of a single individual who has problems which make demands on the single classroom teacher with everything else to do. On the other hand, if the problem is one of learning to speak English, the lone individual may make more progress than the child in a group where there are other children speaking the child's home language.

Almost all language problems involve some work on a one-to-one basis and it is clearly impossible for a teacher with a normal class to provide this on any scale. You therefore need to consider what other help you can muster and, if you can find it, how you can organise the work so that the time is well used. You may be fortunate enough to have a support assistant for a child with language difficulties and you will probably have a general classroom assistant. You may also have the help of parents who may be willing to come in and talk to children who need practice in English. It may also be helpful to invite in parents if there are any, who are bilingual in the child's home language who can read or tell stories in that language and then translate them into English.

In dealing with children with a limited knowledge of English it is important to use the same phrases many times in the same contexts. In managing the day-to-day work of the classroom there are many occasions for this. Phrases such as 'put your things away', 'put your coats on', 'wash your hands for lunch' and so on will soon be picked up by children learning English, who will be able to see what the phrases mean from the actions of the other children. You can then get different children to say the phrases so that those learning English get practice in speaking.

Individual work with such children might involve work with recordings and pictures or slides designed to teach the names of everyday objects and actions.

Work with children with other language disabilities should involve advice from a speech therapist. This is likely to vary from one child to another according to individual need.

Children with undiagnosed learning problems

You may also have children whose problems have not yet been diagnosed, particularly if you teach very young children. You may become aware of a child who appears to be having difficulty in seeing the board or a child who holds his head in an unusual position in what seems to be an effort to hear what you are saying. You can check sight by asking a child for details of what he or she can see close to and at a distance and you can check hearing by standing behind a child and saying something in a normal voice and asking him or her to repeat it. Children who appear to have reading difficulties may also have poor sight. Your recognition of such problems will mean that the first steps to help the child can be taken and he or she can be checked for sight and hearing problems.

Successful work with children with learning problems

It may be helpful to look at the factors associated with successful work with children with learning difficulties. Many of these factors also apply to children with outstanding ability. You are most likely to be successful in teaching such children if you do the following.

- Study them as individuals with interests and a preferred style of working and make a careful diagnosis of the nature of their problems.

- Devise a programme for each child to meet the needs revealed by the diagnosis and involve the child in setting and achieving realistic short-term goals.
- Break down the necessary learning into steps which are small enough for the child to take successfully, but which also have purpose in his or her eyes and involve decision-making and thinking and are not over-dependent on memory.
- Enable each child to see his or her own progress and reinforce learning, including the behaviour you want, by specific praise and encouragement and perhaps by charting progress in some way so that the child can see how he or she is doing.
- Provide opportunities for each child to take responsibility and become more independent.
- Provide genuine opportunities for these children to contribute to the life and work of the class.
- Gain the co-operation of the child's family and work with the parents to help them to find specific ways of helping their child.
- Keep careful records and review progress regularly, usually involving the children themselves.
- Maintain a positive attitude in all circumstances and provide many opportunities that are more likely to lead to success than failure.

It is also important to remember that a child with a disability may have very low self-esteem, which tends to be confirmed very frequently when the child constantly demonstrates that he or she is not as clever as other children. You need to seek out ways to boost his or her self-esteem whenever you can.

It is possible to take a positive approach even in the areas in which a child is weak. Most children at the primary stage are anxious to do well, and if you can get a child to join you in setting targets and achieving them in an agreed time you enable that child to work positively to improve and add to achievement.

For example, suppose you want a child to improve his or her knowledge of multiplication facts. One way forward would be to agree a target day by which he or she would try to learn a specific range of facts and then discuss all the possible ways of working to achieve this. Children might, for example, dictate tests onto a disc or tape for themselves and then play them back when they think they know them, writing down the answers so that they can check them. Another possibility would be to work with another child playing games designed to teach the learning needed and so on.

Schools are now likely to contain more children with disabilities than formerly because fewer are in special schools. This has advantages for the children concerned and it is valuable for them to have the opportunity to learn alongside other children. Conversely, it is useful for the other children to learn alongside children with disabilities but it also poses problems because children with serious disabilities will be expected to cope with as much of the normal school programme as possible and to follow the National Curriculum.

It is probably true to say that many people with disabilities can, if motivated, do more than other people often think they can and this view should be encouraged. Older children, in particular, need to be encouraged to be helpful to, but not 'make pets' of, children with physical disabilities and to treat them as they would other children except where their disability requires particular attention. In the main, the way children with special needs are treated by other children will come from the example set them by the staff. It is important that you demonstrate that you hold high expectations for such children and that they have your full support.

Children with and without particular disabilities may pose problems in school. Difficulties such as poor sight or motor control problems, hyperactivity and others may make the normal programme of work inappropriate or lead to problems of understanding which result in disruptive behaviour. Maladjusted children may create a range of disturbances and may have difficulty in relating to others. You may have to teach specific interpersonal skills and discuss ways of relating to others with such children and also to encourage normally developing children to be ready to help those with special needs.

There may also be some children who have difficulty in school because personal problems from home occupy their minds to the exclusion of everything else. You may only hear of this by chance, but if you find that a child who used to work well is quite suddenly doing very badly, not really attending in class and giving the impression of being pre-occupied, it may be worth trying to explore further, perhaps by talking with the child and checking with other teachers to see if they have heard anything that might be causing such a problem.

From your point of view, while it is valuable to know what causes a particular difficulty, the more important question is how to deal with it. Part of knowing how to deal with it is knowing enough about it to know what is possible and what is impossible. It is easy to be so concerned by what you discover about a child's background and so sympathetic towards him or her that you give too little attention to his or her learning needs. The fact that Jackie lives daily with violence and family rows may make you sympathetic when she finds it difficult to concentrate, but it may be that the most helpful thing you can do is to help her succeed in learning to read. Every teacher needs to be a sympathetic human being, but no teacher has time to be a psychologist as well. However, it may be wise to let your headteacher know when you hear or see something in relation the background of a particular child that makes you concerned about his or her home life. It will still be important to show such children that they have your full support in school.

Review 19.1 Working with children with special needs

1   Which children in my class need to be treated individually for some of the time because of their special needs?
2   Do I know enough about the problems of each of them? How can I find out more?
3   Have I provided suitable programmes for each of them designed to meet their particular needs?
4   Am I aware of all the children who have problems of sight or hearing? Could there be some children with these problems which have not been diagnosed?
5   Have I any children who are colour blind? If so, what am I doing to help them?
6   How well am I coping with children who have behaviour problems? Have I strategies for dealing with the problems they create?
7   Am I creating situations in which children with special needs experience success?
8   Does my organisation enable me to spend time with these children? Have I organised their work so that they do not waste time?
9   Is my assistant able to help me with some of these children?
10 How satisfactory is my overall provision for children with special needs? Are they making as much progress as possible given their problems?

The child with outstanding ability

In any class there will be some children who are more able than the majority in some or all of the work of the class, who will need individual programmes for some work. From time to time you may encounter a child who is so far ahead of the group that he or she needs an individual programme for almost everything or at least a variation of the class or group programme. This group is beginning to be more considered at a national level and schools are being encouraged to try to make adequate provision for them. In one sense these too are children with special educational needs of a quite different kind.

You need to be aware of any children who have outstanding ability of some kind, maybe in most areas of work or in some particular area, such as writing, mathematics, art or music or any other subject. You need to try to provide opportunities for such children perhaps to work at their own ideas or at a more advanced level whenever you consider the work you are asking from the rest of the class is too easy for them. You need to be aware of their needs and look for ways of helping them to fulfil their promise.

It is tempting to believe that such children are easy to identify and don't need any extra help because they can get on by themselves. The evidence from a number of studies suggests that this is not the case. Some gifted children use their ability to hide their gifts so that they are like their peers and not all of their gifts are known to their teachers, particularly if they are disinclined to conform and do as they are told.

Different forms of giftedness

There are a number of ways in which a child can be gifted and you need to be fully aware of the nature of a child's gifts if you are to be able to provide the right support for him or her.

Outstanding ability in using language

A child may be able to speak and write using an unusually wide vocabulary and much more advanced sentence constructions than his or her contemporaries. S/he may also choose to write and talk about unusual subjects for his or her age. Such a child should be encouraged to read widely and be given a good deal of choice in subjects for writing.

Outstanding creative ability

This may manifest itself in a variety of ways. It may show itself in writing, drawing and painting, technology, musical ability or more generally in being an 'ideas person'. You need to give such a child encouragement in whichever of these areas s/he appears to show talent and provide opportunities for him or her to develop the ideas and skills s/he has.

Outstanding mathematical ability

The future mathematician is likely to show interest in whatever aspect of mathematics s/he meets. You need to encourage such a child to work at increasingly difficult problems. S/he is likely to be well ahead of the class more generally and you may need to offer him or her an individual programme in this subject.

Outstanding physical ability

From an early stage such a child will be able to try physical movements well in advance of his or her classmates. There may even be a problem that the child's keenness leads to attempts to do things which are rather beyond his or her ability.

The importance of encouragement

In all these cases your encouragement of the child will be important as it is for all of us, and you also need to be aware that sometimes very able children try to disguise their abilities in order not to antagonise their contemporaries. If you single out such children too much in front of others, this is a likely possibility.

If you want to be sure that you are catering for such children you need to do the following.

- Develop your skill in identifying children of outstanding ability. Look particularly for the child who is unusual in some way, who asks unusual questions, has original ways of looking at things, or shows particular talent in an area of curriculum. Where you have serious queries about such a child, it may be a good idea to ask if s/he can be seen by an educational psychologist.
- Make sure your overall programme is rich and varied enough for latent gifts to emerge. Some people reveal their gifts only if the circumstances are right and when something strikes a chord for them.
- Consider possible teaching approaches for a child of outstanding ability. Try to ensure that you ask questions and present material at a variety of levels and that you include open-ended questions in any questioning session. Try to give him or her some personal time so that you can construct a more appropriate programme which enables the child to work at his or her real level of ability. Your assistant may be able to help here by spending individual time with the child encouraging wider exploration of ideas. Computers also offer opportunities for more individual exploration and for personalising learning.
- Assess carefully the levels of ability and stages of development within the class. Examine the ways in which you check on the abilities and stages of development of your children. Is it possible that you have a child who could do much more demanding work than you are giving him or her? It may be a good idea to go through the register asking yourself this question and then check up on any children whom you think may have more ability than is apparent, by talking further with them and looking again at their work.
- Organise work at different levels. With any topic work you plan to do with the whole class, see that there are, within the plan, opportunities for doing more or doing work which is more demanding. Very able children don't necessarily need the next stage of the work which is in hand, although it may sometimes be appropriate to go on to the next level of the National Curriculum. They are often able to do more than their peers and can enjoy a richer programme involving their own investigations or ideas which you or they suggest. It is a waste of any child's time to do

more of work already mastered, although it can sometimes be difficult to avoid this. Research has tended to find that teachers are inclined to underestimate the most able children, who are often given tasks which were practice of what they already knew rather than consolidation of new learning.

- Consider the basic curriculum in relation to such a child. Since able children learn quickly, their basic learning can be more concentrated than that for other children. It may be a good idea to look through the books and materials you are using to see whether there are short cuts or ways in which a child who grasps things easily can get through the essential work more quickly than the majority. Try building a collection of material for the faster workers. It multiplies the material if a group of teachers collaborate in making and collecting such material and share it.

- Consider how you can exploit and develop a child's gifts. A child who works quickly has time for other work. Try to find some genuine problems or tasks which are within the capacity of such a child and if possible enlist help from parents, students and others who may be interested. For example, an older child might undertake the production of a story book for younger children. Such project material must actually be used, however, and the child or children must be aware of this from the outset; otherwise the discipline of working in a real situation will be lost. A further project might be to evaluate the effect of this work. The story book might be given to one or two younger children who could be asked to read it and say what they thought of it.

Children of high ability have a particular need to acquire study skills so that they are able to work independently and are not too dependent on a busy teacher.

Review 19.2 Providing for children with outstanding ability

1   Have I any children of outstanding ability in my class? What distinguishes them from the rest of the class?
2   What particular abilities do they appear to possess?
3   Can I recognise the signs of different kinds of outstanding ability even when the child in question tries to disguise it?
4   Am I making adequate provision for each very able child? Is he or she making as much progress as his/her ability suggests?
5   How independent in their work are these children?
6   What balance of work with the class and individual programmes should I try to achieve with them?
7   What can my assistant do to help these children?

Work with gifted children is gradually taking a more important place on the national agenda. Industry and different professions are looking for people of high ability and creative ideas, who will be able to make a very positive contribution. It seems likely that there will be increasing pressure on schools to take their needs as seriously as we now take the needs of those with learning difficulties.

Children from ethnic minorities

Many schools now have children from different ethnic backgrounds and this poses particular problems for teachers. Schools in some areas now have a long history of working successfully with such children and dealing with some of the problems it raises.

The need for an agreed policy and ethos

It is essential that all staff at a school which is ethnically mixed take a firm stand on an anti-racist view. Diversity should be respected and celebrated and everyone involved needs to feel part of a community which values all its members equally and in which all teachers and other staff and children try to be sensitive to other people, especially if they don't speak much English or have a different coloured skin.

Differences in the performance of these groups

There has been concern about this for a number of years, and some of the differences are long-standing. Some researchers suggest that a certain amount of stereotyping is going on and is influencing both children and teachers to their disadvantage. It is also the case that very often children's social background is not taken into account and this affects ethnic minority children as well as white children although probably not in the same way.

Gillborn and Mirza (2000) note the differences in attainment of different ethnic groups. While the attainment of these groups is slowly improving, 'African-Caribbean, Pakistani and Bangladeshi pupils are markedly less likely to attain five higher grade GCSE passes than their white and Indian peers nationally'. Indian pupils have made the greatest gains since 1990 but the gap between African-Caribbean and Pakistani pupils and their white peers has increased.

The London Development Agency in 2004 listed the following key issues about Afro-Caribbean pupils in London schools:

- low teacher expectation of academic success;
- high teacher expectation for challenges to teacher authority;
- unfair behaviour management practices with Afro-Caribbean youth

receiving harsher reprimands than pupils from other ethnic groups for the same incidents/misbehaviour;
- high levels of pupil–teacher conflict with teachers attempting to exert excessive and insensitive levels of control;
- repression of positive pupil attempts to contribute to classroom thinking and environment;
- repression of Afro-Caribbean cultural expression;
- failure to tackle institutional racism systematically;
- failure to deliver an inclusive curriculum.

LEAs where there is concern about racism in the schools do their best to ensure that schools are given guidance on this issue. Berkshire, a county in which people of other races are a small minority, produced this policy statement back at that time.

The Council is opposed to racism in all its forms. It wishes therefore:

1   To promote understanding of the principles and practices of racial equality and justice, and commitment to them.
2   To identify and remove all practices, procedures and customs which discriminate against ethnic minority people and to replace them with procedures which are fair to all.
3   To encourage ethnic minority parents and communities to be fully involved in the decision-making processes which affect the education of their children.
4   To increase the influence of ethnic minority parents, organisations and communities by supporting educational and cultural projects which they themselves initiate.
5   To encourage the recruitment of ethnic minority teachers, administrators and other staff at all levels, and the appointment of ethnic minority governors.
6   To monitor and evaluate the implementation of County Council policies and to make changes and corrections as appropriate.

The Inner London Education Authority, whose schools contained many pupils of other races, produced a somewhat similar policy and also a classroom check-list which suggests ways in which teachers might evaluate the way they were catering for their mixed-race class community.

1   *A welcoming ethos*   Is the general ethos of the classroom welcoming to diversity? Do the teaching and learning styles encourage collaborative working among children? Is there opportunity for children to voice feelings without threat or risk? Are children able to learn from each other and is the teacher able to learn from them?

2 *A multicultural, multilingual content* Is there a multicultural, multilingual content throughout the curriculum and the visual environment of the classroom? Is it possible to apply the 'acid test' of entering the classroom when the children have gone home and know from the displays, children's work, signs and resources that the teacher has a commitment to cultural diversity?

3 *Valuing children's and parents' experience* Do the children and their families feel that what they have to offer is recognised and valued in the classroom? Do they feel confident about bringing their knowledge, skills and experience to the fore and sharing these with others?

4 *Lifting taboo about discussing race and racism* Is there a taboo surrounding discussion of race difference and racism? Do the children feel that these are subjects which are not to be aired in the class-room? Or do they have opportunity to express views and recount experiences? Are the children encouraged to think critically about bias and prejudice in what they see, hear and read?

5 *Learning about and experiencing other cultures* Are the children able to learn about and experience cultural systems and styles of living other than their own? Is there opportunity for them to become more fully informed about people from other ethnic groups?

Equal opportunities

One school with a mixed population set out its equal opportunities policy as follows:

- all pupils to achieve their full potential;
- expectations of all pupils are equally high;
- all pupils have access to and can make use of the school's facilities and resources;
- the school reflects the local community and responds to their needs;
- all pupils are prepared for life in a diverse and multi-ethnic community;
- all pupils understand what prejudice means, how discrimination occurs and how they can take a stand against all forms of racism.

Ethos

- a positive ethos and environment is developed within the school;
- the school challenges and deals effectively with racist incidents;
- targets for different groups are systematically identified and included in the school development plan;
- planning and teaching of the National Curriculum interact with the school's policy on inclusion.

Providing a welcoming environment

This is, of course, important for any school, but one serving an ethnic minority population has a particular responsibility to help children and parents who speak very little or no English to find out all they need to know about children's education in Britain and about their local primary school. The LEA should make provision for information for ethnic minority parents about primary education and with local schools provide opportunities for them to visit and see some of the school's activities, preparatory to their child or children starting there. It will be important in such cases to find interpreters and also to try to provide material for such parents in their own language(s).

If such interpreters are available, the school should have an initial interview with parents giving them the chance to ask questions and telling them about the school and what their son or daughter will do there. This will also be an opportunity for the school to find out about the child's background and personality.

Review 19.3 Providing for ethnic minority children

1   How many ethnic minority children in my class speak English really well? How many have very little knowledge of English?
2   How can I best organise so that it is usually clear where things are and what is going to happen next, perhaps by using pictures or labels in both English and also a more familiar language?
3   What bits of the language of the majority of non-English-speaking children in my class would it be useful for me to learn? How can I do this?

Chapter 20

Working with parents

Many schools have developed excellent work with parents but research suggests that there is still quite a way to go if schools are to create the kind of co-operation with parents which will truly support their children's learning. Children spend much more of their time at home than in school and their parents are their first teachers from whom they continue to learn throughout childhood. There is a wide variation in how effectively parents contribute to children's learning and the more a school works with them, the more they may understand the value of their contribution to their children's education.

Schools will also need to recognise that many women who would previously have been at home all day may now be working and their time to spend with their children may be much more limited than in the past. This makes it all the more important to help them to use the time they have with their children in profitable ways.

Atkin *et al.* (1988) suggest that when parents understand what the school is trying to do, identify with its goals and support its efforts, understand something of their role as educators and take an interest in and provide support for their children's school work then the effects can be dramatic and long-lasting. Parents are a valuable resource and have unique opportunities to contribute to their children's education. The school needs to harness this resource for children's learning.

Supporting work with parents

If the school is large enough it may be a good idea to make relationships with parents the particular responsibility of one member of staff. This person could be responsible for planning and arranging contact with parents and ensuring that all parents are involved with the school as far as possible. S/he would agree with colleagues about meetings to be arranged and material to be sent out to parents. S/he would also encourage everyone to find out as much as possible about each child's home background and generally foster really useful and profitable parent–staff relationships. This could be a role for an assistant or a teacher.

How teachers and parents view each other

Both parents and teachers tend to have stereotypes of each other, and the parents' views of teachers will have been largely formed by their own experience and level of education. This has left some people very hesitant about entering a school and talking with their children's teachers. Parents may see teachers as the fount of all knowledge and wisdom, as intimidating figures or as rather underpaid employees. Teachers, for their part, often blame parents for the problems that their children create in school and frequently comment that it is the parents who do not come to school whom they would most like to see. Teachers may also hold the view that working-class parents are not particularly interested in their children's progress at school. This is often not true and such parents may be hesitant about coming into school, because of their own experience of schooling which they may remember as a rather unhappy one. They may be shy of talking to teachers and may also have some difficulty in finding time to come into school, either because of the demands of younger children or those of their work.

One rather old study of teachers' views of parents noted that many held negative views, particularly about black parents: mainly that they were 'over-concerned with their children's education', 'had too high expectations', 'lacked understanding of British education' and so on. A more recent study of inequalities in education of race, class and gender (Gillborn and Mirza 2000) found that although Afro-Caribbean children started school with some of the highest attainment levels of any group, they left school with the lowest attainment. This suggests that perhaps the black parents' high expectations may have had some justification.

Tizard et al. (1988), in their study, found that virtually all parents said they gave their children help with school work and more black than white parents started to teach their children to read before they started school. It would seem that there are really very few parents who are not interested in their children's education but some are hesitant about coming to the school.

The information parents need

In another rather old study, Atkins et al. (1988) suggest that schools do not give parents sufficient of the right sort of information. Parents get their ideas of what the school is doing mainly from what their children say about it and from looking at and hearing about the work their children are doing. They will probably not be aware of the educational philosophy of the school, its policies and teaching strategies. Teachers too rarely explain what the term's work will cover and suggest ways in which parents might help. Nor do they always explain the processes by which they are helping children to learn. In general parents tend to get the message that teachers would rather they left the business of educating children to them. In practice most parents try to help and this is a resource which should be harnessed more often.

Feedback on children's progress and behaviour

Tizard *et al.* (1988) found that teachers did not give parents a great deal of feedback on children's progress. In the reception classes they studied, 41 per cent of white parents and 16 per cent of black parents had been told how their child's reading compared with that of other children. In the middle infants these figures were 44 per cent and 23 per cent. They were concerned to find that only 20 per cent of parents had been told that their child was having difficulties when testing suggested that the overall figure was considerably higher. Only 12 per cent of parents had been told that their child posed behaviour problems in school, although the teachers said that 26 per cent of children posed such problems. There was also a feeling on the part of some parents that teachers tended to be defensive about problems rather than being prepared to discuss them openly. This study too is now old and we must hope that the situation is now rather better. Parents really need to know what their children are doing in school and many will welcome real involvement. Even the least well-educated parent has something to offer his or her children and schools need to seek and welcome their support.

Parents as partners

Research suggests that there is much to be gained by treating parents as partners in the education of their children. If, as studies suggest, the large majority of parents are keen to help their children, this is a resource which teachers would do well to use. Atkin *et al.* (1988: 59) note that evidence suggests that parental familiarity with the school tends to:

- sharpen their sense of parenting, rather than blurring the distinctions from teaching;
- promote a positive view of school life which is nevertheless sanguine about its weaknesses and limitations;
- serve as a stimulus to the development of home-made, compensatory strategies to tackle perceived difficulties, as they affect their children.

There have been a number of studies of parents hearing their children read on a regular basis and in all cases this has been found to be beneficial. Children's interest in reading has been found to increase and they become more motivated towards school learning. There are also gains in that there are closer relationships between teachers and parents as a result of this development.

Parental contributions to the child's learning

Parents contribute life experience as well as accumulating knowledge of their own child's (or children's) development and individual characteristics and have the advantage of experiencing minute-by-minute child contact in a variety of situations. They too can appraise their child's responsiveness; they can make predictions as to outcomes and make a match between what the child needs and what can be done with whatever resources and support the home has to offer.

The success of programmes for parents reading with their children suggests that there is scope for similar programmes in mathematics. There are many opportunities available to parents in the home for helping children to learn basic mathematical skills in practical situations. Parents may also help by playing games with their children which involve knowledge of number facts. This is a resource which schools would do well to use, perhaps by sending home books and suggestions.

Nursery and reception class teachers are well aware that children's home backgrounds make a difference to the way children settle into school. Wells (1985) found that the strongest association with reading attainment at age seven was the child's knowledge of written language at entry to school. Tizard et al. (1988) found that letter identification at nursery stage was a stronger predictor of reading ability at top infant level than concepts about print or word-matching. They also found that the children of parents who tried to teach them to read and used books scored higher at later stages. The number of books a child had access to was also a predictor of good performance.

Tizard et al. (1988) also found that families with high incomes did no more than other families to help their children, but gave them more experience with books. They were also likely to have greater knowledge of schools and believe that success was due to family influence. Mothers with higher educational qualifications were more likely to have positive attitudes towards helping their children but did not give their children significantly more help. Progress in reading and writing through the infant school was significantly related to parental contact with the school.

Hughes (1986) investigated the mathematical knowledge possessed by pre-school children and found that when children were asked to work in practical situations their knowledge was considerably greater than might be expected. He found that, even at this early stage, there was about a year's difference in performance between children from working-class and those from middle-class homes. This suggests that schools need to do all they can to help parents to prepare their children for school. A number of schools have developed packs of material which parents of pre-school children can use at home with their children in preparation for school. These encourage parents to use opportunities for children's learning and help them to understand what the school may want later.

Home–school links

There are a number of ways in which a school can facilitate home–school links, including the obvious ones like establishing a parents', teachers' and friends' association and making use of the home–school agreement. Schools can also:

- provide social functions where parents, teachers and other interested parties can mix on an informal basis;
- organise parents' meetings in a flexible way so that everyone has a chance to come;
- provide opportunities for parents in small groups to discuss with teachers common problems. This requires skill on the teacher's part but could be helpful to parents and also to teachers in understanding how different parents view things;
- if there is space in the school, establish a parents' room where parents can meet, make coffee, look at books and undertake work for the school's benefit;
- develop a plan in which a parent is responsible for involving other parents in each particular road in the catchment area, welcoming new parents and visiting parents who don't come to meetings;
- develop shared reading plans where the parents agree to hear the child read at home and note what has been read;
- involve parents in work in mathematics, suggesting ways in which they could help their children practise necessary skills;
- involve parents in topic work or work in history and geography, perhaps asking for stories about their youth or inviting them to help with an outing or with collecting material and information;
- ask parents to help by recording stories for children to follow with text;
- ask parents who can do so to type stories by children at their dictation; these stories can then become reading material for the child who has written them and others.

Communication with parents

Parents have a unique view of their children which is much more comprehensive than a teacher's can possibly be. Teachers have therefore a good deal to learn from parents about the children they teach, but it is not always easy to provide an opportunity for doing this. What is needed is a meeting during the course of the first term of the year, if possible where you meet with the parents of each child and you inform each other about the particular child. The parents inform you about their child and how they view what seems to be happening in school and you inform the parents about the child's work and behaviour and tell them about the work the class will be doing in the near future and how they can help. You and the parents can also use the opportunity to discuss frankly any problems they or their child seem to be encountering and discuss how you and they can work together to overcome them. It is also important in talking with parents to try to keep the discussion positive. Even if there are some very negative things about the child you need to try to talk about them as something which together you can overcome.

This kind of parent–teacher relationship is an ideal to be aimed at which might, in some circumstances, be rather difficult to achieve in practice. Your headteacher may not agree with this way of working, some parents may not wish to be involved to this extent or could not spare the time to come to talk to you, or you feel that you are just so busy that you can't spare the time either. What you need to remember as teacher is that there is so much to be learned from parents about the children in your class that you should use any opportunity which occurs to find out more about them. This is particularly true if you teach the youngest children.

Studies suggest that there are two further ways in which teachers are not always effective in communicating with parents.

Problems with teachers' professional language

Teachers are inclined to use what parents see as educational jargon. The problem about jargon is that one person's jargon is another person's technical language. Teachers quite properly have ways of talking about what they do which are particular to the education profession but may be confusing to other people. It is a good idea for a group of teachers to try to think of all the words and phrases they use which may be seen by others as jargon. For example, core subjects, Key Stages, SATs, SENCOs, attainment levels and many other words and phrases are unfamiliar to parents because they have come in since the parents were at school themselves. You need to either avoid using them when talking to parents or explain them.

The appearance and content of communications

The appearance of communications to parents is also important and now all schools have computers anyone can produce good-looking material. General communications to parents should be short and laid out so that they are easy and quick to read, perhaps with large headings which stand out. The language needs to be friendly and jargon-free; complicated sentences should be avoided. Parents have usually a good deal to distract their attention and anything complicated or long will probably not be read. Where appropriate, communications will need to be in more than one language so that they are intelligible to all parents. Parents themselves may be able to help with translating and rewriting documents in other languages.

Working in partnership

If parents are really going to be partners in their children's education they need to be taken into the confidence of the school to a large extent.

Discuss plans for children's learning

Many of the plans for learning should be discussed with parents. School policies should also be discussed and be made available on request. At the level of the individual class the teacher needs to inform parents about the work being planned. There is much to be said for holding class meetings at which the teacher talks to parents about the work that the children will be doing in the coming term and suggests ways in which they can help. Methods need to be explained as well as outcomes so that parents learn how to work with their children in ways which complement the work the teacher is doing.

Class newsletter

You may also like to consider a regular class newsletter, perhaps one each term, which informs parents about the work in hand and suggests ways in which they can help. This might also include information about school journeys and visits and what is needed for them and what should be gained from them as well as what may be needed for different aspects of other work. A newsletter may be a good place to ask for specific help with particular activities, such as helping with a school trip or making costumes for a play. It will, of course, be important not to cover the same ground as any school newsletter and again it may be necessary to enlist the help of certain parents to translate the document into other languages.

Information about their child's progress

Most teachers will regard it as important that children see their progress as improving on their own performance and will want to limit the extent to which children are discouraged by comparison with the progress of other children, particularly where less able children are concerned. However, parents will certainly want to know not only where their child stands currently but also how he or she compares with other children of the same age. In most cases this will be a fairly complex picture with children being well up with the age group or beyond it for some work and doing less well in others. You will need to explain to parents the way in which the Standard Assessment Tasks give the results in different levels for children at the appropriate stages.

How parents can help their child

Discussion about the stage a child is at needs to be followed up by discussion of what the teacher and the parents can do to help a child in the areas where he or she is at the lower levels. Try to have some really positive suggestions about ways in which the parents can help and give them a clear idea of what you are planning to do.

It is important in these discussions to keep a positive view of all that is being said. Try to emphasise the areas in which the child is doing well and be positive about the action to be taken where he or she is doing less well. Try also to avoid stressing what not to do and concentrate instead on what the parents can do.

Discussing behaviour

Discussion with each child's parents needs to go further than discussion about the core subjects. Progress in other areas needs to be discussed along with any problems of behaviour or other problems which worry you or the parent. Teachers, not unnaturally, feel that this is a very delicate area which could imply they are not doing their job or that the parents are not doing their job. Tizard *et al.* (1988) report that, in the one in four cases in their study where teachers actually discussed behaviour with parents, about one-third of parents responded positively, another third agreed with the teacher, about one-quarter responded negatively and the remainder couldn't see the problem. This suggests that children often differ in their behaviour between home and school and that there is everything to be gained from parents and teachers each knowing about the problems the other finds and working together to overcome them. Parents are also often grateful for the opportunity to discuss with someone else the problems they encounter.

Home visiting

It has been customary for most discussion about children to take place on the school premises. However, there is a great deal to be said for visiting the children's homes to discuss them with their parents. Parents feel more confident on their own ground and are usually very appreciative that a teacher has taken the trouble to come and see them. This kind of meeting can be more relaxed than a meeting in school, where there may be others waiting to see you, and it gives the opportunity for you to learn about the parents' view of the child. You can also learn a great deal about a child by seeing his or her home setting and the discussion tends to go better than it sometimes does at school. This takes time, which tends to be a problem for busy teachers, but is very rewarding. It is important to develop techniques for finishing a meeting so that you do not spend too long in any one home. Usually putting papers together and making summarising statements give an indication that the meeting is ending. These are also useful techniques for concluding meetings in school.

School reports

All schools must now send parents a written report on their child's progress, stating where the child has reached in the National Curriculum and giving information about skill development, behaviour, attitudes and any problems as well as information about the average class performance. It is important to be positive as well as honest and there is much to be said for a form of report which allows the parents and possibly older children to comment.

Parents in the classroom

It is fairly common practice in primary schools to invite parents to help in the classroom or about the school. This has a lot of advantages in that parents begin to see how teaching takes place and this not only helps them to support their own children but may well also make them good advocates for the school. The teacher is also helped in many of the tasks which take time from the more professional aspects of teaching.

There are also problems. The first and most difficult problem is that of whether you select the parents who come in to help or take all comers. Where parents are selected this can lead to a good deal of bitterness and upset, but avoids the problem of the parent who wants to take over or the parent who is not very literate. On the other hand, the kinds of parent who are not selected may be just those who would benefit most from being in the school and working with teachers. The problem of the parent who wants to take over may disappear if you are clear what you want and the problem of literacy may be largely a matter of allocating the right tasks to the right people. However, this too may be a problem because inferences can be made from the tasks allocated to parents. It is also important to stress to parents the need for confidentiality about the work of children other than their own.

Another problem arises from the fact that there are now more paid assistants in most schools and parents may find it difficult to accept that one person is paid for supporting the teacher in the classroom and another is expected to be a volunteer. This can be partly dealt with by the tasks each group is asked to do.

In inviting parents to work in the school, you will need to discover what any individual parent has to offer. A parent may have special knowledge and skills which could be widely used in the school. It is also important to plan the work of parents and any other ancillary staff in considerable detail. Bennett and Kell (1989), studying the work of infant classes, make the point that in many of the classes they observed ancillary workers and parents who were left to their own devices and in some cases were not supporting the teacher in a very satisfactory way because the teacher had not thought out how to use their services in sufficient detail.

If you have parents or assistants hearing reading, for example, you should make it clear what the listener should do if a child is stuck for a word or makes a mistake. If parents are supervising children working with sand and water, or working at cooking, they need to know how they can introduce appropriate language and encourage children to experiment and discover. Play is more effective for learning when an adult takes part, but the adult needs to know what he or she is doing. Some parents will do these things instinctively. Others will need help, but in helping them to see what is needed in the classroom you will also be helping them to see what it is important to do in the home. This all suggests that teachers need tactfully to give parents some training in some aspects of helping in the classroom. It may be best to start with asking them to undertake tasks such as preparing materials in the first instance and gradually involving them with the children. A summary of working with parents is given in Review 20.1.

Review 20.1 Working with parents

1 Do I know all the parents of the children in my class by sight and by name?

2 How often do I meet parents as individuals to discuss their children's progress?

3 Do I listen to what parents can tell me about their children and take note of it as well as telling them about my own observations?

4 When I discuss each child with his or her parents do I discuss behaviour as well as academic and other progress?

5 Do I explain to parents the way I am trying to teach their children?

6 Do I keep parents informed about the work we are doing in class?

7 Do I make positive suggestions about ways in which parents can help their children in different aspects of the curriculum?

8 Do I try to avoid jargon and explain the terms we are using in school?

9 Am I ever too defensive about what I am doing?

10 Do I know about and am I making use of any particular skills and knowledge among the parents of the children in my class?

11 Am I making good use of parents in the classroom?

12 Do I plan what parent helpers will do each day, so that they reinforce my work?

13 Have I seriously considered visiting my children's parents in their home? How could I use such an opportunity?

Chapter 21

Evaluation and assessment

Evaluation and assessment have become more important aspects of teachers' work in recent years, especially as a result of the requirement to assess children at the end of each Key Stage. Teachers and schools have been under too much pressure because of national tests and it is hoped that this will be eased a little if the suggested change is adopted of giving these tests when the teacher thinks each child is ready for it. This would be a much more useful arrangement than the present situation where children's wider education tends to be neglected for a period while they are being prepared for the tests.

Normal living involves us all in the process of making judgements about people and events in order to predict what may happen and decide what to do next. We do this from a very early age and it becomes our response to many situations. This is evident when you go to a course or if you are on holiday and meet new people. You listen to them, look at them and ask questions to discover ways in which they are like you and the ways in which they differ and what their interests are and so on. The judgements you make may not always be accurate, but this may not matter in such circumstances, particularly if you are aware that you are making judgements on inadequate evidence.

Educational assessment

As a professional teacher, however, you need to be much more sure of your evidence because much depends upon the outcome of your judgements. You therefore need to extend the everyday practice of making judgements in order to be sure that the judgements you make are as valid as possible.

The Assessment Reform Group (1999: 2) studied assessment in a number of schools and concluded that 'assessment which is explicitly designed to promote learning is the single most powerful tool we have for raising standards and empowering lifelong learners'. They suggest that:

Teachers must be involved in gathering information about pupils' learning and encouraging pupils to review their work critically and constructively.

They do this by:

- observing pupils – this involves listening to how they describe their work and their reasoning;
- questioning, using open questions, phrased to invite pupils to explore their ideas and their reasoning;
- setting tasks in a way which requires pupils to use certain skills or apply ideas;
- asking pupils to communicate their thinking through drawings, artefacts, actions, role play, concept-mapping as well as writing;
- discussing words and how they are being used.

(Assessment Reform Group Report 1999: 8)

As a teacher, irrespective of external tests, you need to check and test and observe children, question them and explore their thinking about what they are doing, so that you can lead them on from the point they have reached. Assessment is one of the most powerful factors for improving learning. The following are important aspects of classroom assessment:

- effective feedback to children on their performance;
- their active involvement in their own learning;
- using the results of assessment to plan teaching;
- recognising that assessment has an important influence on children's motivation and self-esteem;
- the need to train children to assess themselves.

Criteria for assessment systems

The report of the Task Group on Assessment and Testing (Ofsted 1988: 2), which set out the ideas on which the present systems of national testing are based, gave four criteria which it felt that any system of assessment should satisfy.

- The assessment should give direct information about pupils' attainment in relation to objectives: they should be criterion referenced.
- The results should provide a basis for decisions about pupils' learning needs.
- The scales or grades should be capable of comparison across classes and schools if teachers, pupils and parents are to share a common language and common standards: so the results should be calibrated or moderated.
- The ways in which the criteria or scales are set up and used should relate to expected routes of educational development, giving some continuity to a pupil's assessment at different ages: the assessment should relate to progression.

Effective teacher assessment for raising standards

Ofsted (1998: 5) lists the following main findings about schools where teacher assessment was used effectively to raise standards.

- Teachers decide how and when they will assess pupils' attainment at the same time as they plan the work.
- Teachers are proficient in using a range of assessment techniques in the classroom, such as asking questions, observing pupils and setting tasks or tests at the end of a series of lessons.
- Manageable written recording systems are used alongside retention of evidence.
- Teachers make accurate judgements of pupils' work based on reliable sources of evidence.
- There are effective arrangements for moderating teachers' judgements about pupils' work.
- There are effective procedures for reporting on pupils' progress and attainment.

Good assessment systems

Ofsted (1998) found that the best systems involved teachers selecting a piece of work from each child each term, annotating it with a note of the level reached and noting future targets which had been discussed with the pupil. They found that teachers were generally accurate in their judgements about pupils' standards of attainment and undertook regular moderation of work with other teachers which contributed to this. There was often sampling of pupils' work by year group co-ordinators and subject co-ordinators. They were critical of the fact that teachers seldom shared attainment objectives with their pupils and the pupils were not generally aware of the criteria by which they were being assessed.

The process of evaluation and assessment is continuous. It starts before the children come to you and must be there at every stage, sometimes as part of a formal process, but more often as part of your day-to-day observation of children at work. It is important that you are on the lookout for children who are underachieving and that you note pupil attitudes and the effect of these on how they learn.

Marking work

The way you mark work is also important. Children should be made aware of the criteria you are using to make judgements and be encouraged to use these criteria to judge their own work and sometimes that of their peers. A number of studies suggest that although this happens from time to time, very often children still tend to think that the presentation of their work is more important than the content. It is also important in marking work to comment on those aspects where you think the child has done well and to suggest ways in which the work could be improved.

School assessment systems

Many schools have built up assessment materials for use at various stages in the school. These complement the Standard Assessment Tasks and may include standardised tests of various kinds as well as teacher-developed materials. There is also value in noting incidental occurrences such as unusual behaviour or movement or odd facial expression in the classroom as they occur.

Self-evaluation by teachers

You also need to evaluate your own performance, skills and abilities as well as those of the children and appraisal should help with this. Many of the chapters in this book suggest questions you might ask yourself and provide tools for assessing yourself.

The language of assessment and evaluation

The words 'assessment' and 'evaluation' are frequently used as if they were interchangeable. They are not really quite the same. There have been many definitions of these two words and they tend to mean slightly different things in different contexts. For the purposes of this book, assessment refers to the process of gathering and collating evidence; evaluation occurs when you make judgements based on that evidence.

If you are to decide what evidence to look for in making an assessment, it is important that you have in mind criteria against which you will weigh the evidence you find. This means that if, for example, you are checking to see whether a child can add numbers to ten, you are clear on what evidence you will base your judgement. Are you looking for this ability as mental arithmetic? Are you prepared for the child to use apparatus of some kind to help in the calculation? What about counting on the fingers? It will depend upon the age of the child which of these is acceptable, but you need to know what you are looking for before you set out to check in each situation.

There are a number of other words used in the process of evaluation which it may be helpful to define.

- *Formative evaluation*   Assessment of work while it is being carried out.
- *Summative evaluation*   Assessment carried out when a piece of work is completed.

- *Process/product* In any evaluation you can look at what children are getting out of doing something (process) or at what they finally achieve (product).
- *Validity* A test or assessment can be regarded as valid if it can be shown to test what it sets out to test. Thus a written intelligence test given to a child who cannot read might be said to be an invalid test of his or her reasoning ability.
- *Reliability* To be reliable a test needs to give similar results when given to the same person on different occasions.
- *Criterion referencing* A criterion-referenced test is one in which the results are compared with previously defined criteria or objectives.
- *Norm referencing* A norm-referenced test is one in which the results are compared with norms for children of a particular age. Norms are usually established by extensive testing on large samples of the population.
- *Sampling* We can never know everything that is in a child's mind. Any test is only a sample of what the child knows, understands and can do at that particular time and may not be a true representation of that child's ability or achievement. It is no more than the best information we can obtain.

Assessment by observation

The basic method of assessing children is that of observation. This may be observation of the child's performance or of his or her work. Observations may be extended by testing. There is a sense in which all forms of assessment are a kind of observation. Tests and examinations, records and check-lists are devices to make observation more systematic and therefore more likely to be accurate. But you can only assess what is evident. A child may know and be able to do more than he or she can demonstrate in a test situation. You need to be continually asking yourself whether a child's performance is representative of what he or she knows and whether the sample piece of work or behaviour you are considering is typical and whether the result would be the same on another occasion.

The same is true when you want to make assessments of the class as a whole. One reason why a teacher's assessment may sometimes be more accurate than a test is because the teacher helps the child to demonstrate what he or she knows and can do in all sorts of situations, whereas a test only reveals the child's unsupported performance in one situation. The sample of the child's performance which the teacher sees is thus rather more likely to be a valid one and to reflect his or her potential, but your judgement will nevertheless be helped by comparing your conclusions with test results.

Observation in the normal sense has the advantage that you can take into account at the same time many features acknowledged to be important but not easy to test. For example, in hearing a child read, you may note the words he or she is able to recognise, the ability to put them together into sentences, the child's understanding of what he or she is reading, his or her ability to make inferences from and make sense of the text and the mistakes made and their possible significance. It would be difficult to find a test which could do all those things at once with any validity, and while you may be mistaken in your judgements you are in a position to follow up your findings and check them further.

Observation and experience

One disadvantage of this kind of assessment is that you will only see what your experience, background and frame of reference will allow. You may miss things which an observer with different background experience would see because you have not experienced them before. For example, if, in hearing a child read, you have had no experience of considering the significance of the types of errors made by children, you will probably miss some of the particular clues being offered. Perhaps the really significant point to note here is that the skill of observation is one of the most important skills a teacher can have and it is one that you need to work to improve all the time.

Developing your observation skills

One way of improving your own skill in observation is to look at children and their work with other teachers, who, because they are different people who bring different experience to bear on the situation, will see differently from you and may thus enlarge your seeing. This is particularly important at the beginning of your teaching career when you are learning what to expect from children at a particular age and stage of schooling, although it is also true that experience can sometimes make a teacher look at situations less sensitively if some aspects of teaching have become a matter of habit. Many schools use various forms of moderation to make judgements about their children and this benefits everyone.

It is also helpful to teachers to have an assistant who, while she has not your professional knowledge and skills, may see things differently in a way which will stimulate your own thinking, even if her views may seem to you to be a bit amateur. Just having the opportunity to talk things over with someone who also knows the children can be very helpful to you both.

Checking observation and considering what can be recorded

It should also be noted that observation is not confined to what one can see. It involves checking by questioning and discussion and exploring how children see things. Observation is also the main way in which we assess children's progress in more nebulous areas such as personal and social development. Such areas need as much thought and care in assessing them as in making assessments of academic work. Teachers are sometimes reluctant to make formal judgements about more personal aspects of a child's development, but actually do it informally all the time. While it is natural to be hesitant about putting statements about such matters as a child's ability to relate to others on record, it should be remembered that personal development happens and teachers affect it whether it is recorded or not; it may be better to give it careful consideration, thinking about the needs and problems of each child, rather than leaving it to chance. You don't avoid making assessments by not discussing or considering them.

Formal and informal observation

You can assess by observation formally or informally. In the course of your everyday work there will be points which arise which you may need to note. A child will give an answer which makes it clear that he or she has understood something important and made a major step forward. There will be other situations where the opposite happens and a child whom you thought had grasped something demonstrates a lack of understanding. There will be situations where you discover that you have over- or underestimated a child's ability in the work you have allocated and it will be important to remember this and make a change for the next piece of work. There may also be critical incidents in the classroom when you learn something about the way certain children react to particular situations or discover that your organisation or planning was not as good as you thought.

It is not easy to find time to note such incidents, yet they may offer you valuable information. It may be that you try to reserve a few minutes at lunch time and at the end of the day to note down anything of the kind which you have noticed in the course of the day. Your assistant may also be encouraged to look out for such incidents and doing this will not only be helpful to you but will also help her development.

There may also be some opportunities during class time when you can enter a note. It is important that these notes are made in places where you will link them with the notes you make when you are checking on particular children's learning. Having a page in a loose-leaf file for each child for odd notes is valuable and this can be filed when completed alongside notes for each child about other progress. It is also worth remembering that we are not far off being able to record speech with a computer which will translate it into print. This will make record-keeping a quite different activity, in which you will probably need to guard against recording more than you will ever have time to read.

Observation can also be carried out more formally to check specific aspects of learning. This may be the observation of a group or an individual.

Here you need to decide in advance exactly what you are looking for and the way you are going to check it or whether you are simply going to observe or enter into conversation with the child or children to see what their thinking may be. You may also need to decide in advance whether you are going to use the opportunity to extend thinking or whether you are simply observing. Then you need to decide after the observation whether the children in question have grasped the work or whether you need to observe and teach further.

Assessing children's learning ability

You may sometimes be assessing not only the actual learning that has taken place but also the children's learning ability. When you are observing a group, you may be looking at how the children share group tasks, the kind of discussion that takes place, the involvement of the group members, the emergence of leaders within the group, time spent off-task and so on.

It is worth trying to reserve some time for this kind of observation each week. If you plan to observe a small number of children in detail each day you can gradually work round the class and spend time observing every child in some detail. If you encourage your assistant to do this too, the activity will not only be useful to you, but will also be a learning opportunity for her.

Involving children in assessing their work

As children grow and develop they gradually learn to assess many things about themselves and their work. They can make a useful contribution to your knowledge of how well they are learning and developing if you involve and encourage them in assessing various aspects of their work. Their ability to do this should increase as they grow older.

It can be useful to arrange for children in pairs to exchange the written work they have each done, look at their partner's work critically (but being careful not to overdo it!) and report to each other. Looking critically at someone else's work can help you to look critically at your own. A number of the ideas in this chapter lend themselves to involving the children.

Another idea for helping them to look critically at their work is to spend some time discussing with them what they think you take into account when you mark their work. You could then go on to ask them to go through a particular piece of work before they hand it in and write at the bottom of it what they think you will say about it. This can be very revealing, both in their views of what you look for in marking work and also their accuracy in applying the same criteria to their own work.

Testing

A test might be regarded as one way of making observation rather more objective. Teachers need to give tests for a variety of reasons and there is certainly a place for both teacher-made and standardised tests as well as SATs.

Teachers often feel that there is something special about standardised tests which makes the results of a child's performance in such a test much more reliable than a teacher's judgement. While it is certainly true that occasionally a test result will make a teacher think again about a child, the judgement of an experienced teacher is also a very good guide, as was noted in the Ofsted (1998) survey of teacher assessment at Key Stage 2.

One of the reasons for feeling that standardised tests give special information is that they are the nearest thing we have to an objective assessment and subjective judgement is often doubted. There is a sense, however, in which all assessment must be subjective. In the first instance there are subjective views involved somewhere in the choice of test, whether chosen by the DfES, an LEA, the head or the teacher. There is also an element of subjective judgement in interpreting the results.

A particular point to note about testing is that there is a difference between testing for mastery and testing for other purposes. When you give children a test on something they have learned in order to see how well they know it, you should expect a high proportion of good answers from everyone if the teaching and learning have been adequate. If you are testing to discover how each child stands relative to his or her peers or to help you make decisions about grouping children, you need a spread of scores, with some children getting very high scores and others very low scores, because the purpose of the exercise is to differentiate among the children.

It is important to distinguish between testing for mastery and testing for discrimination since the overuse of discriminatory tests is very discouraging to children who do badly. Generally speaking success leads to success and the teacher's task is to organise so that every child is able to succeed at some level.

A diagnostic test which is planned to discover problems may have any kind of score for any child because it is designed to discover difficulties. The SATs are mainly designed as mastery tests, although it will obviously be possible to identify children who have problems which need to be explored further.

Purposes of tests and observation

Teachers normally use tests and observations to find answers to the following questions.

Is this child or are these children ready for the next stage or for a particular form of learning or teaching?

In this context you might also test to discover what a child can do and what he or she already knows. You might be interested too in how the child sets about the task. Intelligence tests of various kinds might be said to come into this category, which may include some diagnostic tests. The SATs are intended to serve this purpose among others.

Has this child or have these children learned what I wanted them to learn?

This is probably the most common reason for testing in school and teachers usually make their own tests for this purpose. It may be a good idea gradually to develop a set of test materials for work in specific areas of curriculum, which can be given to individuals or groups when you feel they are ready to have their work checked. If you regard each test you give as feeding into a test system over a period and code and store it carefully, you will in due course build up a body of material to use in this way. This also means that the time spent on devising tests is used to full advantage. Some schools do this on a year-group or school basis.

How does this child perform relative to others of the same age?

Most primary teachers like to encourage children to work to improve their own performance and discourage too much rivalry. There is, nevertheless, a need to know how a child is doing relative to norms of some kind and you may want to make this clear to parents in a tactful way. This will emerge clearly from National Curriculum testing, but you need to explain to parents and others that the relationship is a complex one, perhaps with a child doing well in one aspect and less well in another. This should also make it clear to both children and parents in which areas there is a need for improvement.

There may be a case for occasional use of a standardised test which gives national norms to check whether there are children who are underachieving. It is very easy to regard the group you teach as the norm and accept some underachievement without realising it.

What particular difficulties is this child experiencing?

When a child fails to make normal progress, you need to discover why. You also need to discover just what it is the child doesn't understand or can't do. You may therefore need diagnostic material as well as your own observation. There is some published diagnostic material, but you really need to develop your own alongside this. You need spelling tests which identify gaps in phonic knowledge and lack of knowledge of spelling rules. You also need tests of mathematics which include knowledge of number bonds and tables and identify difficulties with particular operations. Such tests may be on paper or recorded or on computer and can be used by individuals, groups or the whole class and can be especially useful at the beginning of the year when you are finding out what children know and can do. Here again, if you work over a period developing test material, you can gradually build up a kit of diagnostic tests. It is helpful not only to collect test material but also material for teaching and practising the learning which the diagnosis identifies as being necessary.

Record-keeping

Record-keeping has always been an important part of the teacher's work but the assessment required by the National Curriculum has made even greater demands. Teachers now need evidence of children's work which enables them to decide the level each child has reached in the core subjects. There is also a need for long-term records which follow a child through the school and for records of your own input to work and the corresponding output from the children. The teacher or the school which will be providing for a particular child later on will also need information from you and you need to remember this as time goes by.

Purposes of record-keeping

There are many reasons for record-keeping besides those of recording progress in the National Curriculum. An important reason for record-keeping is continuity. If you should happen to have a long illness or leave your present school in mid-year, all that you have learned about your children may be lost if you do not leave appropriate records so that someone else can take up where you left off.

Records may help you to match work to individual children and help them to overcome learning problems. Something a child does once may not appear to be significant, but if it happens several times it may give you important clues to the nature of a difficulty. You may not notice this if you do not keep appropriate records. It would be difficult to keep this kind of record for all the children all the time but you can do it for a small number who have difficulties.

Value of background information

Important items from a child's background over a period may help you to understand his or her difficulties and put you in a better position to help. For example, a child who has changed schools a number of times may be insecure and need help in filling gaps in learning. A child whose sibling has some kind of disability may find it difficult to cope with the extra attention that the sibling needs from his or her parents. Background information of this kind is sensitive and you or your headteacher may need to ask the parents concerned if they mind having it recorded so that teachers are aware of any difficulties the child may have. There is much to be said for involving parents in some cases in compiling background records of children.

Records of your teaching

You also need to keep records which show what worked and what didn't work with individuals and with the group. This means keeping records of what you have tried and with what success. Such information is important for your development as a teacher as well as that of the children. Here again it is very enlightening occasionally to ask children for their views on a particular lesson.

Records to inform others

Your records are also important information for the teacher who takes your class after you and for your headteacher and possibly for a year-leader or co-ordinator who may be relying on you for information about children and the success of the programme planned for the year group. You may also need to provide information for other services from time to time such as the school psychological service, the health service or social services.

Assessing the National Curriculum (SEAC 1990) makes the following points about the records of children's progress. They should:

- be simple to complete so that they do not cause too much interference in classroom activities and practice;
- include all the relevant information so that they may readily inform decisions about future action;
- be meaningful to others who may need to have access to them;
- be accessible to pupils so that they can enhance pupils' understanding of the teaching, learning and assessment process.

What needs to be recorded

Every school should keep long-term records giving relevant information about each child's background and you should be able to turn to such records to discover what you need to know about your children. Background records ought to give some health information. You need to know about disabilities or other problems, particularly when they are not very obvious. You need to be aware of children who should wear glasses, children with inadequate hearing, children who are colour blind and so on. You also need to know of any children with problems, such as a weak heart, or asthma or epilepsy, which could affect what you do with them in school or any children who have had long absences through illness. You also need some background information about the child's family.

If you are to take on where a previous teacher left off, you need to know the facts about work covered in the previous year. The National Curriculum makes this easier in some ways even though it demands a great deal from teachers by way of recording. It should be possible to review a child's progress right the way through schooling.

School records or records to be passed on need to contain only what might be described as considered records. Your own day-to-day notes, which may contain comments about individual children and the success or otherwise of particular pieces of work, are recorded for your benefit alone. These notes will inform your final records but be different from them.

We have already noted that it is helpful to keep a loose-leaf file with a page for each child. You can then add material and put the page into a longer-term record when it is full. You need to find time for talking with each child about his or her individual progress and agree targets for future work. The loose-leaf file will provide useful material for discussion.

Types of record

Recording is a time-consuming process and it is therefore important to find forms of recording which can be completed easily. Records can be classified as follows.

Notes of observations

These can be notes of things that occur which you feel are of interest and can be made day by day as things happen. You can make this kind of observation more systematic by observing and talking with a few children each week and recording these observations in greater detail. Notes of this kind, kept over a period, provide insight into a child's development.

Records of achievement

Primary schools are expected to keep records of achievement for children. SEAC (1990) describes a record of achievement as:

- a cumulative record of an individual child's achievements in school;
- compiled by the pupils, the teacher and others who are involved in the learning process;

- usually confined to positive achievement;
- the place to note personal and social attributes and a wider range of activities and experiences.

SEAC goes on to state the purposes which records of achievement might serve:

- to involve the child and parents more closely in planning and reviewing the child's progress;
- to enable teachers and parents to help pupils to develop as individuals;
- to ensure planned continuity and learning development across points of transition in the child's school career;
- to identify with parental help a child's strengths and weaknesses.

It is easy to see the benefits that might result from this kind of record. It encourages the child to develop the habit of self-assessment and involves parents and child in considering development. Parents thus become involved in what is happening to the child in school and aware also of the value of some of the child's out-of-school activities. It also involves teachers in considering how best to carry out this work, which will add to their understanding of the individual child.

A collection of specific information about each child's work and behaviour

You may make observations against a check-list of specific items such as the ability to work with others towards a particular goal or the ability to use the class library to find particular information. It is useful to identify a series of items and look for different things weekly, monthly or termly. Part of this record might be some form of profile. A profile has been described as a competency map which shows areas of weakness or strength, as can be seen in Review 21.1. Profile recording is particularly useful for non-measurable aspects of development. When a profile is used for personal characteristics it is important to see it as a starting point for improvement rather than a description of inborn characteristics. The example in Review 21.1 would be useful to discuss with a child and consider his or her view of how it should be completed.

Results of tests and assessments

Test scores and assessments are part of the process of implementing the National Curriculum and over a period they will show patterns which will be of interest. You need to be systematic in reviewing this kind of information about children. One way of doing this is to look particularly at the records of a small group of children each week so that over the term you look carefully at all the records of children's work. This can link up with individual discussions with children about their progress and the targets they might set for themselves.

A collection of samples of each child's work over a period

Many schools now collect samples of work in order to assess the levels each child is achieving, and if these are collected over a period they can give a good picture of a child's progress. While the collection of samples is not very time-consuming it is easy to collect more material than you really need and have difficulty in keeping it sorted. It can be useful to involve children in selecting work for their record folder. It is also useful to mark each item with the level you think it has achieved.

A record of progress through schemes with clear stages

A scheme which has clear stages, whether a published scheme or the teacher's own, provides a record of the stage each child has reached in the particular work concerned. This may be simply a matter of noting the page or chapter that a child has reached or the books he or she has read; children can very often keep this kind of record for themselves.

Check-lists

It can be helpful to use check-lists of such things as phonic knowledge and knowledge of number facts, ticking off the items as you check them.

Collection of errors made by an individual

Errors in reading, writing and number work provide a teacher with important clues to a child's thinking. These clues become increasingly informative if lists of errors are kept over a period. Children can help by doing some of this for themselves.

Lists of work covered or attempted

This is another record which children can keep for themselves. It may also be useful to make a duplicated sheet for each child of work done by the class over a term or year and then add a note of individual variations. These lists can then go into the children's record folders.

Notes made by children of work done

It will depend to some extent on the way you work and the age of your children whether and how you use this kind of record. It is helpful, on completing a project, for each child to note down the things he or she did as part of the work. It can also be useful to ask children to record what they did at the end of each session in a notebook kept for this purpose. If you review these notes they can give you some idea of how much work individuals are actually doing and the notebooks may suggest targets which individuals should try to achieve.

Notes of discussions held with children and their parents

We have already noted that it is valuable to have regular meetings with each child at which work is discussed and targets set. The information from these meetings then feeds into the meetings with parents. It is important to make notes of what is said at both these meetings for future reference. It can also be valuable to review each child's work with another teacher in order to check on your own conclusions.

Reports to parents

Schools are required to provide reports to parents on their children's attainment and progress at all stages including reception. The Qualifications and Curriculum Authority (1999: 32) suggests that these should contain the following information:

- brief comments on the child's progress in each subject and activity studied as part of the school curriculum – these should highlight strengths and development needs;
- the child's general progress;
- arrangements for parents to discuss the report with a teacher at the school;
- total number of sessions (half-days) since the child's last report or since the child entered the school, whichever is the later, and the percentage missed through unauthorised absence.

There should also be comparative data about children in the same age group, the same school and nationally. The Qualifications and Curriculum Authority (QCA) paper suggests that parents want to know how their child's performance compares with previous performance, the strengths and weaknesses, areas for development and improvement, how they can help and whether the child appears to be happy, settled and behaving well. They also suggest that it is important not to obscure low achievement or underachievement by the use of faint praise or by avoiding any mention of the problem.

Records to be passed on to the next school

Whether a child is transferring to a new school at the normal transfer age or transferring because the parents are moving him or her, the sending school has a responsibility to send on records. These should include:

- personal information about the child;
- the primary school record of achievement;
- National Curriculum assessment test records and teacher assessment;
- a folder of written work which represents the best the child can do;
- information about special educational needs or giftedness where this is applicable.

General points about records

In deciding what records to keep, bear in mind that you want records that are not only easy to maintain but also easy to use. Records which give you information at a glance are more likely to be used than long pieces of writing. Look, too, to see how much recording the children might do themselves. A factual record can be kept by children in some simple form from an early stage. Even five-year-olds can make a mark in a box when they finish something.

A school has to decide who has access to the records of an individual teacher. Ideally, records should be kept in a form that can be shared with children, parents and other teachers. This avoids having to make additional records for discussion with others or for passing on to the next teacher or school. However, it may be necessary to summarise records for passing on and there will need to be agreement about how much should be passed on to the next school.

There must also be agreement about for how long records which are not passed on should be kept. There may be queries long after a child has left the school and this suggests that the records of an individual child should probably be kept until he or she reaches school-leaving age.

Evaluation of the work of the teacher

Schools should monitor the performance of staff through providing regular appraisal and target-setting. All teachers need to reflect on and review their own performance and appraisal should help with this. Targets will reflect those the school has agreed with the LEA and the school's own target-setting. Monitoring will include observation of classroom teaching by team leaders, or, in small schools, the headteacher or deputy, giving feedback on previously agreed issues. It is also valuable, as we noted earlier, if it can be arranged, for teachers to observe each other. Arrangements for classroom observation should always be discussed beforehand, with the teacher whose work is being observed explaining the plans for the lesson, what he or she hopes the children will learn and the aspects of the lesson on which it would be helpful to have feedback. There should also be discussion as soon afterwards as possible.

Preparation for the appraisal interview should also involve you in self-evaluation, trying to identify the areas in which work seems to be successful and other areas in which there are problems which might benefit from discussion. The interview itself should be supportive and identify any training needs you may have and should conclude with a small number of agreed objectives for the coming period. Advice on target-setting suggests that targets should be SMART: Specific, Measurable, Achievable, Relevant and Time-related. There should be follow-up discussions later to discuss how things are going and whether there is a need to modify any of the targets agreed. Where appropriate there should be coaching to help develop any new approaches being considered. You may also need to update your job description.

Pupil progress is the next area in which you need to demonstrate effectiveness. You may have evidence from baseline assessments, SATs or internal and standardised tests to show that your pupils are making good progress.

Wider professional effectiveness is concerned with professional development and making an active contribution to achieving the aims of the school. It may be useful in this context to list any courses you have attended and any work you have done to develop work in the school more generally.

Finally, you will be judged on professional characteristics, such as motivating pupils, analysing and reflecting on work, teamwork and so on. Your headteacher will make an initial judgement on your application to the work and it will be checked by an external adviser. You may make your own initial self-evaluation and self-assessment using Review 21.1.

At a less formal level, your teaching assistant should be able to give you some feedback on a day-to-day basis, helping you to assess the effect your teaching had on particular children, or the way in which different children interpreted your instructions. You will, of course, be observing such things yourself, but it is always useful to have another person's observations and here again, this can be a learning opportunity for your assistant.

Teacher self-evaluation

This book has included a number of reviews to help you to determine your style and preferences and to assess your own performance.

Problems about assessment

Time

Every primary school teacher will be aware that the major problem about assessment is finding sufficient time to do it. You need to seek out ways of assessing which are part of your normal work and do not require any special activity. The time problem looms less large if you break it down into a small number of children to check each day and each week so that, in time, you get round the entire class. It also helps, particularly with older children, if you explain what you are doing and invite children's co-operation in not interrupting you when you are making checks on other children's progress. Here again, you should be training your assistant to help.

Provision for children with special educational needs and the very able

Children with special needs, in particular, will need work broken down into smaller steps than most children. Statements in the National Curriculum about what children should be able to do will need to be broken down to meet the needs of individuals and your evaluation of their work should be against targets which they are able to meet.

You should also consider the needs of the very able and the kind of targets you might set for them and how you will assess their progress.

Children whose home language is not English

It will obviously depend a good deal on how good a child's English is whether this poses a problem or not. There are likely to be some problems of understanding, even with older children. It may be possible to reword what is being asked in such a way that the child understands. As we saw earlier, it also helps if you try to say things using the same words when you are telling the children as a class what to do and it is also worth learning a few important words in the language which a number of the class speak. You may also have the benefit of some bilingual adults who may be ready to help and it may be necessary to enlist the help of a bilingual parent to translate questions from time to time. Other children may also be able to help in translating. In addition, it may be possible to make judgements from what the child does rather than what he or she says.

Children may be upset by not attaining as well as others

This is undoubtedly a danger but may to some extent be met by giving each child targets within his or her reach. Your attitude of expectancy that a child will achieve at a given level is also important – you need to convey to children that you believe in their ability to achieve.

Review 21.1 Evaluation and assessment

1 Do I plan assessment and evaluation at the same time as I plan programmes of work?

2 Do I use a range of assessment techniques to enable me to judge, not only each child's work, but also to ensure that the assessments I make are valid?

3 How do I make judgements about each child's performance? What evidence do I use? Does this give a fair and useful picture of the child in question?

4 Do the records I keep about individual children give a fair picture of each child in my class?

5 Do I discuss my assessments of children with other teachers? What could I learn from this?

6 Do I share with children the purposes of my teaching and the criteria by which I judge their work?

7 Do I encourage my children to evaluate their own work and perhaps discuss it with a partner and help them to do this by suggesting criteria?

8 Are my records both useful and manageable?

9 Do I give parents a sufficiently full picture of their child's progress and behaviour?

10 Could another teacher take my class on from where they are now using my records?

Chapter 22

Conclusion

We have now looked at all the main aspects of teaching and learning which are part of the difficult professional task of educating children. We have discussed all the factors involved in teaching a group of children and you should now be in a position to make decisions about all the issues involved in organisation and how you like to teach. You may like to look back at your answers to Reviews 5.1 and 5.2 and at some of the other reviews after a period of time and consider how things are working out.

Each decision you make at the beginning of the school year has implications for how you set about your task and for your long-term plans. You also need to consider how you will work towards the organisation you want and what you will do to train your children to work in the way you choose. If this is very different from their previous experience it may take time and you would be wise to introduce changes very gradually and one at a time. If the change you envisage is considerable, it may take half a term or more before you begin to see results. Be prepared for this and be prepared also to stop and consolidate or even go back if something isn't working.

A particular picture of the well-organised classroom has been implicit in much that has been said in this book. It would therefore seem appropriate to conclude with a description of what such a classroom might look like.

The well-organised classroom

The well-organised classroom is attractive and welcoming. There is colour and interest and it makes a visual impact on the visitor. At the same time, it is clear that it is a workshop in which many activities take place. It is therefore functional with materials and tools carefully arranged and labelled so that they are easy to find, use and keep in good order.

Children are comfortable and at home in this classroom and it is easy to see that it is as much their base as the teacher's. Their work is much in evidence. It is carefully and attractively displayed, sometimes with work chosen and displayed by the children themselves, who are encouraged to think about the way things can be mounted and shown. There is never too much display at the same time, however, and there is discussion of what is shown and it is frequently changed. Display is also used frequently used by the teacher as a starting point and stimulus for work.

The classroom assistant is well employed in this classroom. She and the teacher talk every morning about the work for the day and plan how it will be carried out. This gives the assistant a clear idea of what the teacher is expecting of her as well as what the children will be doing. The teacher very often asks his or her assistant to look out for certain things, such as the reactions of particular children to what they have been asked to do, or how children who are working in pairs or groups are listening to each other and learning to work together.

The teacher is very conscious of the need to take into account the training that the assistant has had and the knowledge of various kinds that she brings to the job and to make good use of this as well as helping her to acquire further knowledge and develop skill. The teacher takes as many opportunities as s/he can to talk to the assistant about what she is doing and the things she should look out for in helping the children. S/he also finds that the assistant provides some very useful feedback from her observations. They have become a good team, working together for the good of the children. They try to meet first thing every morning to discuss the day's work and again at the ending of the school day to discuss how it all went.

Children in this classroom feel secure in knowing what they may and may not do and this means that the day runs easily with children moving from one task to the next. They start work as soon as they come into the classroom and it is unusual to see a long queue of children waiting for attention from the teacher. There are very few enquiries to the teacher about minor matters of organisation because they are largely taken care of by arrangements about the classroom and the assistant also helps with queries. Children talk sensibly about what they are doing and learn from one another.

There is a sense of purpose in this classroom. The teacher has discussed with each child what s/he should be aiming to achieve and children have been trained to do a good deal of planning and organising of their own work and are well on the way to becoming independent learners. Many children become so absorbed in what they are doing that they are prepared to continue with it at home and would choose to work through breaks in the day. They are confident in their ability to learn and do things and have many ideas which they are well able to follow up. The teacher suggests ideas for homework and also involves children in suggesting ideas. The children have also become self-critical in a way which helps them to further their own learning. In consequence the standards of work achieved by all the children are extremely high.

The curriculum followed by the class is broad. The literacy and numeracy hours give rise to much interesting work and there are many opportunities for using the core subjects in other work. The differing needs of children have been carefully considered, with good provision made for children with special educational needs and for the very able and for those who are learning English as a second language.

The teacher is very conscious of the need for first-hand experience and frequently takes the children out of school and brings objects, materials and people into school to extend the children's experience. The teacher also listens to children and encourages discussion, both as a class and also in pairs and small groups, using questions which extend the children's thinking, and considers carefully how best to develop skills of all kinds, seeking out situations in which the children can communicate for a genuine purpose rather than as an exercise.

The teacher is very clear about the objectives of any given piece of work and shares this information with the assistant and also with the children so that they are clear what is the expected outcome. The teacher also shares with them the criteria by which each piece of work will be assessed and encourages them to assess their own performance and discuss it with the person who sits next to them.

The work of the classroom is planned to include class work, group work and individual work and these approaches are chosen very carefully to match the teacher's intentions and the needs of the children. The teacher is skilled at holding the interest of the whole class and uses whole-class teaching very effectively.

This classroom is well supplied with computers which are in use by children almost all day. They are very competent with them and are able to use the internet. They also correspond with children in another school, emailing each other stories they have written and telling their correspondent about what they are doing in school.

The school also now has a number of interactive whiteboards and the teacher in this classroom makes very good use of this facility, involving children in many different ways in working with it.

Work in groups is well used. This is sometimes a matter of children of similar ability being taught as a group or given similar work and sometimes a group working co-operatively to agreed ends. The ability to work as a group has been carefully nurtured by the teacher and many children are now competent group leaders as well as being able to contribute to the work in hand, sharing and taking turns and trying hard to further agreed goals. There is also work in pairs with children helping each other and checking each other's work.

The teacher is also well-organised with work that is carefully planned, but at the same time provides flexibility and the opportunity to pick up children's questions or interests if they look as if they would be valuable to follow up. The teacher has clear aims and regularly reviews work in the light of them, demonstrating an enjoyment of learning which is communicated to the children in many areas of work.

It is evident that the teacher and the assistant both like children and enjoy their company, respecting them as individuals without dominating them. The ideas and suggestions the children offer are received in a positive and encouraging way because the teacher has the ability to see things from the point of view of each individual child and is thus able to motivate children and match work to each one. Each child has the opportunity to enjoy the challenge of work which is just within his or her capacity but at the same time is able to succeed.

The teacher in this classroom uses time to good advantage and is relaxed. As the children have become more independent it has become possible to turn attention to longer discussion and work with individuals and small groups, making them think through ideas and helping them to plan work and evaluate. There is also time to discuss how children feel about things and to consider the development of their emotions.

Parents are welcomed to this classroom and the teacher takes time to talk with them and find out about their children. They are given positive suggestions about ways in which they can help their children with the work in hand and their contributions are welcomed. Some parents also come to help in the classroom.

The teacher is involved in the wider professional setting of the school and also more generally as a professional educator. This means working to keep up with what is happening in education and seeing whether research findings and knowledge of how children develop and learn have any relevance to his/ her classroom situation.

The relationships between the teacher, the assistant and the children are reflected in the relationships of the children with one another. There is always a sense of caring in this class and it is evident in many of the day-to-day activities.

Many of us would like to aspire to this picture, and it is greatly to the credit of teachers and assistants in British primary schools that so many achieve something like it.

References

Alexander, R. (1992) *Policy and Practice in Primary Education*, London: Routledge.

Alexander, R., Rose, J. and Woodhead, C. (1992) *Curriculum Organisation and Classroom Practice in Primary Schools*, London: Department of Education and Science.

Askew, M. and Wiliam, D. (1995) *Recent Research in Mathematics Education 5–16*, London: HMSO for Ofsted.

Askew, M., Brown, M., Rhodes, V., Johnson, D. and Wiliam, D. (1997) *Effective Teachers of Numeracy*, London: Kings College for the Teacher Training Agency.

Assessment Reform Group (1999) *Assessment for Learning: Beyond the Black Box*, Cambridge: Cambridge School of Education.

Atkin, J., Bastiani, J., and Goode, J. (1988) *Listen to Parents*, London: Croom Helm.

Barnes, R. (1999) *Positive Teaching, Positive Learning*, London: Routledge.

BECTA (2005) *Evidence on the Progress of ICT in Education*, British Educational Communication and Technology Agency.

Bennett, S.N. (1976) *Teaching Styles and Pupil Progress*, London: Open Books.

Bennett, S.N., Desforges, C., Cockburn, A. and Wilkinson, B. (1984) *The Quality of Pupil Learning Experiences*, London: Lawrence Erlbaum Associates.

Bennett, S.N. and Dunne, E. (1994), Exeter: University of Exeter.

Bennett, S.N. and Kell, J. (1989) *A Good Start? Four-Year-Olds in Infant Schools*, Oxford: Basil Blackwell.

Bennett, S.N., Wragg, E.C., Carre, C.G. and Carter, D.S.G. (1991) 'A longitudinal study of primary teachers' perceived competences and concerns about National Curriculum implementation', *Research Papers in Education* 6(3): 197–233.

BESA (2001) *How is the Interactive Whiteboard Being Used in the Primary School*, report by Julie Cogill, British Educational Suppliers Association.

Brophy, J. and Good, T. (1986) 'Naturalistic studies of teacher expectation effects', in Hammersley, M. (ed.) *Case Studies in Classroom Research*, Buckingham: Open University Press.

Bruner, J.S. (1985) 'Vygotsky: a historical and conceptual perspective', in Wertsch, J.V. (ed.) *Culture, Communication and Cognition: Vygotskian Perspectives*, Cambridge: Cambridge University Press.

Carrington, B. and Short, G. (1989) *Race and the Primary School*, Windsor: NFER-Nelson.

Chazan, M., Laing, A. and Harper, G. (1987) *Teaching Five to Eight-Year-Olds*, Oxford: Blackwell.

Cogill, J. (2003) 'The use of interactive whiteboards in the primary school: effects on pedagogy', Research Bursary Reports, Coventry: BECTA, quoted in Kennewell, S. (2004) *Reflections on the Interactive Whiteboard Phenomenon: a Synthesis of Research From the UK*, Swansea: School of Education.

Cohen, A. and Cohen, L. (eds) (1988) *Early Education: The School Years: A Source Book for Teachers*, London: Paul Chapman Publishing.

Cortazzi, M. (1991) *Primary Teaching: How it is*, London: David Fulton.

Craft, A. (2005) *Creativity in Schools*, Oxon: Routledge.

Cullingford, C. (1995) *The Effective Teacher*, London: Caswell.

Dean, J. (2000) *Improving Children's Learning: Effective Teaching in the Primary School*, London: Routledge.

Delamont, S. (ed.) (1987) *The Primary School Teacher*, London: Falmer.

Department for Education and Employment (1999) *National Numeracy Strategy Framework*, DfEE.

Department of Education and Science (1985) *Education for All*, a summary of the Swan Report, London: Runnymede Trust.

Department for Education and Skills (2004) *Excellence and Enjoyment*: DfES.

Department for Education and Skills (2003) Green Paper *Every child matters*, Norwich: Stationery Office.

Department for Education and Skills (2005) *Harnessing Technology – Transforming Learning and Children's Services*, DfES.

Desforges, C. (1985) 'Matching tasks to children's attainments', in Bennett, N.S. and Desforges, C. (eds) *Recent Advances in Classroom Research*, Edinburgh: Scottish Academic Press for the *British Journal of Educational Psychology*, monograph series no. 2.

Docking, J. (ed.) (1990) *Education and Alienation in the Junior School*, London: Falmer.

Dunne, E. and Bennett, S.N. (1990) *Talking and Learning in Groups: Activity Based In-Service and Pre-Service Materials*, London: Routledge.

Edwards, D. and Mercer, N. (1987) *Common Knowledge*, London: Methuen.

Edwards, A. and Knight, P. (1994) *Effective Early Years Education: Teaching Young Children*, Buckingham: Open University Press.

Galton, M. and Simon, B. (1980) *Progress and Performance in the Primary School Classroom* (The Oracle Study), London: Routledge and Kegan Paul.

Galton, M. (1989) *Teaching in the Primary School*, London: David Fulton.

Gardner, H. (1983) *Frames of Mind: The Theory of Multiple Intelligences*, New York: Basic Books.

Gillborn, D. and Mirza, H.S. (2000) *Educational Inequality: Mapping Race, Class and Gender, a Synthesis of Research Evidence*, London: Ofsted.

Goleman, D. (1996) *Emotional Intelligence*, London: Bloomsbury.

Hargreaves, L. (1990) 'Teachers and pupils in small schools', in Galton, M. and Patrick, H. (eds) *Curriculum Provision in the Small Primary School*, London: Routledge.

Harlen, W. (1985) *Teaching and Learning Primary Science*, London: Paul Chapman Publishing.

Hay McBer (2000) *Research into Teacher Effectiveness*, London: Hay McBer.

HMI (1978) *Primary Education in England: A Survey by HM Inspectors of Schools*, London: HMSO.

HMI (1996–7) *Standards in the Primary Curriculum*, London: Ofsted.

HMI (1999a) *The National Literacy Strategy: An Interim Evaluation*, London: Ofsted.

HMI (1999b) *The National Literacy Strategy: An Evaluation of the First Year*, London: Ofsted.

HMI (2000) *The National Numeracy Strategy: An Interim Evaluation*, London: Ofsted.

Holt, J. (1984) *How Children Fail*, Harmondsworth: Penguin.

Houlton, D. (1988) 'Teachers and diversity', in Cohen, A. and Cohen, L. (eds) *Early Education: The School Years: A Source Book for Teachers*, London: Paul Chapman Publishing.

Hughes, M. (1986) *Children and Number: Difficulties in Learning Mathematics*, Oxford: Basil Blackwell.

Inhelder, B. and Piaget, J. (1958) *The Growth of Logical Thinking from Childhood to Adolescence*, New York: Basic Books.

Jackson, K.F. (1975) *The Art of Solving Problems*, London: Heinemann.

Kelly, A. (1988) 'Gender differences in teacher–pupil interaction: a meta-analytic review', *Research in Education* 39: 1–23.

Kerry, T. (1980) *Effective Questioning*, Teacher Education Project, Nottingham: University of Nottingham School of Education.

Lewin (1951) *Field Theory in Social Science*, New York, NY: Harper.

Mortimore, P., Sammons, P., Stoll, L., Lewis, D. and Ecob, R. (1988) *School Matters*, London: Open Books.

National Advisory Committee on Creative and Cultural Education (1999) *All Our Futures: Creativity, Culture and Education*, London: Department for Education and Employment.

Ofsted (1996–7) *Standards in the Primary Curriculum*, London: Ofsted.

Ofsted (1997) *The Teaching of Number in Three Inner-urban LEAs*, London: Ofsted.

Ofsted (1988) *Teacher Assessment in the Core Subjects at Key Stage 2: Policy and Practice*, London: Ofsted.

Ofsted (2000) *The National Numeracy Strategy: An Interim Evaluation*, London: Ofsted.

Osterman, K. and Kottkamp, R. (1994) 'Rethinking professional development', in Bennett, N., Glatter, R. and Levacic, R. (eds) *Improving Educational Management through Research and Consultancy*, London: Paul Chapman.

Parsons, J.E., Ruble, D.N., Hodges, K.L. and Small, A.V. (1976) 'Cognitive-developmental factors in emerging sex differences in achievement-related expectancies', *Journal of Social Issues* 32 (3): 47–61.

Piaget, J. (1952) *The Origins of Intelligence in Children*, New York: International Universities Press.

Plowden (1967) *Children and their Primary Schools*, Report of the Central Advisory Council for Education in England, London: HMSO.

Pollard, A. and Tann, S. (1987) *Reflective Teaching in the Primary School*, London: Cassell Education.

Primary Strategy and Framework (2006) London: DfES.

Qualifications and Curriculum Authority (1999) *Assessment and Reporting Arrangements at Key Stage 2*, London: QCA Publications.

Rose (2006) *Independent Report of the Teaching of Early Reading*, London, DfES.

SEAC (School Examinations and Assessment Council) (1990) *Assessing the National Curriculum*, London: SEAC.

Somekh, B. and Davis, N. (eds) (2002) *Using Information Technology Effectively in Teaching and Learning*, London: Routledge.

Straker, A. (1999) *Report to National Union of Teachers' Numeracy Task Group*, NUT.

Sylva, K., Roy, C. and Painter, M. (1980) *Child Watching at Playgroup and Nursery School*, London: Grant McIntyre.

Tizard, B. and Hughes, M. (1984) *Young Children Learning: Talking and Thinking at Home and at School*, London: Fontana.

Tizard, B., Blatchford, P., Burke, J., Farquhar, C. and Lewis, I. (1988) *Young Children at School in the Inner City*, London: Lawrence Erlbaum Associates.

Vygotsky, L.S. (1978) *Mind in Society: The Development of Higher Psychological Processes*, Cambridge, MA: Harvard University Press.

Webb, R. and Vulliamy, G. (1996) *Roles and Responsibilities in the Primary School*, Buckingham: Open University Press.

Wegerif and Dawes (1996) *Thinking and Learning with ICT, Raising achievement in primary classrooms*, RoutledgeFalmer; 2nd edn (2004) e-prints Soton: University of Southampton.

Wells, C.G. (1985) *Language, Learning and Education: Selected papers from the Bristol study, Language at home and at school*, Slough: NFER-Nelson.

Wheldall, K. and Glynn, T. (1989) *Effective Classroom Learning*, Oxford: Blackwell.

Wragg, E.C. (1984) *Classroom Teaching Skills*, London: Croom Helm.

Wragg, E.C. and Brown, G. (1993) *Explaining*, London: Routledge.

Index